ENCYCLOPAEDIA OF GLOBAL BANKING THEORY AND APPLICATIONS

ENCYCLOPAEDIA OF GLOBAL BANKING THEORY AND APPLICATIONS

HEMANT SHARMA

CYBER TECH PUBLICATIONS
4264/3, Ansari Road, Daryaganj, New Delhi-110002 (India)
Ph.: 011-23244078, 011-43559448 Fax: 011-23280028
E-Mail: cyberpublicationsdelhi@yahoo.com
Website: www.cybertechpublications.com

ENCYCLOPAEDIA OF GLOBAL BANKING THEORY AND APPLICATIONS

HEMANT SHARMA

First Edition 2011

Published by :

G.S. Rawat for **Cyber Tech Publications**

4264/3, Ansari Road, Daryaganj, New Delhi-110002 (India)

Ph.: 011-23244078, 011-43559448 Fax: 011-23280028

E-Mail: cyberpublicationsdelhi@yahoo.com

Website: www.cybertechpublications.com

Printed at: Asian Offset Printers, Delhi-53

Contents

Preface

The banks make more international loans, many experts believe that there must be greater international cooperation regarding standards and regulations to lower the risk of bank failure and international financial collapse. In 1988 the Basel Committee on Banking Supervision, an international organization of bank regulators based in Basel, Switzerland, took the first steps in this direction with the Basel Capital Accord. The accord established a global standard for assessing the financial soundness of banks and required banks to maintain a minimum ratio of capital to risky assets. Many banking experts believe this accord became the primary tool for strengthening the safety of international banking. The accord was eventually adopted by 100 countries.

In 2001 the Basel Committee recommended a new set of regulations known as the New Basel Capital Accord to replace the 1988 agreement. Banks have historically financed international trade, but a notable recent development has been the expansion of branches and subsidiaries that are physically located abroad, as well as the increased volume of loans to foreign borrowers. In 1960 only eight U.S. banks had foreign offices with a total of 131 branches. By 1998 about 82 U.S. banks had about 935 foreign branches. The expansion of trade in recent decades has been paralleled by the growth of multinational banking.

Similarly, the number of foreign banks with offices in the United States has increased dramatically. In 1975, 79 foreign banks were chartered in the United States, accounting for 5 percent of U.S. bank assets. In 1998, 243 foreign banks had U.S. offices, accounting for 23 percent of U.S. bank assets. Most of these banks are business-oriented banks, but some have also engaged in retail banking. In 1978 the U.S. Congress passed the International Banking Act, which imposed constraints on the activities of foreign banks in the United States, removing some of the advantages they had acquired in relation to U.S. banks.

—Author

1

Theory of the Global Banking

INTRODUCTION

Banks have historically financed international trade, but a notable recent development has been the expansion of branches and subsidiaries that are physically located abroad, as well as the increased volume of loans to foreign borrowers. In 1960 only eight U.S. banks had foreign offices with a total of 131 branches. By 1998 about 82 U.S. banks had about 935 foreign branches. The expansion of trade in recent decades has been paralleled by the growth of multinational banking.

Similarly, the number of foreign banks with offices in the United States has increased dramatically. In 1975, 79 foreign banks were chartered in the United States, accounting for 5 percent of U.S. bank assets. In 1998, 243 foreign banks had U.S. offices, accounting for 23 percent of U.S. bank assets. Most of these banks are business-oriented banks, but some have also engaged in retail banking. In 1978 the U.S. Congress passed the International Banking Act, which imposed constraints on the activities of foreign banks in the United States, removing some of the advantages they had acquired in relation to U.S. banks.

As banks make more international loans, many experts believe that there must be greater international cooperation regarding standards and regulations to lower the risk of bank failure and international financial collapse. In 1988 the Basel Committee on Banking Supervision, an international organization of bank regulators based in Basel, Switzerland, took the first steps in this direction with the Basel Capital Accord. The accord established a global standard for assessing the financial soundness of banks and required banks to maintain a minimum ratio of capital to risky assets. Many banking experts believe this accord became the primary tool for strengthening the safety of international banking. The accord was eventually adopted by 100 countries. In 2001 the Basel Committee recommended a new set of regulations known as the New Basel Capital Accord to replace the 1988 agreement.

INDIAN BANKING: AN INTRODUCTION

The Indian banking can be broadly categorized into nationalized (government owned), private banks and specialized banking institutions. The Reserve Bank of India acts a centralized body monitoring any discrepancies and shortcoming in the system. Since the nationalization of banks in 1969, the public sector banks or the nationalized banks have acquired a place of prominence and has since then seen tremendous progress. The need to become highly customer focused has forced the slow-moving public sector banks to adopt a fast track approach.

The unleashing of products and services through the net has galvanized players at all levels of the banking and financial institutions market grid to look anew at their existing portfolio offering. Conservative banking practices allowed Indian banks to be insulated partially from the Asian currency crisis. Indian banks are now quoting al higher valuation when compared to banks in other Asian countries (viz. Hong Kong, Singapore, Philippines etc.) that have major problems linked to huge Non Performing Assets (NPAs) and payment defaults. Co-operative banks are nimble footed in approach and armed with efficient branch networks focus primarily on the 'high revenue' niche retail segments.

The Indian banking has finally worked up to the competitive dynamics of the 'new' Indian market and is addressing the relevant issues to take on the multifarious challenges of globalization. Banks that employ IT solutions are perceived to be 'futuristic' and proactive players capable of meeting the multifarious requirements of the large customers base. Private banks have been fast on the uptake and are reorienting their strategies using the internet as a medium The Internet has emerged as the new and challenging frontier of marketing with the conventional physical world tenets being just as applicable like in any other marketing medium.

The Indian banking has come from a long way from being a sleepy business institution to a highly proactive and dynamic entity. This transformation has been largely brought about by the large dose of liberalization and economic reforms that allowed banks to explore new business opportunities rather than generating revenues from conventional streams (i.e. borrowing and lending). The banking in India is highly fragmented with 30 banking units contributing to almost 50% of deposits and 60% of advances. Indian nationalized banks (banks owned by the government) continue to be the major lenders in the economy due to their sheer size and penetrative networks which assures them high deposit mobilization. The Indian banking can be broadly categorized into nationalized, private banks and specialized banking institutions.

The Reserve Bank of India act as a centralized body monitoring any discrepancies and shortcoming in the system. It is the foremost monitoring body in the Indian financial sector. The nationalized banks (i.e. government-owned banks) continue to dominate the Indian banking arena. Industry estimates indicate that out of 274 commercial banks operating in India, 223 banks are in the public sector and 51 are in the private sector. The private sector bank grid also includes 24 foreign banks that have started their operations here. Under the ambit of the nationalized banks come the specialized banking institutions. These co-operatives, rural banks focus on areas of agriculture, rural development etc.,

Capital Market

Stock market volatility touches every participant directly/indirectly in the capital market. General feeling is that the stock markets worldwide have become very fragile in the recent past on account of various developments such as Asian crisis. Brazil Real fall and Russian debacle. Many far-reaching stock reforms have been introduced in the Indian market for the last few years. These reforms, in turn, changed market structure. Changing market structure influences nature of stock price behavior.

Primary Securities Market

The primary capital market (PCM) plays an important role in the overall functioning of securities market. Despite several measures the primary market remained lackluster till recently and the pick up is gradual. According to the SEBI annual report fewer number of issues accessed the primary market during the year and the significantly lower than that of the Previous financial year. Share of the equity issues, in terms of number and amount Mobilized, however, was higher in this financial year compared to the previous one. More than three-fourths of the total amount was occupied second and no resources were in the previous years, banks and financial institutions continued for 84.5% of the resourced mobilized compared to 68.1% in 2001-02. All other industries shared the remaining portion.

Capital Raised During 2002-03

During the financial year 2002-03, primary market witnessed a decrease of 46.0% in the amount raised and also a decrease of 25.7% in the number of issues launched compared to the same period in 2001-02. A total of 26 issues (14 public issues and 12 rights issues) opened during the financial year 2002-03 raising Rs. 4070.29 crore (Rs. 3638.6 crore through public issues and 431.6 crore through rights issues). In 2001-02 a total of 35 issues opened for raising Rs. 7543.0 crore (20 public issues-Rs. 6501.8 crore and 15 rights issues-Rs. 1041.2).

Industry Wise Capital Mobilization

Three industries viz. Banks/Fls, Engineering and Telecommunications accounted for 93.2 per cent of the resourced mobilized in 2001-02. In the current year, the same three industries accounted for 84.7 per cent of the funds raised. With the banks and Fls, increasing their share from 68.3 per cent to 84.5 per cent and companies in the Telecommunications sector and raising any resourced. In 2002-03 the three industries which accounted for 95.3 per cent of the resources where Banking/Fls, Information Technology, Paper and Pulp.

SECONDARY MARKET

During 2002-03, performance of Indian Stock market was, by and large, a lackluster one, S&P CNX NIFTY and BSE Sensex both registered

Duration

In exercise of the powers conferred under Section 5 of The Foreign Trade (Development and Regulation Act), 1992 (No. 22 of 1992), the Central Government hereby notifies the Export and Import Policy for the period 2002-2007.

This Policy shall come into force with effect from 1st April, 2002 and shall remain in force upto 31st March, 2007 and will be co-terminus with the Tenth Five Year Plan (2002-2007). However, the Central Government reserves the right in public interest to make any amendments to this Policy in exercise of the powers conferred by Section-5 of the Act. Such amendment shall be made by means of a Notification published in the Gazette of India.

Transitional Arrangements

Any Notifications made or Public Notices issued or anything done under the previous Export/Import policies, and in force immediately before the commencement of this Policy shall, in so far as they are not inconsistent with the provisions of this Policy, continue to be in force and shall be deemed to have been made, issued or done under this Policy. Licence/certificate/permissions issued before the commencement of this Policy shall continue to be valid for the purpose for which such licence/certificate/permission was issued unless otherwise stipulated.

In case an export or import that is permitted freely under this Policy is subsequently subjected to any restriction or regulation, such export or import will ordinarily be permitted notwithstanding such restriction or regulation, unless otherwise stipulated, provided that the shipment of the export or import is made within the original validity of the irrevocable letter of credit established before the date of imposition of such restriction

FOREIGN TRADE POLICY

Objectives

Trade is not an end in itself, but a means to economic growth and national development. The primary purpose is not the mere earning of foreign exchange, but the stimulation of greater economic activity. The Foreign Trade Policy is rooted in this belief and built around two major objectives. These are:

(i) To double our percentage share of global merchandise trade within the next five years; and

(ii) To act as an effective instrument of economic growth by giving a thrust to employment generation.

Strategy

These objectives are proposed to be achieved by adopting, among others, the following strategies:

(i) Unshackling of controls and creating an atmosphere of trust and transparency to unleash the innate entrepreneurship of our businessmen, industrialists and traders.

(ii) Simplifying procedures and bringing down transaction costs.

(iii) Neutralizing incidence of all levies and duties on inputs used in export products, based on the fundamental principle that duties and levies should not be exported.

(iv) Facilitating development of India as a global hub for manufacturing, trading and services.

(v) Identifying and nurturing special focus areas which would generate additional employment opportunities, particularly in semi-urban and rural areas, and developing a series of 'Initiatives' for each of these.

(vi) Facilitating technological and infrastructural upgradation of all the sectors of the Indian economy, especially through import of capital goods and equipment, thereby increasing value addition and productivity, while attaining internationally accepted standards of quality.

(vii) Avoiding inverted duty structures and ensuring that our domestic sectors are not disadvantaged in the Free Trade Agreements/Regional Trade Agreements/Preferential Trade Agreements that we enter into in order to enhance our exports.

(viii) Upgrading our infrastructural network, both physical and virtual, related to the entire Foreign Trade chain, to international standards.

(ix) Revitalising the Board of Trade by redefining its role, giving it due recognition and inducting experts on Trade Policy.

(x) Activating our Embassies as key players in our export strategy and linking our Commercial Wings abroad through an electronic platform for real time trade intelligence and enquiry dissemination.

Partenership

The new Policy envisages merchant exporters and manufacturer exporters, business and industry as partners of Government in the achievement of its stated objectives and goals. Prolonged and unnecessary litigation vitiates the premise of partnership. In order to obviate the need for litigation and nurture a constructive and conducive atmosphere, a suitable Grievance Redressal Mechanism will be established which, it is hoped, would substantially reduce litigation and further a relationship of partnership.

The dynamics of a liberalized trading system sometimes results in injury caused to domestic industry on account of dumping. When this happens, effective measures to redress such injury will be taken.

Roadmap

This Policy is essentially a roadmap for the development of India's foreign trade. It contains the basic principles and points the direction in which we propose to go. By virtue of its very dynamics, a trade policy cannot be fully comprehensive in all its details. It would naturally require modification from time to time. We propose to do this through continuous updation, based on the inevitable changing dynamics of international trade. It is in partnership with business and industry that we propose to erect milestones on this roadmap.

FUNCTIONS OF COMMERCIAL BANKING

A commercial bank is a type of financial intermediary and a type of bank. Commercial bank has two possible meanings:

- Commercial bank is the term used for a normal bank to distinguish it from an investment bank.

  This is what people normally call a "bank". The term "commercial" was used to distinguish it from an investment bank. Since the two types of banks no longer have to be separate companies, some have used the term "commercial bank" to refer to banks which focus mainly on companies.

In some English-speaking countries outside North America, the term "trading bank" was and is used to denote a commercial bank. (After the great depression, the U.S. Congress required that banks only engage in banking activities, whereas investment banks were limited to capital markets activities. This separation is no longer mandatory.)

It raises funds by collecting deposits from businesses and consumers via checkable deposits, savings deposits, and time (or term) deposits. It makes loans to businesses and consumers. It also buys corporate bonds and government bonds. Its primary liabilities are deposits and primary assets are loans and bonds.

- Commercial banking can also refer to a bank or a division of a bank that mostly deals with deposits and loans from corporations or large businesses, as opposed to normal individual members of the public (retail banking).

WHAT ARE CENTRAL BANKS?

The central bank has been described as "the lender of last resort", which means that it is responsible for providing its economy with funds when commercial banks cannot cover a supply shortage. In other words, the central bank prevents the country's banking system from failing. However, the primary goal of central banks is to provide their countries' currencies with price stability by controlling inflation. A central bank also acts as the regulatory authority of a country's monetary policy and is the sole provider and printer of notes and coins in circulation. Time has proven that the central bank can best function in these capacities by remaining independent from government fiscal policy and therefore uninfluenced by the political concerns of any regime. The central bank should also be completely divested of any commercial banking interests.

The Rise of the Central Bank

Today the central bank is government owned but separate from the country's ministry of finance. Although the central bank is frequently termed the "government's bank" because it handles the buying and selling of government bonds and other instruments, political decisions should not influence central bank operations. Of course, the nature of the relationship between the central bank and the ruling regime varies from country to country and continues to evolve with time. To ensure the stability of a country's currency, the central bank should be the regulator and authority in the banking and monetary systems. Historically, the role of the central bank has been growing, some may argue, since the establishment of the Bank of England in 1694. It is, however, generally agreed upon that the concept of the modern central bank did not appear until the 20th century as problems developed in the commercial banking system. Thus, the central bank's modern function emerged in response to an already present commercial banking structure.

Between 1870 and 1914, when world currencies were pegged to the gold standard (GS), maintaining price stability was a lot easier because the amount of gold available was limited. Consequently, monetary expansion could not occur simply from a political decision to print more money, so inflation was easier to control. The central bank at that time was primarily responsible for maintaining the convertibility of gold into currency; it issued notes based on a country's reserves of gold.

At the outbreak of WWI, the GS was abandoned, and it came apparent that, in times of crisis, governments, facing budget deficits (because it costs money to wage war) and needing greater resources, will order the printing of more money. As governments did so, they encountered inflation. After WWI, many governments opted to go back to the GS to try to stabilize their economies. With this rose the awareness of the importance of the central bank's independence from the political machine.

During the unsettling times of the Great Depression and the aftermath of WWII, world governments predominantly favored a return to a central bank dependent on the political decision making process. This view emerged mostly from the need to establish control over war-shattered economies; furthermore, countries with newly-acquired independence opted to keep control over all aspects of their countries-a backlash against colonialism.

The rise of managed economies in the Eastern Bloc was also responsible for increased government interference in the macroeconomy. Soon after the effects of WWII, however, the independence of the central bank from the government came back into fashion in Western economies and has prevailed as the optimal way to achieve a liberal and stable economic regime.

HOW THE BANK INFLUENCES AN ECONOMY

A central bank can be said to have two main kinds of functions: (1) macroeconomic when regulating inflation and price stability and (2) microeconomic when functioning as a lender of last resort.

Macroeconomic Influences

As it is responsible for price stability, the central bank must regulate the level of inflation by controlling money supplies by means of monetary policy. The central bank performs open market transactions that either inject the market with liquidity or absorb extra funds, directly affecting the level of inflation. To increase the amount of money in circulation and decrease the interest rate (cost) for borrowing, the central bank can buy government bonds, bills, or other government-issued notes. This buying can, however, also lead to higher inflation. When it needs to absorb money to reduce inflation, the central bank will sell government bonds on the open market, which increases the interest rate and discourages borrowing. Open market operations are the key means by which a central bank controls inflation, money supply, and price stability.

Microeconomic Influences

The establishment of central banks as lender of last resort has pushed the need for their freedom from commercial banking. A commercial bank offers funds to clients on a first come, first serve basis. If the commercial bank does not have enough liquidity to meet its clients' demands (commercial banks typically do not hold reserves equal to the needs of the entire market), the commercial bank can turn to the central bank to borrow additional funds.

This provides the system with stability in an objective way; central banks cannot favor any particular commercial bank. As such, many central banks will hold commercial-bank reserves that are based on a ratio of each commercial bank's deposits. Thus, a central bank may require all commercial banks to keep, for example, a 1:10 reserve/deposit ratio. Enforcing a policy of commercial bank reserves functions as another means to control money supply in the market. Not all central banks, however, require commercial banks to deposit reserves. The United Kingdom, for example, does not have this policy while the United States does.

The rate at which commercial banks and other lending facilities can borrow short-term funds from the central bank is called the discount rate (which is set by the central bank and provides a base rate for interest rates). It has been argued that, for open market transactions to become more efficient, the discount rate should keep the banks from perpetual borrowing, which would disrupt the market's money supply and the central bank's monetary policy. By borrowing too much, the commercial bank will be circulating more money in the system. Use of the discount rate can be restricted by making it unattractive when used repeatedly.

Transitional Economies

Today developing economies are faced with issues such as the transition from managed to free market economies. The main concern is often controlling inflation. This can lead to the creation of an independent central bank but can take some time, given that many developing nations maintain control over their economies in an effort to retain control of their power. But government intervention, whether direct or indirect through fiscal policy, can stunt central bank development. Unfortunately, many developing nations are faced with civil disorder or war, which can force a government to divert funds away from the development of the economy as a whole. Nonetheless, one factor that seems to be confirmed is that, for a market economy to develop, a stable currency (whether achieved through a fixed or floating exchange rate) is needed. However, the central banks in both industrial and emerging economies are dynamic because there is no guaranteed way to run an economy regardless of its stage of development.

BANKING IN INDIA

Banking in India originated in the first decade of 18th century with The General Bank of India coming into existence in 1786. This was followed by Bank of Hindustan. Both these banks are now defunct. The oldest bank in existence in India is the State Bank of India being established as "The Bank of Bengal" in Calcutta in June 1806. A couple of decades later, foreign banks like Credit Lyonnais started their Calcutta operations in the 1850s. At that point of time, Calcutta was the most active trading port, mainly due to the trade of the British Empire, and due to which banking activity took roots there and prospered. The first fully Indian owned bank was the Allahabad Bank, which was established in 1865.

By the 1900s, the market expanded with the establishment of banks such as Punjab National Bank, in 1895 in Lahore and Bank of India, in 1906, in Mumbai-both of which were founded under private ownership. The Reserve Bank of India formally took on the responsibility of regulating the Indian banking sector from 1935. After India's independence in 1947, the Reserve Bank was nationalized and given broader powers.

Nationalisation

The next significant milestone in Indian Banking occurred on July 19, 1969 when the then Indira Gandhi government nationalized the 14 largest commercial banks. A second nationalization of 6 more commercial banks followed in 1980. The stated reason for the nationalisation was to give the government more control of credit delivery. After this, until the 1990s, the nationalised banks grew at a leisurely pace of around 4%, closer to the average growth rate of the Indian economy.

Liberalisation

In the early 1990s the then Narasimha Rao government embarked on a policy of liberalisation and gave licences to a small number of private banks, which came to be known as New Generation tech-savvy banks, which included banks such as UTI Bank (the first of such new generation banks to be set up), ICICI Bank and HDFC Bank. This move, along with the rapid growth in the economy of India, kickstarted the banking sector in India, which has seen rapid growth with strong contribution from all the three sectors of banks, namely, government banks, private banks and foreign banks.

The next stage for the Indian banking has been setup with the proposed relaxation in the norms for Foreign Direct Investment, where all Foreign Investors in banks may be given voting rights which could exceed the present cap of 10%.

The new policy shook the Banking sector in India completely. Bankers, till this time, were used to the 4-6-4 method (Borrow at 4%; Lend at 6%; Go home at 4) of functioning. The new wave ushered in a modern outlook and tech-savvy methods of working for traditional banks. All this led to the retail boom in India. People not just demanded more from their banks but also received more.

CURRENT SCENARIO

Public Sector Banks

SBI Group: State Bank of India, with its seven associate banks command the largest banking resources in India. SBI and its associate banks are:

- State Bank of India
- State Bank of Bikaner & Jaipur
- State Bank of Hyderabad
- State Bank of Indore
- State Bank of Mysore
- State Bank of Patiala
- State Bank of Saurashtra
- State Bank of Travancore

After the amalgamation of New Bank of India with Punjab National Bank, currently there are 19 nationalised banks in India:

- Allahabad Bank
- Andhra Bank
- Bank of Baroda
- Bank of India
- Bank of Maharashtra
- Canara Bank
- Central Bank of India
- Corporation Bank
- Dena Bank
- Indian Bank
- Indian Overseas Bank
- Oriental Bank of Commerce

- Punjab & Sind Bank
- Punjab National Bank
- Syndicate Bank
- Union Bank of India
- United Bank of India
- UCO Bank
- Vijaya Bank

Private Sector Banks

- Bank of Rajasthan
- Bharat Overseas Bank
- Catholic Syrian Bank
- Centurion Bank of Punjab
- Dhanalakshmi Bank
- Federal Bank
- HDFC Bank
- ICICI Bank
- IDBI Bank
- IndusInd Bank
- ING Vysya Bank
- Jammu & Kashmir Bank
- Karnataka Bank
- Karur Vysya Bank
- Kotak Mahindra Bank
- SBI Commercial and International Bank
- South Indian Bank
- Tamilnad Mercantile Bank Ltd.
- UTI Bank
- YES Bank

Foreign Banks

- ABN AMRO BANK N.V.
- Abu Dhabi Commercial Bank Ltd
- Bank of Ceylon
- BNP Paribas Bank
- Citibank
- China Trust Commercial Bank
- Deutsche Bank
- HSBC
- JPMorgan Chase Bank
- Standard Chartered Bank
- Scotia Bank
- Taib Bank

Currently (2007), overall, banking in India is considered as fairly mature in terms of supply, product range and reach-even though reach in rural India still remains a challenge for the private sector and foreign banks. Even in terms of quality of assets and capital adequacy, Indian banks are considered to have clean, strong and transparent balance sheets-as compared to other banks in comparable economies in its region. The Reserve Bank of India is an autonomous body, with minimal pressure from the government. The stated policy of the Bank on the Indian Rupee is to manage volatility-without any stated exchange rate-and this has mostly been true.

With the growth in the Indian economy expected to be strong for quite some time-especially in its services sector, the demand for banking services-especially retail banking, mortgages and investment services are expected to be strong. M&As, takeovers, asset sales and much more action (as it is unravelling in China) will happen on this front in India.

In March 2006, the Reserve Bank of India allowed Warburg Pincus to increase its stake in Kotak Mahindra Bank (a private sector bank) to 10%. This is the first time an investor has been allowed to hold more than 5% in a private sector bank since the RBI announced norms in 2005 that any stake exceeding 5% in the private sector banks would need to be vetted by them.

Currently, India has 88 scheduled commercial banks (SCBs)-28 public sector banks (that is with the Government of India holding a stake), 29 private banks (these do not have government stake; they may be publicly listed and traded on stock exchanges) and 31 foreign banks.

They have a combined network of over 53,000 branches and 17,000 ATMs. According to a report by ICRA Limited, a rating agency, the public sector banks hold over 75 percent of total assets of the banking industry, with the private and foreign banks holding 18.2% and 6.5% respectively.

DIRECT FINANCE PAYMENT

Definition

Direct Finance Payment refers to payment service where the finance authority issues payment instruction according to fund application by eligible department and ICBC pays the fund directly to the payee account through the treasury's single account system according to the payment instruction.

Products' Target Client

The service mainly serves the finance authorities at each level included in the treasury centralized payment reform and is applicable for the wage expenditure, project procurement, and goods and service procurement of the budgeting units.

Features and Strengths

Large Business Network

ICBC not only has large number of Business Offices in wide distribution, but also possess the largest customer group in the domestic banking sector. It has shaped the banking competitive advantage of highest ratio for efficient fund allocation within system and lowest ratio for cross-bank payment.

Advanced Payment System

All transactions are centralized in one data center for processing. The fund is linked to accounting entries, which effectively prevents the criminal attempts by internal and external personnel taking advantage of time lag between fund activities and accounting entries. The leading "Bank-Finance Link" system in the sector synchronizes the fund flow and information flow. The transaction information is transmitted through encrypted mode. The system achieved the electronic State treasury fund payment clearing, standardized information transmission, and informationalized reporting system management. The system makes ICBC at the leadership position in China in terms of agency State treasury centralized payment service. Therefore, ICBC is capable to promptly respond to the variety of large batch, inter-region, and inter-bank fund payment requests from the finance authorities and budgeting units.

Diversified Information Feedback Platform

In response to the special requirement by finance authority's centralized payment service, ICBC launched automated processing for fund settlement, accounting, information transmission, and reporting. It realized real-time enquiry, collection and sorting, and summary and analysis of information and ensured timely, accurate, and secure feedbacks to the finance authorities and budgeting units at each level. Furthermore, ICBC takes full advantage of its IT and electronic service and makes use of special-line networking, Internet Banking, and other channels to break through the limitation of Business Offices and the business hours. It provides a 24-7 electronic real-time enquiry system for the finance authorities and budgeting units at each level and provides multi-function, convenient and prompt, and safe and reliable electronic enquiry service.

Service Channels

"Bank-Finance Link" system.

Application Condition

The finance authorities at each level that are included in the Treasury centralized payment reform are eligible to apply for direct payment services.

Service Procedure

(I) As per finance authority's notification, ICBC opens the zero-balance account for direct payment and Treasury single account clearing.

(II) The finance authority issues Finance Direct Payment Voucher to ICBC or sends the electronic direct payment instruction to ICBC through special line.

(III) ICBC transfers the fund to the payee or the eligible unit's account on real-time basis through "Bank-Finance Link" system.

(IV) ICBC timely delivers the payment slip to the finance authority and upload the electronic return slip to the finance authority through special line and deliver the Finance Direct Payment Deposit Advice to the budgeting units. It presents the finance direct payment 10-day (monthly) report to the finance authority as per stipulated time and enables the dynamic monitoring service to the finance authority to cover Treasury fund payments.

FINANCE AUTHORIZED PAYMENT

Definition

Finance Authorized Payment is service arrangement where the finance authority allocate the monthly fund limit to the zero-balance account of the budgeting units according to the budget and fund usage plan, whereas the budgeting units make their payments within the allocated fund limit.

Product's Target Client

The service mainly targets to the budgeting units at each level included in the Treasury centralized payment reforms. It is applicable for the procurement payment and random expenditures not yet included in the Finance Direct Payment.

Features and Strengths

Automatic Line Distribution

"Bank-Finance Link" system automatically receives the authorized payment limit transmitted from finance authority to ICBC through special line or other methods and automatically diverts it to the intermediary service platform of each first-tier (direct control) branches and automatically prints the line deposit advice for the budgeting units.

Automatic Line Control

"Bank-Finance Link" system is managed centrally as per first-tier budgeting units for the authorized payment limit. It automatically renew the line after the new line granting or line drawdown; for over-the-limit payment, it automatically stops payment and sends feedback to the budgeting unit; it automatically reinstates the relevant limits when the funds are returned to the Treasury.

Automatic System Resources Retrieval

The teller user only needs to input the few key elements such as receiving account number and is able to retrieve the budgeting unit name, account code, and other voucher data pre-stored in the system, thereby minimizing the data entry volume.

Dynamic Monitoring Service

The system retrieves the finance payment details from the database and retrieves the back office system per minute on real-time basis to generate the real-time monitoring file saved under the designated folder for real-time monitoring by the finance authority.

Automatic Generation of Various Payment Information

The "Bank-Finance Link" system automatically generates electronic return slip and all sorts of reports that are fed back to the finance authority through special line or other means and automatically print the reconciliation breakdown and monthly reconciliation sheet for the budgeting unit.

Service Channels

"Bank-Finance Link" system.

Application Condition

The budgeting units at each level that are included in the Treasury centralized payment reform and who holds approval by the finance authority permitting the unit to open zero-balance account and relevant materials stipulated in Administrative Methods on Bank Account are eligible for Authorized Payment services.

Service Procedure

(I) ICBC opens zero-balance account for the budgeting unit.

(II) The finance authority passes the electronic Detailed Finance Authorized Payment Limit Advice through special line or other means to ICBC's "Bank-Finance Link" system.

(III) "Bank-Finance Link" system automatically breaks down the authorized payment limit and the administering Business Offices enquires and prints Finance Authorized Payment Line Deposit Advice to be sent to the basic budgeting units.

(IV) The budgeting unit presents the payment application and the administering Business Office generates the authorized payment transaction through "Bank-Finance Link" system.

For over-the-limit payments, the system automatically stops payment and provide payment stop feedback to the budgeting unit. For payment within line, the system transfers the fund to the payee account on real-time basis.

(V) "Bank-Finance Link" system automatically generates the Finance Authorized Payment electronic return slip and daily, ten-day, and monthly report to be fed back to Ministry of Finance, the People's Bank of China, and the budgeting units; the system automatically generates monthly reconciliation sheet and detailed reconciliation sheet to be delivered to the budgeting units by administering Business Offices.

NON-TAX REVENUE COLLECTION

Definition

The Non-Tax Revenue Collection refers to service where ICBC opens non-tax revenue special account, fund collection, remittance and transfer clearing, and information feedback for the finance authorities, State authorities, public utilities, and non-government organizations at each level.

Product Target Client

The service is applicable for the collection and payment management for State authorities, public utilities, and non-government organizations at each level including: administrative fee collection, centralized receipts by supervisory department (incl. sector organizations with government function), and other non-tax revenues.

Features and Strengths

Large Business Network

ICBC has a large number and wide distribution of Business Offices. Its Business Office distribution pattern can match with the non-tax income-receiving units' characteristics of wide distribution, highly systematic organization, and wide dispersion of payers. It is capable to provide services for the payers and the receiving units all over China. All its Business Offices accept the finance non-tax fund collection requests and formed powerful network coverage advantage.

Advanced Business System

All transactions are centralized in one data center for processing. The fund is linked to accounting entries, which effectively prevents the criminal attempts by internal and external personnel taking advantage of time lag between fund activities and accounting entries. The leading "Bank-Finance Link" system in the sector synchronizes the fund flow and information flow. The transaction information is transmitted through encrypted mode. The system achieved the electronic State non-tax fund payment clearing, standardized information transmission, and informationalized reporting system management. The system makes ICBC at the leadership position in China in terms of agency State treasury non-tax revenue collection service.

Diversified Information Feedback Platform

In response to the special requirement by finance authority's non-tax revenue information feedback, ICBC launched automated processing for fund settlement, accounting, information transmission, and reporting. It realized real-time enquiry, collection and sorting, and summary and analysis of information and ensured timely, accurate, and secure feedbacks to the finance authorities, supervisory departments, and the receiving units at each level.

Furthermore, ICBC takes full advantage of its IT and electronic service and makes use of special-line networking, Internet Banking, and other channels to break through the limitation of Business Offices and the business hours. It provides a 24-7 electronic real-time enquiry system for the finance authorities, supervisory departments, and the receiving units at each level and provide multi-function, convenient and prompt, and safe and reliable electronic enquiry service.

Convenient Service Process

It adopts the leading and revolutionary technology in the sector that optimizes services procedure, shortens the hierarchy of accounting, realizes the flat management, and simplifies the system search and visit procedures to the maximum extent, thereby increasing the speed of service processing. The teller only needs to input the few key elements such as amount and receiving account number, the system can retrieve the corresponding voucher element resources pre-stored in the system for automated data processing, thereby minimizing the data entry volume.

Diversified Fee Payment Platform

ICBC takes the full advantage in Internet Banking to enable customers' fee payment services through Internet Banking. The administering personnel of the supervisory departments or receiving units and the payers may pay fees and enquire relevant information behind the doors. The payer may also enquire fee payment information at any time through Telephone Banking or cell phone SMS.

Service Channels

"Bank-Finance Link" system.

Application Condition

The finance authorities, supervision departments, and receiving units at each level who holds relevant materials stipulated in Administrative Methods on Bank Account are eligible for Non-tax Revenue Collection services.

Service Procedure

Account Opening

ICBC sets up finance special account for the finance authorities as per the finance authority's notice and relevant regulations. ICBC opens the finance remittance and payment special account at ICBC branch institutions for the receiving unit as per the stipulated procedures.

Payment

The payers or the receiving units make payment at ICBC Business office and presents General Non-Tax Revenue Payment Advice ("Payment Advice" hereinafter). ICBC's Business Offices that accept non-tax revenue payment include finance special account bank, finance payment special account bank, and the associate bank (all Business offices other than remittance and payment special account banks).

Fund Remittance and Transfer

ICBC Business Office double-checks the key elements in Payment Advice and input the relevant information into "Bank-Finance Link" system. The system automatically verifies the check code and transfers the non-tax revenue to the finance special account of finance remittance and payment special account on real-time basis through real-time clearing system. It then passes the key information in the Payment Advice to the special account bank on real-time basis through "Bank-Finance Link" system.

Fund Sweeping

By the close of each working day, each finance remittance and payment account sweep the fund deposited in the finance remittance and payment special account to the finance special account through real-time clearing system. It also passes the relevant non-tax revenue collection information to the finance special account bank through "Bank-Finance Link" system. The finance remittance and payment account balance is back to zero after sweeping.

Diversion to Treasury or Fund Allocation

ICBC finance special account bank diverts the fund in finance special account to the Treasury unified account or fund allocation as per instruction of the finance authority.

Feedback

Electronic Feedback: By the end of each day, ICBC "Bank-Finance Link" system pools the non-tax revenue collection information and sends feedback to the finance authority as per stipulated format through data transmission special line or other methods and deliver Non-Tax Revenue Reconciliation

Statement to the finance authority upon the next day. The "Bank-Finance Link" system's dynamic monitoring system can also provide the finance authority with ICBC's real-time monitoring and control service for all non-tax revenue collection accounts.

The finance authority can enquire the combination information for non-tax revenue collection details, total, and number of payments as per department, account, time period, and other criteria. Meanwhile, ICBC Internet Banking system provides feedback to the supervisory departments for the non-tax revenue collection of its subordinate receiving units and provides feedback to the receiving units for account information of finance remittance and payment special account.

Report Feedback: "Bank-Finance Link" system can automatically generate all sorts of income reports and accounting statements. ICBC finance special account banks double-check the fund data each day and present the finance special account fund collection, payment, balance daily reconciliation statement to the finance authority in the next day and reconcile the finance special account fund account with the finance authority by the next day following the close of the month.

Each account bank will print ICBC Ten-Day (Monthly) Statement of Agency Non-Tax Revenue Collection as per stipulated format to the finance authority, supervisory department, and receiving units within 2 days after each ten-day period of the month and within 4 days after each month and reconcile accounts with the finance authority, supervisory department, and receiving units within 4 days after each month

Revenue Refund

As per instruction from the finance authority, ICBC finance special account bank inputs the relevant revenue refund information in "Bank-Finance Link" and process the revenue refund through finance special account. ICBC transfers the fund into the payer's account bank and sends feedback to the finance authority through "Bank-Finance Link" system. The revenue refund is generally completed through account transfer, and there is no cash refund. For refund needing cash, ICBC processes the refund strictly as per relevant regulations by the finance authority.

More Money in Circulation Means more Trade

Many of the mercantilists, some of whom also used the arguments already discussed, wanted more money because they regarded money, not merely as a passive medium of exchange, but as a force acting through its circulation from hand to hand as an active stimulus to trade. An increased amount of money in circulation, they believed, meant (or caused) an increased volume of trade, and since men would produce only what they could sell a quickening of trade meant an increase of production and therefore a wealthier country. Here, it should be noted, money is valued as an instrument or stimulus of trade rather than for its own sake. The writers who stressed "circulation" as the valuable service of money often shifted, however, from the concept of money circulating as a medium of exchange to money passing from the hands of a lender to those of a borrower, and rarely distinguished clearly between them. The underlying reasoning is often presented in the form of analogies, especially with the circulation of the blood, which William Harvey had discovered not long before.

Stress on the importance of an abundance of money in circulation if trade was to flourish is already to be found in very early writers. The most elaborate expositions of the "circulation" argument were made by William Potter and John Law. Potter's argument seems to reduce to this: The wealth of a country is equal to the value of the goods of all sorts therein, money being valuable only as it serves to bring about the production of more goods. The more money men have, the more they spend and the faster they spend it. If men acquire more money and spend it as fast as they receive it, the sales of merchants and manufacturers will increase proportionately. If they sell five times as much in money value, they will produce five times as much, and even more, in physical quantities, since they can afford to charge lower prices on the greater volume of sales.

In reference to a commonwealth, or any society of men, the greater quantity there is amongst them, of money, credit, or that which is taken by them for commodities, the more commodity they sell, that is, the greater is their trade. For whatsoever is taken amongst men for commodity, though it were ten times more than now it is, yet if it be one way or other laid out by each man, as fast as he receives it, it must needs come to pass, that (resting nowhere) it doth occasion a quickness in the revolution of commodity from hand to hand, that is trade, proportionable to the greatness of its quantity.

John Law's argument is essentially the same, although stated more conservatively. The most enthusiastic advocates of the circulation argument, Potter and Law included, were advocates of paper money. But if paper money were accepted as of equal value to metallic money, the great reason for desiring a favorable balance of trade, that it results in an inflow of bullion, should lose its force. Such in fact was the case with some of them, as the following extracts show:

For whether a nation have any silver amongst them or no, yet if they can trade as well without it, what need they care? for their estates in vendible commodities (and consequently their credit) is of as real value as if it were in money.

Whatsoever quantity of credit shall be raised in this office, will be as good, and of as much use, as if there were so much money in specie added to the present stock of the nation...'tis more prudent and advantageous to a nation, to have the common standard or medium of their trade within their power, and to arise from their native product, than to be at the mercy of a foreign prince for his gold and silver, which he may at pleasure behold.... Credit can neither be hoarded up, nor transported to the nation's disadvantage; which consequently frees us from the care and necessity of making laws to prevent exportation of bullion or coin, being always able to command a credit of our own,...as useful, and as much as shall be necessary.

The only necessity of a foreign trade for England is because we make a foreign commodity (gold and silver) the standard of all ours, and the only medium of commerce, which (as long as it continues so) if we want, all trades must cease; but if we can find out another and safer medium of exchange (as this credit) appropriated to the place where we live and not subject to such obstruction as the other, why should we not readily embrace it?

And if the proprietors of the bank can circulate their funds of twelve hundred thousand pounds, without having more than two or three hundred thousand pounds lying dead at one time with another, this bank will be in effect, as nine hundred thousand pounds, or a million of fresh money, brought into the nation.

Whether in any one year half a million is brought into a commercial country by trade, or issued out by banks, in notes, upon good security, it will serve for the same purposes.

Some advocates of paper money made little or no reference to the balance of trade or to trade policy in their tracts. This freedom from the prevailing obsession with the state of the balance of trade may have been due to a loss of interest in a policy of securing laboriously through the complicated regulation of trade the increase of money which could be secured more quickly, with greater certainty, and with less effort, by means of the printing press. But some of the advocates of paper money displayed loyalty to the current belief in the importance of a favorable balance of trade, either because of blind acceptance of traditional doctrine, or on the basis of the store of wealth argument or the analogy from personal finance that one should buy less than one sells, and these writers claimed that an increase of paper money would not drive bullion out of the country, but on the contrary would make the balance of trade more favorable through its beneficial effect on production and trade.

2

Quantity Theory of Money

INTRODUCTION

Those mercantilists who sought an increase in the supply of money because they wanted more circulation or more invested capital clearly wanted genuine physical increases in trade or capital and not merely nominal increases in terms of a depreciated monetary unit. Their doctrines, therefore, would seem to come into sharp conflict with any theory of the value of money which makes it vary inversely with its quantity, whether proportionately or not. Only for those mercantilists who wanted an increase of money for use as hoards or stores of wealth would acceptance of a quantity theory of money involve no problem of reconciliation. Many of the mercantilist writers gave no evidence of recognition of the dependence of the value of money upon its quantity. A few of them, in fact, wanted more money as a cure for the evils resulting from high prices. But, although Locke is sometimes credited with the first clear English formulation of the quantity theory, many of the mercantilists, from the beginning of the seventeenth century on, did present, in one connection or another, some simple version of the quantity theory, although in most cases they failed to incorporate it as an integral part of their foreign-trade doctrine and failed also to show any concern about its consistency with the rest of their doctrine. There follow quotations from writings antedating Locke by some forty to ninety years which present some form of quantity theory of the value of money:

Plenty of money maketh generally things dear, and scarcity of money maketh likewise generally things good cheap. Whereas things particularly are also dear or good cheap according to plenty or scarcity of the things themselves, or the use of them.

Even as plenty of money maketh things dear, and scarcity of money maketh things good cheap: even so plenty or scarcity of commodities maketh the price thereof to rise and fall according to their use more or less.

It is a common saying, that plenty or scarcity of money makes all things dear or good or cheap.

Gold and silver...in the intrinsic...are commodities, valuing each other according to the plenty or scarcity; and so all other commodities by them; and that is the sole power of trade.

Money through want or plenty raises or diminishes the price of all things.

In those countries where monies are scarce, there the lands and native wares are cheap, so likewise where money doth abound, there the lands and wares are dear.

Several mercantilists faced squarely the apparent conflict between the quantity theory of money and their doctrines and attempted to meet the issue either by arguing that they could be reconciled or by denying the truth of the quantity theory. Apparently the first of these was William Potter, who has not received the attention which he deserves in this connection. Potter, as has been shown, claimed that an increase of money in circulation would result in an even more than proportionate increase in trade and production, or in goods in circulation. In order to refute it, he states a quantity theory of money in its simplest one-sided form:

If then, in opposition to what is thus undertaken to be proved, it should be objected, that an increase of money would occasion an increase in the price of commodities, proportionable to such increase of money, (that is, if the money were twice as much, commodity would be twice as dear) consequently (going never the further in commodity by the increase thereof) would not occasion any increase in the sale of commodity: therefore not any increase of trade; and yet (by causing the price of commodities to rise) incur an inconvenience, contrary to what is before affirmed.

His answer is elaborate and not always intelligible. He assumes the basis of the theory of money he is attacking to be that an increase of money increases prices by increasing the (physical) volume of sales (by increasing the demand for commodities). He replies that if, when money is doubled, the prices of commodities are also doubled, there will be no increase in the (physical) amount of sales.

The theory therefore involves a contradiction. He then attempts to meet it by another line of reasoning. Quick trade permits of a small profit, and therefore a lower price. Quick sales enable artisans and others to produce more quickly, and if they sell more they can afford to charge a lower price. The increase in the amount of commodities resulting from the stimulus to trade of an increase in money, instead of raising prices, will therefore lower them. Prices will rise only if the increase in commodities is proportionately less than the increase in money, which is not likely to be the case. But even if prices should rise somewhat, it is better to have an abundance of comforts, though dear, than a smaller amount thereof, though never so cheap.

Another advocate of paper money, John Asgill, denied the truth of the quantity theory of money on different and exceedingly slender grounds: an increase in money would lower the rate of interest and therefore raise land values, but not the prices of commodities in general, because "the price of corn and cattle don't rise and fall with the interest of money." John Law attacked it, partly by arguments closely resembling those of Potter, partly on reasoning peculiarly his own. The stimulus to trade and industry resulting from an increase in money would result in an increase in commodities. Because money would be easier to borrow, merchants would be able to increase the extent of their operations and to sell at lower rates of profit, and therefore the value of the money would not fall, *i.e.*, prices would not rise. Money falls in value only when given to a people in greater quantity than there is demand for; if the money is issued only as there is demand for it, its value will not depreciate, "the quantity and demand increasing and decreasing together. Law concedes that if the quantity of money in any particular country "should increase beyond the proportion that country bears to Europe," prices would rise there, but the rise of prices would spread elsewhere, so that the value of money would become the same, or about the same, everywhere. The country which had acquired the increase of money would profit greatly thereby, "for that country would have the whole benefit of the greater quantity, and only bear a share of the lesser value, according to the proportion its money had to the money of Europe. What would make the prices rise elsewhere, he does not explain.

Another writer, James Hodges, who complained of scarcity of money, wanted plate called in and coined and the monetary value of the English standard coin raised as a remedy for this scarcity. He claimed that these measures would result in higher prices only after they resulted in an increase in the number of coins in circulation. The effect on prices would therefore be gradual, and meanwhile there would be a stimulus to trade. After a short time the value of the coin could be gradually lowered, and the surplus bullion returned to be made into plate again if its owners so desired. His argument is interesting as an anticipation of Hume's doctrine that rising prices are a stimulus to trade, and for its endeavor to find a method of obtaining this stimulus without involving a permanent increase in the price level. The difficulty with the scheme, granting its logic, is, of course, that the period of stimulus would be followed by a period of at least corresponding depression.

Both Potter and Law claimed that an increase of (paper) money would make the balance of trade more favorable and would lead to an inflow of bullion. Potter argued that the beneficial effects of an increased quantity of money would enable England to outsell other countries, for "the greater trade of one country hath a capacity of undermining and eating out the lesser trade of other countries. For reasons not explained, unless it be the fall in English prices alleged to result from an increase in the quantity of money, both foreign and English commodities would fall in price in England, but not abroad. Exports would therefore be paid for with bullion (and presumably imports would be paid for with English commodity exports), and the bullion could be coined into English money without loss. But with unusual consistency Potter admits that when paper money or credit is available as a substitute, metallic money would be of little importance to England. Law showed more concern than did Potter about the state of the balance of trade, but he also claimed that an increased amount of money through the issue of paper money would make the balance favorable: "Most people think scarcity of money is only the consequence of a balance due; but 'tis the cause as well as the consequence, and the effectual way to bring the balance to our side, is to add to the money." More money, by employing more people, would make a surplus of goods available for export, and if sufficient money was issued production would reach a level at which more would be exported than imported. Conversely, if the amount of money was reduced, some of the laborers would be rendered idle, the domestic output would shrink, exports would fall, and an unfavorable balance would result. These results of a change in the quantity of money he would apparently expect not to be transitory but to persist as long as the new quantity of money persisted.

The Mercantilists on Hoards and Plate

Because the mercantilists differed among themselves as to the character of the benefit which resulted from an increase in the amount of bullion in a country, they also differed in their attitudes toward the miser, the collector of gold or silver plate, the usurer, and the spendthrift. Those mercantilists for whom the chief virtue in an increased supply of bullion lay in its stimulus to circulation condemned private hoards as an evil, and also regarded other practices which kept bullion from circulating as money, such as its use in the manufacture of plate, as objectionable. Vaughan condemned hoarding and the use of plate as contributing factors to the scarcity of money, and recommended sumptuary legislation to check the melting of money and its manufacture into plate. An anonymous writer criticized the Established church on the ground that it hoarded riches which should circulate, so that "the money that before ran current in trading, is dammed up in their coffers."

Another pamphlet, written as an answer to this one, condemned the excess of silver plate for the same reason, but claimed that there was no occasion for alarm about hoarding, as there was not much of it, and urged in the defense of the church that it could be charged with responsibility for the prevailing scarcity of money only if the clerics kept "banks of money dead by them, which was not the case. Complaint against the usurer as a hoarder of money was likewise without basis, since "his money walks, though upon other legs, either serving the tradesman or the gentleman, for preparing commodities to export, or to buy what is imported for his expenses.

Manley found fault with the miser, because "money locked up in the miser's coffers is like dung in a heap, it does no good, but being dispersed, and orderly disposed abroad, enricheth the land." An anonymous writer wanted misers' hoards taxed, in order to draw some of their money into circulation, especially in time of war when trade was slack. "I know no difference," he wrote, "betwixt bringing treasure out of an iron chest by a good law, and plowing the seas by long and dangerous voyages" in order to secure bullion through foreign trade.

One of Locke's objections to the reduction of the interest rate by law was that it would result in men keeping their money "dead" by them, instead of lending it, with resultant loss to trade. Petty expressed a preference for money over plate, because it served trade better, as did also Hugh Chamberlain: "Money is living riches, plate but dead; that being capable of turning and improving trade, when this is not."

Hodges's scheme for a forced three-year surrender of plate in return for "raised" money, with prohibition of ownership of plate in the interval, in order for a time to secure relief from the prevailing scarcity of money, and to obtain the stimulus to trade of slowly rising prices, has already been referred to. Another writer urged a similar scheme for raising money 5 per cent, in order to draw hoards of the old, and therefore undervalued, coins into circulation.

One writer made the same sort of contrast between hoarded and circulating money, hoarded credit being the exchequer bills which, because of the high rate of interest they carried, were held instead of being used as money: "...in the frequent passing of credit from hand to hand, consists its great usefulness in trade; for when either money or credit is hoarded up, it may more properly be said to stagnate, than to circulate." Postlethwayt, in a curious argument, claimed that lending of money at interest involved hoarding and therefore on circulation grounds was to be condemned.

If some money is hoarded, the volume of trade will fall. In order to bring the hoarded money back into trade, those in great need of it will offer interest ("profit") for its loan. The result will be that other moneyed men, instead of "circulating their money" in trade, will "lock it up," while awaiting the opportunity to lend it, preferring to get their income by usury instead of by trade. Eventually the money so withdrawn from trade would be lent and would thus return to trade, but bearing an interest charge which would act as a restraint on trade.

Some writers objected, on similar grounds, to the establishment of banks, holding that they monopolized money, and kept it from circulating. Child, for example, maintained that "principally this seeming scarcity of money proceeds from the trade of bankering, which obstructs circulation." Strangely enough, considering his views on the effect of lending at interest on monetary circulation, Postlethwayt made the most effective rejoinder to this argument which I have found:

It may be here requisite to take notice of that erroneous notion entertained by some, that banks and bankers engross the money, hoard it up, and hinder its circulation in trade; but, if such will consider this matter in its true light, they will easily be convinced, that the money lodged in banks, and in the hands of bankers, is the most constantly employed of any; for, though the specie should lie still till called for, yet the notes given out for its value, are continually circulating; whereby is done abundantly more service to trade, than if the same lay dormant in private hands; and yet the necessities of the depositors are effectually answered.

Once hoarding and the use of coin or bullion in the making of plate were attacked, there were few to come to their defense, and the use of gold and silver in the making of thread or in gilding met with almost general condemnation. Mun, however, opposed restrictions on the melting-down of coin into plate on the ground that gold and silver were more apt to be carried out of the kingdom in payment of purchases of foreign goods if in the form of coin than if kept in the form of plate, and Misselden before him, while conceding that too much plate in the kingdom would cause scarcity of money, nevertheless held that it was better to have bullion kept in the form of plate than to turn it into coin and thus turn it out of the kingdom because of the undervaluation of coin which he alleged then prevailed in England.

A sixteenth-century writer condoned the use of bullion for plate, because it resulted in the formation of a sort of secondary national reserve for emergencies, upon which the king, in case of a great war, could draw "without any grouching of the Commons." The same argument is to be found occasionally in the later literature, and is made by Briscoe to serve as a defense of private hoards. Hoarded treasure, bullion and coin, is part of the "capital stock of national treasure" and can be drawn upon in a national emergency. Private hoarding is as good as having treasure stored by the king. Toward the end of the seventeenth century there appeared a new doctrine of the existence of a "due proportion" between money and goods, and therefore of the possibility of excess of money as far as trade needs were concerned.

The quantity theory of money also tended to lead to the conclusion that an increase in the amount of money by increasing prices would reduce exports and thus eventually be lost to the country. Writers who on "due proportions of money to trade" or on quantity-theory grounds conceded that there was under any given set of circumstances a maximum amount of money which could be kept in circulation, and who still attached special importance to the precious metals, were likely to approve of turning the money into plate or of its hoarding as a means either of stimulating the further import of bullion or of, checking an outflow. It was doubtless such reasoning which led John Houghton to the conclusion that "if the King should hoard up much money, it would for the present make it dearer, that dearness would make it be brought in more plentifully, and that would make it more plentiful than it was before." Petty wrote: "For there may be as well too much money in a country, as too little. I mean, as to the best advantage of its trade; only the remedy is very easy, it may be soon turned into the magnificence of gold and silver vessels."

On similar grounds another writer would tolerate the increased use of plate if there was more money than was necessary to carry on trade and "defray the expense of living," and Vanderlint, who accepted the quantity theory and wanted low prices but at the same time wanted a favorable balance of trade payable in specie, recommended as a means of attaining these apparently conflicting objectives that the private hoarding of gold and silver and their use in plate, and even in gold and silver cloth and gilding, be encouraged. He cited with approval the practice of the East Indians of hoarding the silver they receive, with the result that prices remained low there, exports continued to exceed imports, and the balance was paid in still more silver. Harris presents a similar solution of the same dilemma. If the inflow of bullion resulting from a favorable balance of trade is kept:

> *as a dead stock, either by turning it into plate or by any other method, so as to prevent its getting into trade as money; it may continue to go on increasing in more bullion, which in this case will be a real increase of wealth.... Let an increased stock of bullion get out again into trade, and it will soon turn the balance the other way.*

But gold and silver can be best stored up in the form of plate:

But people in general will not hoard up cash; all like to display their wealth, and to lay out their superfluities in some costly things. There seems then no method so effectual for the securing of a dead stock of treasure in any country, as the encouraging the use of plate, by making it fashionable, preferable to more brittle or more perishable commodities. Plate would be a national resource in case of emergency, and not the less so, because the precious metals had not as yet received the shape of coins.

Hume in 1752 claimed that state hoarding was the only expedient by which a country could raise its supply of the precious metals above the equilibrium level, but commented that this was "a practice which we should all exclaim against as destructive, namely, the gathering of large sums into a public treasure, locking them up, and absolutely preventing their circulation."

Henry Home accepted so whole-heartedly the lesson of the quantity theory of money that he looked upon an export surplus alike with an import surplus as dangerous to the country. The latter meant an outward drain of money, with a consequent fall of prices and stoppage of industry. The former meant an influx of specie, extravagance, rise in prices, and finally a fall in exports, rise in imports, an unfavorable balance again, and a recurrence of the drain of specie. What was to be desired was an even balance. Therefore, "let the registers of foreign mints be carefully watched, in order that our current coin may not exceed that of our industrious neighbors." But it was not the quantity of gold and silver in a country that determined the price level, but the quantity of money in circulation. Still retaining some traces of the mercantilist attachment for the precious metals, he therefore advocated the conversion of money into plate and even, under favorable circumstances, the formation of a state treasure.

3

History of Global Banking

INTRODUCTION

Many of today's banking services were first practiced in ancient Lydia, Phoenicia, China, and Greece, where trade and commerce flourished. The temples in Babylonia made loans from their treasuries as early as 2000 BC. The temples of ancient Greece served as safe-deposit vaults for the valuables of worshipers. The Greeks also coined money and developed a system of credit. The Roman Empire had a highly developed banking system, and its bankers accepted deposits of money, made loans, and purchased mortgages. Shortly after the fall of Rome in AD 476, banking declined in Europe.

The increase of trade in 13th-century Italy prompted the revival of banking. The money-changers of the Italian states developed facilities for exchanging local and foreign currency. Soon merchants demanded other services, such as lending money, and gradually bank services were expanded.

The first bank to offer most of the basic banking functions known today was the Bank of Barcelona in Spain. Founded by merchants in 1401, this bank held deposits, exchanged currency, and carried out lending operations. It also is believed to have introduced the bank check. Three other early banks, each managed by a committee of city officials, were the Bank of Amsterdam (1609), the Bank of Venice (1587), and the Bank of Hamburg (1619). These institutions laid the foundation for modern banks of deposit and transaction.

For more than 300 years, banking on the European continent was in the hands of powerful statesmen and wealthy private bankers, such as the Medici family in Florence and the Fuggers in Germany. During the 19th century, members of the Rothschild family became the most influential bankers in all Europe and probably in the world. This international banking family was founded by German financier Mayer Amschel Rothschild (1743-1812), but it soon spread to all the major European financial capitals.

The Bank of France was organized in 1800 by Napoleon. The bank had become the dominant financial institution in France by the mid-1800s. In Germany, banking experienced a rapid development about the middle of the 19th century with the establishment of several strong stock-issuing, or publicly owned, banks.

Banking in the British Isles originated with the London goldsmiths of the 16th century. These men made loans and held valuables for safekeeping. By the 17th century English goldsmiths created the model for today's modern fractional reserve banking-that is, the practice of keeping a fraction of depositors' money in reserve while extending the remainder to borrowers in the form of loans. Customers deposited gold and silver with the goldsmiths for safekeeping and were given deposit receipts verifying their ownership of the gold deposited with the goldsmith. These receipts could be used as money because they were backed by gold. But the goldsmiths soon discovered that they could take a chance and issue additional receipts against the gold to other people who needed to borrow money. This worked as long as the original depositors did not withdraw all their gold at one time. Hence, the amount of receipts or claims on the gold frequently exceeded the actual amount of the gold, and the idea that bankers could create money was born.

Bank of North America

The first important bank in the United States was the Bank of North America, established in 1781 by the Second Continental Congress. It was the first bank chartered by the U.S. government. Other banks existed in the colonies prior to this, most notably the Bank of Pennsylvania, but these banks were chartered by individual states. In 1787 the Bank of North America changed to a Pennsylvania charter following controversy about the legality of a congressional charter. Other large banks were chartered in the early 1780s by the various states, primarily to issue paper money called bank notes. These notes supplemented the coins then in circulation and assisted greatly in business expansion. The banks were also permitted to accept deposits and to make loans.

Because there were no minimum reserve requirements on deposits, bank notes were secured by the assets of the issuing banks. Most assets took the form of business loans. The only restraint on a bank's ability to extend loans was the public's unwillingness to accept its notes. Acceptance of a bank's notes usually was determined by the bank's record in exchanging the notes for coins when called upon to do so. Since most of them were able to do this, the early banks enjoyed wide latitude in granting loans.

In 1791 the federal government chartered the Bank of the United States, commonly referred to as the "First" Bank of the United States, to serve both the government and the public. One-fifth of the bank's capital was supplied by the federal government. The bank was a repository of government funds and a source of loans for individuals and the federal and state governments. The charter of the "First" Bank of the United States was allowed to lapse in 1811, in part because half of its stock was owned by foreigners but also because of opposition to the bank by more than 80 state-chartered banks. The main reason for the conflict between state banks and the "First" Bank of the United States was that the public preferred the notes of the Bank of the United States because of the bank's excellent reputation. This made it difficult for state banks to attract customers.

Second Bank of the United States

During the War of 1812, hard currency (coins) became scarce and many state banks stopped redeeming their notes for coins. This brought into question the underlying value of bank notes and limited their use as money. At the same time, however, banks began increasing the amount of notes they issued. This rapid increase in paper money caused prices to rise and created inflation. These developments created a demand for establishing the "Second" Bank of the United States, which was chartered in 1816. The bank had a stormy career. Many local bankers who had to compete with this government-sponsored bank opposed it, as did President Andrew Jackson. As a result of Jackson's opposition, the federal government withdrew its deposits in 1833, and three years later, when the bank's charter was not renewed, it went out of existence.

FREE BANKING AND THE SAFETY FUND SYSTEM

In 1838 New York State passed a free banking law. Before this date all incorporated banks had been chartered by states and had been granted the note-issuing privilege. Under free banking, charters could be obtained without a special act of the state legislature. The main requirement for new banks was that they post collateral of government bonds equal in value to the notes to be issued. In principle, noteholders were protected because, if the bank failed, proceeds from the sale of the collateral would be used to reimburse them. Free banking was soon adopted by other states. Because there was little regulation of new banks, many banks failed and bank fraud occurred. The free-banking years of 1837 to 1863 are also known as the Wildcat Banking era.

In New England, however, the Suffolk Bank in Boston, Massachusetts, had redeemed bank notes of out-of-town banks only if they kept on deposit amounts large enough to cover the redemptions. Since Boston was a trade center, the pressure was great on all New England banks to accept this system, known as the Suffolk banking system. Practically all New England banks had joined the system by 1825.

In the early 1800's New York State also developed the safety fund system, under which each member bank contributed a small percentage of its capital annually to a state-managed fund. The purpose of the fund was to protect noteholders in the event of bank failure. In 1842 Louisiana enacted legislation to limit the number of banks and to require them to maintain one-third of their assets in cash and two-thirds in short-term obligations.

THE NATIONAL BANKING ACT OF 1863

The Civil War (1861-1865) brought about the National Banking Act of 1863, and with it a fundamental change in the structure of commercial banking in the United States. Originally named the National Currency Act, but later amended and renamed, the National Banking Act created the system known as dual banking, in which banks could have either a state or federal charter.

This system still exists in the United States. The act established the Office of the Comptroller of the Currency in the Department of the Treasury and gave it the power to issue national bank charters to any bank that met minimum requirements. The philosophy of relatively "free banking" continued until 1935 when Congress made it more difficult to obtain a bank charter. The 1863 act allowed nationally chartered banks to issue a uniform bank note backed by U.S. government bonds. The amount of the notes was not to exceed 90 percent of the value of the bonds. Officials hoped that the issuance of uniform bank notes backed by the U.S. government would guarantee the value of bank notes and thereby produce a useful nationwide currency, while also inducing state banks to take out national charters.

However, because the regulations accompanying a national charter were much stricter than state charters, a movement toward federal charters did not happen as planned. In 1865 the U.S. Congress enacted a 10 percent tax on any bank or individual paying out or using state bank notes. As a result of the tax, many banks converted to national charters, but many others simply stopped issuing their own notes. Instead, these state banks began to issue their customers demand deposit money-that is, checking accounts, instead of bank notes.

By the 1870's, deposits were well established as a substitute for paper or coin currency, and state banks experienced a revival. State charters contained several advantages over federal charters. State-chartered banks were allowed to hold lower cash reserves relative to deposits, and less capital. State-chartered banks had more flexible branching opportunities and fewer restrictions on the types of loans that could be made.

The National Banking Act was successful in correcting some failings of the pre-Civil War commercial banking system. It produced a unified national paper currency consisting primarily of national bank notes. Bank crises, however, did not disappear. Panics occurred in 1873, 1884, 1893, and 1907, although the causes of these crises varied. Between 1873 and 1907, demand deposits far outweighed bank note circulation. At times some banks were unable to make immediate payment of demands on these deposits. Consequently these banks failed, and their depositors suffered losses of all or part of the money in their accounts.

FEDERAL RESERVE ACT OF 1913

The financial panic of 1907 resulted in the Federal Reserve Act of 1913. This act went further than any earlier legislation in recognizing the importance of stable money and credit conditions to the health of the national economy. Under the Federal Reserve Act, a central bank was reestablished for the United States, the first since the "Second" Bank of the United States. The new bank was charged with maintaining sound credit conditions. To achieve this goal, the Federal Reserve System was given control over the minimum amount of reserves that member banks must hold for each dollar of deposits. It also obtained the power to lend money to member banks and regulate the types of assets they can hold. Members of the Federal Reserve System include national banks, whose membership is required, and state banks, whose membership is optional. Membership requires a bank to buy stock in the Federal Reserve System. Most large banks under state charter have joined the system. World War I (1914-1918) brought about inflation and a sharp postwar recession (economic slowdown). Although the banks had bought large quantities of U.S. government bonds during the war, they also lent large amounts of money to individuals engaged in stock market speculation. By investing in bonds, banks helped finance government expenditures during the war and the attendant expansion of American productive resources in the decade following World War I. By lending money to speculators, they became a major factor in the climb of stock prices and the wave of speculation that resulted in the crash of 1929.

BANKING DURING THE GREAT DEPRESSION

The Great Depression of the 1930s dealt a severe blow to the commercial banking industry. Many banks failed (went out of business) when their loans could not be repaid. The number of commercial banks declined from 26,000 in 1928 to about 14,000 in 1933. Total deposits in these banks declined by about 35 percent. Depositors rushed to retrieve their money, a process known as a run on the banks, and the federal government was forced to close all the banks for four days in 1933 to stem the panic. It became apparent to observers that the Federal Reserve System had not solved all the problems of bank stability.

Consequently, during the Great Depression, Congress recognized the importance of a sound banking system and created a number of agencies to restore public confidence in the banking system. Among the first of these was the Federal Housing Administration, which was created in 1934 to insure payment on home loans made by private lending institutions. The guarantee helped preserve the value of bank loans and enabled banks to continue to lend money to home-buyers.

The Banking Act of 1933, also known as the Glass-Steagall Act, created the Federal Deposit Insurance Corporation (FDIC) to insure bank deposits, increase the confidence of depositors, and therefore prevent bank runs. Federal Reserve member banks were required to join the FDIC. Membership was optional for other banks. The Glass-Steagall Act also set interest rate ceilings on deposits to reduce competition among banks, which was considered a cause of bank failures during the Great Depression. It also prevented banks from becoming too involved in investment-banking activities, such as underwriting stocks or bonds for companies. Underwriting, which typically involves selling stocks or bonds at a guaranteed price, can be risky and can cause banks to fail. The act also prevented banks from buying stock, which is a risky activity if the stock market crashes. This prohibition on investment-banking activities lasted until the 1980s.

The banking system began to recover in 1934. By 1937 deposits had reached pre-Depression levels. During World War II (1939-1945), deposits increased rapidly and more than doubled from 1941 to 1946. For the next 40 years the U.S. banking system went through a continuous expansion and modernization. In particular, there was an enormous increase in lending to consumers, through installment loans (loans for a fixed amount repaid in equal monthly payments) and credit card loans (loans for a varied amount repaid more flexibly).

BANKING AFTER WORLD WAR II

Some of the legislation enacted during the Great Depression and in the immediate postwar period began to have negative repercussions on the banking industry by the 1970s, according to some experts. Interest ceilings on deposits, which were required by the Glass-Steagall Act, prevented banks from competing with unregulated money market funds or even bonds issued by the U.S. Treasury. As people withdrew deposits to earn higher interest elsewhere (a process known as disintermediation), SLAs found it increasingly difficult to raise funds to make mortgage loans. Many SLAs went out of business. Disintermediation was not the only problem SLAs faced, however. Many SLAs decided to venture into business lending in the early 1980s with drastic consequences as commercial real estate markets collapsed. Many business loans went bad and forced even more SLAs out of business. In 1980, 3,998 SLAs existed in the United States. By 1992 the number had dwindled to only 2,039. There were 672 SLA failures from 1989 to 1992 alone and over 1,200 overall. The SLA crisis ultimately led to the collapse of the Federal Savings and Loan Insurance Corporation. It necessitated a restructuring of deposit insurance in the United States and a government bailout of the SLA industry that cost taxpayers an estimated $200 billion.

Restrictions on how banks could expand geographically also affected the industry. The Bank Holding Company Act of 1956 prohibited bank holding companies from acquiring banks across state lines. As a result of geographic limitations on expansions, banks were forced to operate primarily in local markets, which made banks particularly susceptible to local economic downturns. This act also restricted the activities of bank holding companies, limiting them to only those activities that were closely related to banking.

Legislation enacted in the 1980s and 1990s began to address these issues. The Depository Deregulation and Monetary Control Act of 1980 eliminated ceilings on interest rates. The 1994 Riegle-Neal Interstate Banking and Branching Efficiency Act legalized interstate banking, allowing banks to diversify geographically.

The most sweeping legislation, however, took place in 1999 when Congress removed most of the remaining provisions of the Glass-Steagall Act and replaced it with the Gramm-Leach-Bliley Act, named after Republican Party sponsors Phil Gramm, Jim Leach, and Thomas Bliley, Jr. The act also removed some of the restrictions of the Bank Holding Company Act of 1956 by permitting bank holding companies to engage in the full range of financial services, including lending, deposit taking, investment advising, insurance, stock and bond underwriting, and other investment banking services. The act did not, however, allow bank holding companies to own nonfinancial businesses. Many observers believe that the new law will increase the dominance of bank holding companies and lead to the establishment of so-called universal banks that offer a full array of financial services, including traditional banking services, insurance, investment advice, and stock and bond brokerage services. Critics of the law, however, caution that the new law, combined with the provisions of the 1994 act that ended restrictions on branching and allowed nationwide banking, may ultimately diminish competition for financial services in the United States.

E-BANKING: INTRODUCTION

This booklet, one of several comprising the FFIEC Information Technology Examination Handbook (IT Handbook), provides guidance to examiners and financial institutions on identifying and controlling the risks associated with electronic banking (e-banking) activities. The booklet primarily discusses e-banking risks from the perspective of the services or products provided to customers. This approach differs from other booklets that discuss risks from the perspective of the technology and systems that support automated information processing. To avoid duplication of material, this booklet refers the reader to other IT Handbook booklets for detailed explanations of technology-specific issues or controls.

Examiners may use the examination procedures and request letter items included in this booklet in appendix A to review risks in the electronic delivery of financial products and services. These procedures address services and products of varied complexity. Examiners should adjust the procedures, as appropriate, for the scope of the examination and the risk profile of the institution. The procedures may be used independently or in combination with procedures from other IT Handbook booklets or from agency handbooks covering non-IT areas.

Definition of e-banking

For this booklet, e-banking is defined as the automated delivery of new and traditional banking products and services directly to customers through electronic, interactive communication channels. E-banking includes the systems that enable financial institution customers, individuals or businesses, to access accounts, transact business, or obtain information on financial products and services through a public or private network, including the Internet. Customers access e-banking services using an intelligent electronic device, such as a personal computer (PC), personal digital assistant (PDA), automated teller machine (ATM), kiosk, or Touch Tone telephone. While the risks and controls are similar for the various e-banking access channels, this booklet focuses specifically on Internet-based services due to the Internet's widely accessible public network. Accordingly, this booklet begins with a discussion of the two primary types of Internet websites: informational and transactional.

Informational Websites

Informational websites provide customers access to general information about the financial institution and its products or services. Risk issues examiners should consider when reviewing informational websites include:

Potential liability and consumer violations for inaccurate or incomplete information about products, services, and pricing presented on the website;

Potential access to confidential financial institution or customer information if the website is not properly isolated from the financial institution's internal network;

Potential liability for spreading viruses and other malicious code to computers communicating with the institution's website; and

Negative public perception if the institution's on-line services are disrupted or if its website is defaced or otherwise presents inappropriate or offensive material.

Transactional Websites

Transactional websites provide customers with the ability to conduct transactions through the financial institution's website by initiating banking transactions or buying products and services. Banking transactions can range from something as basic as a retail account balance inquiry to a large business-to-business funds transfer. E-banking services, like those delivered through other delivery channels, are typically classified based on the type of customer they support. The following table lists some of the common retail and wholesale e-banking services offered by financial institutions.

Table 1: Common E-Banking Services

Retail Services	Wholesale Services
Account management	Account management
Bill payment and presentment	Cash management
New account opening	Small business loan applications, approvals, or advances
Consumer wire transfers	
Investment/Brokerage services	Commercial wire transfers
Loan application and approval	Business-to-business payments
Account aggregation	Employee benefits/pension administration

Since transactional websites typically enable the electronic exchange of confidential customer information and the transfer of funds, services provided through these websites expose a financial institution to higher risk than basic informational websites. Wholesale e-banking systems typically expose financial institutions to the highest risk per transaction, since commercial transactions usually involve larger dollar amounts. In addition to the risk issues associated with informational websites, examiners reviewing transactional e-banking services should consider the following issues:

Security controls for safeguarding customer information;

Authentication processes necessary to initially verify the identity of new customers and authenticate existing customers who access e-banking services;

Liability for unauthorized transactions;

Losses from fraud if the institution fails to verify the identity of individuals or businesses applying for new accounts or credit on-line;

Possible violations of laws or regulations pertaining to consumer privacy, anti-money laundering, anti-terrorism, or the content, timing, or delivery of required consumer disclosures; and

Negative public perception, customer dissatisfaction, and potential liability resulting from failure to process third-party payments as directed or within specified time frames, lack of availability of on-line services, or unauthorized access to confidential customer information during transmission or storage.

E-banking Components

E-banking systems can vary significantly in their configuration depending on a number of factors. Financial institutions should choose their e-banking system configuration, including outsourcing relationships, based on four factors:

Strategic objectives for e-banking;

Scope, scale, and complexity of equipment, systems, and activities;

Technology expertise; and

Security and internal control requirements.

Financial institutions may choose to support their e-banking services internally. Alternatively, financial institutions can outsource any aspect of their e-banking systems to third parties. The following entities could provide or host (i.e., allow applications to reside on their servers) e-banking-related services for financial institutions:

Another financial institution,

Internet service provider,

Internet banking software vendor or processor,

Core banking vendor or processor,

Managed security service provider,

Bill payment provider,

Credit bureau, and

Credit scoring company.

E-banking systems rely on a number of common components or processes. The following list includes many of the potential components and processes seen in a typical institution:

Website design and hosting,

Firewall configuration and management,

Intrusion detection system or IDS (network and host-based),

Network administration,

Security management,

Internet banking server,

E-commerce applications (e.g., bill payment, lending, brokerage),

Internal network servers,

Core processing system,

Programming support, and

Automated decision support systems.

These components work together to deliver e-banking services. Each component represents a control point to consider.

Through a combination of internal and outsourced solutions, management has many alternatives when determining the overall system configuration for the various components of an e-banking system. However, for the sake of simplicity, this booklet presents only two basic variations. First, one or more technology service providers can host the e-banking application and numerous network components as illustrated in the following diagram.

In this configuration, the institution's service provider hosts the institution's website, Internet banking server, firewall, and intrusion detection system. While the institution does not have to manage the daily administration of these component systems, its management and board remain responsible for the content, performance, and security of the e-banking system.

Second, the institution can host all or a large portion of its e-banking systems internally. A typical configuration for in-house hosted, e-banking services is illustrated below. In this case, a provider is not between the Internet access and the financial institution's core processing system. Thus, the institution has day-to-day responsibility for system administration.

E-banking Support Services

In addition to traditional banking products and services, financial institutions can provide a variety of services that have been designed or adapted to support e-commerce. Management should understand these services and the risks they pose to the institution. This section discusses some of the most common support services: weblinking, account aggregation, electronic authentication, website hosting, payments for e-commerce, and wireless banking activities.

Weblinking

A large number of financial institutions maintain sites on the World Wide Web. Some websites are strictly informational, while others also offer customers the ability to perform financial transactions, such as paying bills or transferring funds between accounts.

Virtually every website contains "weblinks." A weblink is a word, phrase, or image on a webpage that contains coding that will transport the viewer to a different part of the website or a completely different website by just clicking the mouse. While weblinks are a convenient and accepted tool in website design, their use can present certain risks. Generally, the primary risk posed by weblinking is that viewers can become confused about whose website they are viewing and who is responsible for the information, products, and services available through that website. There are a variety of risk management techniques institutions should consider using to mitigate these risks. These risk management techniques are for those institutions that develop and maintain their own websites, as well as institutions that use third-party service providers for this function. The agencies have issued guidance on weblinking that provides details on risks and risk management techniques financial institutions should consider.

Account Aggregation

Account aggregation is a service that gathers information from many websites, presents that information to the customer in a consolidated format, and, in some cases, may allow the customer to initiate activity on the aggregated accounts. The information gathered or aggregated can range from publicly available information to personal account information (e.g., credit card, brokerage, and banking data). Aggregation services can improve customer convenience by avoiding multiple log-ins and providing access to tools that help customers analyze and manage their various account portfolios. Some aggregators use the customer-provided user IDs and passwords to sign in as the customer. Once the customer's account is accessed, the aggregator copies the personal account information from the website for representation on the aggregator's site (i.e., "screen scraping"). Other aggregators use direct data-feed arrangements with website operators or other firms to obtain the customer's information. Generally, direct data feeds are thought to provide greater legal protection to the aggregator than does screen scraping.

Financial institutions are involved in account aggregation both as aggregators and as aggregation targets. Risk management issues examiners should consider when reviewing aggregation services include:

Protection of customer passwords and user IDs-both those used to access the institution's aggregation services and those the aggregator uses to retrieve customer information from aggregated third parties-to assure the confidentiality of customer information and to prevent unauthorized activity,

Disclosure of potential customer liability if customers share their authentication information (i.e., IDs and passwords) with third parties, and

Assurance of the accuracy and completeness of information retrieved from the aggregated parties' sites, including required disclosures

Additional information regarding management of risks in aggregation services can be found in appendix D.

Electronic Authentication

Verifying the identities of customers and authorizing e-banking activities are integral parts of e-banking financial services. Since traditional paper-based and in-person identity authentication methods reduce the speed and efficiency of electronic transactions, financial institutions have adopted alternative authentication methods, including:

Passwords and personal identification numbers (PINs),

Digital certificates using a public key infrastructure (PKI),

Microchip-based devices such as smart cards or other types of tokens,

Database comparisons (e.g., fraud-screening applications), and

Biometric identifiers.

The authentication methods listed above vary in the level of security and reliability they provide and in the cost and complexity of their underlying infrastructures. As such, the choice of which technique(s) to use should be commensurate with the risks in the products and services for which they control access. Additional information on customer authentication techniques can be found in this booklet under the heading "Authenticating E-Banking Customers."

The Electronic Signatures in Global and National Commerce (E-Sign) Act establishes some uniform federal rules concerning the legal status of electronic signatures and records in commercial and consumer transactions so as to provide more legal certainty and promote the growth of electronic commerce. The development of secure digital signatures continues to evolve with some financial institutions either acting as the certification authority for digital signatures or providing repository services for digital certificates.

Website Hosting

Some financial institutions host websites for both themselves as well as for other businesses. Financial institutions that host a business customer's website usually store, or arrange for the storage of, the electronic files that make up the website. These files are stored on one or more servers that may be located on the hosting financial institution's premises. Website hosting services require strong skills in networking, security, and programming. The technology and software change rapidly. Institutions developing websites should monitor the need to adopt new interoperability standards and protocols such as Extensible Mark-Up Language (XML) to facilitate data exchange among the diverse population of Internet users.

Risk issues examiners should consider when reviewing website hosting services include damage to reputation, loss of customers, or potential liability resulting from:

Downtime (i.e., times when website is not available) or inability to meet service levels specified in the contract,

Inaccurate website content (e.g., products, pricing) resulting from actions of the institution's staff or unauthorized changes by third parties (e.g., hackers),

Unauthorized disclosure of confidential information stemming from security breaches, and

Damage to computer systems of website visitors due to malicious code (e.g., virus, worm, active content) spread through institution-hosted sites.

Payments for E-commerce

Many businesses accept various forms of electronic payments for their products and services. Financial institutions play an important role in electronic payment systems by creating and distributing a variety of electronic payment instruments, accepting a similar variety of instruments, processing those payments, and participating in clearing and settlement systems. However, increasingly, financial institutions are competing with third parties to provide support services for e-commerce payment systems.

Among the electronic payments mechanisms that financial institutions provide for e-commerce are automated clearing house (ACH) debits and credits through the Internet, electronic bill payment and presentment, electronic checks, e-mail money, and electronic credit card payments. Additional information on payments systems can be found in other sections of the IT Handbook.

Most financial institutions permit intrabank transfers between a customer's accounts as part of their basic transactional e-banking services. However, third-party transfers-with their heightened risk for fraud-often require additional security safeguards in the form of additional authentication and payment confirmation.

Bill Payment and Presentment

Bill payment services permit customers to electronically instruct their financial institution to transfer funds to a business's account at some future specified date. Customers can make payments on a one-time or recurring basis, with fees typically assessed as a "per item" or monthly charge. In response to the customer's electronic payment instructions, the financial institution (or its bill payment provider) generates an electronic transaction-usually an automated clearinghouse (ACH) credit-or mails a paper check to the business on the customer's behalf. To allow for the possibility of a paper-based transfer, financial institutions typically advise customers to make payments effective 3-7 days before the bill's due date.

Internet-based cash management is the commercial version of retail bill payment. Business customers use the system to initiate third-party payments or to transfer money between company accounts. Cash management services also include minimum balance maintenance, recurring transfers between accounts and on-line account reconciliation. Businesses typically require stronger controls, including the ability to administer security and transaction controls among several users within the business.

This booklet discusses the front-end controls related to the initiation, storage, and transmission of bill payment transactions prior to their entry into the industry's retail payment systems (e.g., ACH, check processing, etc.). The IT Handbook's "Retail Payments Systems Booklet" provides additional information regarding the various electronic transactions that comprise the back end for bill payment processing.

The extent of front-end operating controls directly under the financial institution's control varies with the system configuration. Some examples of typical configurations are listed below in order of increasing complexity, along with potential control considerations.

Financial institutions that do not provide bill payment services, but may direct customers to select from several unaffiliated bill payment providers.

Caution customers regarding security and privacy issues through the use of on-line disclosures or, more conservatively, e-banking agreements.

Financial institutions that rely on a third-party bill payment provider including Internet banking providers that subcontract to third parties.

Set dollar and volume thresholds and review bill payment transactions for suspicious activity.

Gain independent audit assurance over the bill payment provider's processing controls.

Restrict employees' administrative access to ensure that the internal controls limiting their capabilities to originate, modify, or delete bill payment transactions are at least as strong as those applicable to the underlying retail payment system ultimately transmitting the transaction.

Restrict by vendor contract and identify the use of any subcontractors associated with the bill payment application to ensure adequate oversight of underlying bill payment system performance and availability.

Evaluate the adequacy of authentication methods given the higher risk associated with funds transfer capabilities rather than with basic account access.

Consider the additional guidance contained in the IT Handbook's "Information Security," "Retail Payment Systems," and "Outsourcing Technology Services" booklets.

Financial institutions that use third-party software to host a bill payment application internally.

Determine the extent of any independent assessments or certification of the security of application source code.

Ensure software is adequately tested prior to installation on the live system.

Ensure vendor access for software maintenance is controlled and monitored.

Financial institutions that develop, maintain, and host their own bill payment system.

Consider additional guidance in the IT Handbook's "Development and Acquisition Booklet."

Financial institutions can offer bill payment as a stand-alone service or in combination with bill presentment. Bill presentment arrangements permit a business to submit a customer's bill in electronic form to the customer's financial institution. Customers can view their bills by clicking on links on their account's e-banking screen or menu. After viewing a bill, the customer can initiate bill payment instructions or elect to pay the bill through a different payment channel.

In addition, some businesses have begun offering electronic bill presentment directly from their own websites rather than through links on the e-banking screens of a financial institution. Under such arrangements, customers can log on to the business's website to view their periodic bills. Then, if so desired, they can electronically authorize the business to "take" the payment from their account.

The payment then occurs as an ACH debit originated by the business's financial institution as compared to the ACH credit originated by the customer's financial institution in the bill payment scenario described above. Institutions should ensure proper approval of businesses allowed to use ACH payment technology to initiate payments from customer accounts.

Cash management applications would include the same control considerations described above, but the institution should consider additional controls because of the higher risk associated with commercial transactions. The adequacy of authentication methods becomes a higher priority and requires greater assurance due to the larger average dollar size of transactions. Institutions should also establish additional controls to ensure binding agreements-consistent with any existing ACH or wire transfer agreements-exist with commercial customers. Additionally, cash management systems should provide adequate security administration capabilities to enable the business owners to restrict access rights and dollar limits associated with multiple-user access to their accounts.

Person-to-Person Payments

Electronic person-to-person payments, also known as e-mail money, permit consumers to send "money" to any person or business with an e-mail address. Under this scenario, a consumer electronically instructs the person-to-person payment service to transfer funds to another individual. The payment service then sends an e-mail notifying the individual that the funds are available and informs him or her of the methods available to access the funds including requesting a check, transferring the funds to an account at an insured financial institution, or retransmitting the funds to someone else. Person-to-person payments are typically funded by credit card charges or by an ACH transfer from the consumer's account at a financial institution. Since neither the payee nor the payer in the transaction has to have an account with the payment service, such services may be offered by an insured financial institution, but are frequently offered by other businesses as well.

Some of the risk issues examiners should consider when reviewing bill payment, presentment, and e-mail money services include:

Potential liability for late payments due to service disruptions,

Liability for bill payment instructions originating from someone other than the deposit account holder,

Losses from person-to-person payments funded by transfers from credit cards or deposit accounts over which the payee does not have signature authority,

Losses from employee misappropriation of funds held pending access instructions from the payer, and

Potential liability directing payment availability information to the wrong e-mail or for releasing funds in response to e-mail from someone other than the intended payee.

Wireless E-banking

Wireless banking is a delivery channel that can extend the reach and enhance the convenience of Internet banking products and services. Wireless banking occurs when customers access a financial institution's network(s) using cellular phones, pagers, and personal digital assistants (or similar devices) through telecommunication companies' wireless networks. Wireless banking services in the United States typically supplement a financial institution's e-banking products and services.

Wireless devices have limitations that increase the security risks of wireless-based transactions and that may adversely affect customer acceptance rates. Device limitations include reduced processing speeds, limited battery life, smaller screen sizes, different data entry formats, and limited capabilities to transfer stored records.

These limitations combine to make the most recognized Internet language, Hypertext Markup Language (HTML), ineffective for delivering content to wireless devices. Wireless Markup Language (WML) has emerged as one of a few common language standards for developing wireless device content. Wireless Application Protocol (WAP) has emerged as a data transmission standard to deliver WML content.

Manufacturers of wireless devices are working to improve device usability and to take advantage of enhanced "third-generation" (3G) services. Device improvements are anticipated to include bigger screens, color displays, voice recognition applications, location identification technology (e.g., Federal Communications Commission (FCC) Enhanced 911), and increased battery capacity. These improvements are geared towards increasing customer acceptance and usage. Increased communication speeds and improvements in devices during the next few years should lead to continued increases in wireless subscriptions.

As institutions begin to offer wireless banking services to customers, they should consider the risks and necessary risk management controls to address security, authentication, and compliance issues. Some of the unique risk factors associated with wireless banking that may increase a financial institution's strategic, transaction, reputation, and compliance risks are discussed in appendix E.

4

International Law of Banking

INTRODUCTION

According to the President of the International Court of Justice, Rosalyn Higgins, international law is a normative system "harnessed to the achievement of common values-values that speak to us all, whether we are rich or poor, black or white, of any religion or none, or come from countries that are industrialized or developing". Higgins R, Problems and process: international law and how we use it (Oxford: Clarendon Press, 1994) at 16. International Law also called public international law to distinguish from "private international law", i.e. resolution for conflict of laws in its most general sense, "consists of rules and principles of general application dealing with the conduct of states and of international organizations and with their relations inter se, as well as with some of their relations with persons, whether natural or juridical." Columbia Law School, McKeever, 2003-

Definition of International Law International law concerns the structure and conduct of states, international organizations, and, to a certain degree, also multinational corporations and individuals. While both are supranational systems of law, the term "public international law" should be distinguished from "private international law". Public international law regulates the relationship between states and international entities, regulates competing demands, and establishes the framework for predictable and agreed behaviour among parties. Private international law selects between conflicting municipal systems of law to regulate the relationship between persons, as defined both legally and naturally. Columbia Law School, McKeever, 2003-Institutions Involved in the Process The necessity for international law arose in the context of increased international communication, trade, and conflict.

THE SCOPE OF INTERNATIONAL LAW

International law establishes the framework and the criteria for identifying states as the principal actors in the international legal system. As the existence of a state presupposes control and jurisdiction over territory, international law deals with the acquisition of territory, state immunity and the legal responsibility of states in their conduct with each other. The law is similarly concerned with the treatment of individuals within state boundaries.

There is thus a comprehensive regime dealing with group rights, the treatment of aliens, the rights of refugees, international crimes, nationality problems and human rights generally. It further includes the important functions of the maintenance of international peace and security, arms control, the pacific settlement of disputes and the regulation of the use of force in international relations. Even when the law is not able to stop the outbreak of war, it has developed principles to govern the conduct of hostilities and the treatment of prisoners. International law is also used to govern issues relating to the global environment, the global commons such as international waters and outer space, global communications, and world trade.

Whilst municipal law is hierarchical or vertical, with the legislature enacting binding legislation, international law is horizontal, with all states being sovereign and theoretically equal. Because of this, the value and authority of international law is dependent upon the voluntary participation of states in its formulation, observance, and enforcement. Although there may be exceptions, most states enter into legal commitments to other states out of enlightened self-interest rather than adherence to a body of law that is higher than their own. As D. W. Greig notes, "international law cannot exist in isolation from the political factors operating in the sphere of international relations". Greig, D. W., International Law, 2nd edn (Butterworths: London, 1976)

Where there are breaches of the law, international law has no established compulsory judicial system for the settlement of disputes or coercive penal system. That is not to say that there are no judicial or quasi-judicial tribunals in international law. The formation of the United Nations, for example, created a means for the world community to enforce international law upon members that violate its charter.

Traditionally, states were the sole subjects of international law. With the proliferation of international organizations over the last century, they have in some cases been recognized as relevant parties as well. Recent interpretations of international human rights law, international humanitarian law, and international trade law have been inclusive of corporations, and even individuals.

FUNDAMENTAL CONFLICTS OVER INTERNATIONAL LAW

The 17th, 18th and 19th centuries saw the growth of the concept of a "nation-state", which comprised nations controlled by a centralized system of government. The concept of nationalism became increasingly important as people began to see themselves as citizens of a particular nation with a distinct national identity. Until the beginning of the 20th century, relations between nation-states were dictated by Treaty, unenforceable agreements to behave in a certain way towards another state. Many people now view the nation-state as the primary unit of international affairs.

States may choose to voluntarily enter into commitments under international law, but they will often follow their own counsel when it comes to interpretation of their commitments. As the 20th century progressed, a number of violent armed conflicts, including WWI and WWII, exposed the weaknesses of a voluntary system of international treaties. In an attempt to create a stronger system of laws to prevent future conflicts, a vehicle for the application of international law was found in the creation of the United Nations, an international law making body, and new international criminal laws were applied at the Nuremberg trials. Over the past fifty years, more international laws and law making bodies have been created.

Many people feel that these modern developments endanger nation states by taking power away from state governments and ceding it to international bodies such as the U.N. and the World Bank. Some scholars and political leaders have recently argued that international law has evolved to a point where it exists separately from the mere consent of states. There is a growing trend toward judging a state's domestic actions in the light of international law and standards. A number of states, notably the United States vehemently oppose this interpretation, maintaining that sovereignty is the only true international law and that states have free reign over their own affairs. Similarly, a number of scholars now discern a legislative and judicial process to international law that parallels such processes within domestic law. Opponents to this point of view maintain that states only commit to international law with express consent and have the right to make their own interpretations of its meaning; and that international courts only function with the consent of states. Because international law is a relatively new area of law its development is uncertain and its relevance and propriety is hotly disputed.

SOURCES OF INTERNATIONAL LAW

International law has three primary sources: international treaties, custom, and general principles of law (cf. Art. 38 of the Statute of the International Court of Justice). International treaty law is comprised of obligations states expressly and voluntarily accept between themselves in treaties. Customary international law is derived from the consistent practice of States accompanied by opinio juris, i.e. the conviction of States that the consistent practice is required by a legal obligation. Judgments of international tribunals as well as scholarly works have traditionally been looked to as persuasive sources for custom in addition to direct evidence of state behavior. Attempts to codify customary international law picked up momentum after the Second World War with the formation of the International Law Commission (ILC). Codified customary law is made the binding interpretation of the underlying custom by agreement through treaty. For states not party to such treaties, the work of the ILC may still be accepted as custom applying to those states. General principles of law are those commonly recognized by the major legal systems of the world. Certain norms of international law achieve the binding force of peremptory norms (jus cogens) as to include all states with no permissible derogations. Legal principles common to major legal systems may also be invoked to supplement international law when necessary.

INTERPRETATION OF INTERNATIONAL LAW

Where there are disputes about the exact meaning and application of national laws, it is the responsibility of the courts to decide what the law means. In international law as a whole, there are no courts which have the authority to do this. It is generally the responsibility of states to interpret the law for themselves. Unsurprisingly, this means that there is rarely agreement in cases of dispute. Insofar as treaties are concerned, the Vienna Convention on the Law of Treaties writes on the topic of interpretation that:: "A treaty shall be interpreted in good faith in accordance with the ordinary meaning tc be given to the terms of the treaty in their context and in the light of its object and purpose." (article 31(1) This is actually a compromise between three different theories of interpretation:

* The textual approach is a restrictive interpretation which bases itself on the "ordinary meaning" of the text, the actual text has considerable weight.
* A subjective approach considers the idea behind the treaty, treaties "in their context", what the writers intended when they wrote the text.
* A third approach bases itself on interpretation "in the light of its object and purpose", i.e. the interpretation that best suits the goal of the treaty, also called "effective interpretation". These are general rules of interpretation; specific rules might exist in specific areas of international law.

Enforcement by States

Apart from a state's natural inclination to uphold certain norms, the force of international law has always come from the pressure that states put upon one another to behave consistently and to honor their obligations. As with any system of law, many violations of international law obligations are overlooked. If addressed, it is almost always purely through diplomacy and the consequences upon an offending state's reputation. Though violations may be common in fact, states try to avoid the appearance of having disregarded international obligations. States may also unilaterally adopt sanctions against one another such as the severance of economic or diplomatic ties, or through reciprocal action. In some cases, domestic courts may render judgment against a foreign state (the realm of private international law) for an injury, though this is a complicated area of law where international law intersects with domestic law. States have the right to employ force in self-defense against an offending state that has used force to attack its territory or political independence. States may also use force in collective self-defense, where force is used against another state. The state that force is used against must authorize the participation of third-states in its self-defense. This right is recognized in the United Nations Charter.

Enforcement by International Bodies

Violations of the UN Charter by members oi the United Nations may be raised by the aggrieved state in the General Assembly for debate. The General Assembly cannot make binding resolutions, but under the "Uniting for Peace" resolution (GA/RES/0377) it declared it could authorize the use of force if there had been Breaches of the Peace or Acts of Aggression, provided that the Security Council due to a negative vote of a permanent member failed to act. It could call for other collective measures (such as economic sanctions) given a situation constituted the milder "threat to the Peace". The legal significance of such a resolution is unclear, as the General Assembly cannot issue binding resolutions.

They can also be raised in the Security Council. The Security Council can pass resolutions of the UN Charter to recommend "Pacific Resolution of Disputes." Such resolutions are not binding under international law, though they usually are expressive of the council's convictions. In rare cases, the Security Council can pass resolutions of the UN Charter related to "threats to Peace, Breaches of the Peace and Acts of Aggression," and these are legally binding under international law, and can be followed up with economic sanctions, military action, and similar uses of force through the auspices of the United Nations.

It has been argued that resolutions passed outside can also be binding; the legal basis for that is the Council's broad powers under Article 24(2), which states that "in discharging these duties (exercise of primary responsibility in international peace and security), it shall act in accordance with the Purposes and Principles of the United Nations". The mandatory nature of such resolutions was upheld by the International Court of Justice in its advisory opinion on Namibia. The binding nature of such resolutions can be deduced from an interpretation of their language and intent.

States can also, upon mutual consent, submit disputes for arbitration by the International Court of Justice (ICJ), located in The Hague, Netherlands. The judgments given by the Court in these cases are binding, although it possesses no means to enforce its rulings. The Court may give an advisory opinion on any legal question at the request of whatever body may be authorized by or in accordance with the Charter of the United Nations to make such a request. Some of the advisory cases brought before the court have been controversial with respect to the courts competence and jurisdiction.

Often enormously complicated matters, ICJ cases (of which there have been less than 150 since the court was created from the Permanent Court of International Justice in 1945) can stretch on for years and generally involve thousands of pages of pleadings, evidence, and the world's leading specialist public international lawyers. As of 2005, there are twelve cases pending at the ICJ. Decisions made through other means of arbitration may be binding or non-binding depending on the nature of the arbitration agreement, whereas decisions resulting from contentious cases argued before the ICJ are always binding on the involved states.

Though states (or increasingly, international organizations) are usually the only ones with standing to address a violation of international law, some treaties, such as the International Covenant on Civil and Political Rights have an optional protocol that allows individuals who have had their rights violated by member states to petition the international Human Rights Committee.

THE BACKDROP

Through the ages a code developed for the relations and conduct between nations. Even when nations were at war, envoys were often considered immune to violence. The first formal attempts in this direction, which over time have developed into the current international law, stem from the era of the Renaissance in Europe. In the Middle Ages, it had been considered the obligation of the Church to mediate in international disputes. During the Council of Constance (1414) Pawel Wlodkowic, rector of Jagiellonian University (Krakaw,

Poland), theologian, lawyer and diplomat, presented the theory that all, including pagan, nations have right to self-govern and to live in peace and possess their land.

At the beginning of the 17th century, several generalizations could be made about the political situation. Self-governing, autonomous states existed. Almost all of them were governed by monarchs. The Peace of Westphalia is often cited as being the birth of the modern nation-states, establishing states as sovereigns answering to no-one within its own borders. Land, wealth, and trading rights were often the topics of wars between states.

Some people assert that international law developed to deal with the new states arising, others claim that the lack of influence of the Pope and the Catholic church gave rise to the need for new generally-accepted codes in Europe.

The French monk Emeric Cruce (1590-1648) came up with the idea of having representatives of all countries meeting in one place to discuss their conflicts so as to avoid war and create more peace. He suggested this in his The New Cyneas (1623), choosing Venice to be the selected city for all of the representatives to meet, and suggested that the Pope should preside over the meeting. Of course, during the Thirty Years' War (1618-1648), this was not acceptable to the Protestant nations. He also said that armies should be abolished and called for a world court. Though his call to abolish armies was not taken seriously, Emeric Cruce does deserve his place in history through his foresight that international organizations are crucial to solve international disputes.

The statesmen of the time believed no nation could escape war, so they prepared for it. King Henry IV's Chief Minister, the Duke of Sully, proposed the founding of an alliance of the European nations that was to meet to arbitrate issues and wage war not between themselves but collectively on the Ottoman Turks, and he called it the Grand Design, but was never established.

After World War I, the nations of the world decided to form an international body. U.S. President Woodrow Wilson came up with the idea of a "League of Nations". However, due to political wrangling in the U.S. Congress, the United States did not join the League of Nations, which was one of the causes of its demise. When World War II broke out, the League of Nations was finished.

Yet at the same time, the United Nations was being formed. On January 1, 1942, US President Franklin D. Roosevelt issued the "Declaration by United Nations" on behalf of 26 nations who had pledged to fight against the Axis powers. Even before the end of the war, representatives of 50 nations met in San Francisco to draw up the charter for an international body to replace the League of Nations. On October 24, 1945, the United Nations officially came into existence, setting a basis for much international law to follow.

Modern international law is often affirmed as the product of modern European civilization.

The seafaring principalities of India established legal rules for ocean navigation and regional commerce.

The Greek system of independent city-states bore a close resemblance to contemporary nation-state system. The Aetolian and Achaean leagues of the 3rd century BC represented early organisational efforts at international cooperation and facilitated the development of arbitration as a dispute settlement technique.

INTERNATIONAL LEGAL THEORY

The intellectual seeds of modern international law germinated in the 16th and 17th centuries, when the influence of the Roman Catholic Church in international affairs gradually weakened. Many early international legal theorists were concerned with axiomatic truths thought to be reposed in natural law. Among the early natural law writers, Francisco de Victoria, Dominican professor of theology at the University of Salamanca, examined the question of just war and Spanish authority in the Americas. He did so while Spain was at the height of its power, after the violent Spanish conquest of Peru in 1536.

Eclectic School

Central in the development of modern international law was Hugo Grotius a Dutch theologian, humanist and jurist. In his principal work De jure Belli ac Pacis Libri Tres ("Three Books on the Law of War and Peace"; 1625), Grotius claimed that nations as well as persons ought to be governed by universal principle based on morality and divine justice. Much of Grotius's content drew from the Bible and from classical history (just war theory of Augustine of Hippo). Drawing also from domestic contract law, he also noted that relations between polities were governed by jus gentium, the law of peoples, which had been established by the consent of the community of nations.

The fundamental facets of the Grotian or eclectic school, especially the doctrines of legal equality, territorial sovereignty, and independence of states, became definitive to international law in Europe. These principals were recognised in the Peace of Westphalia and became the foundation for the treaties of Osnabrack and Manster.

Another eclectic thinker, German philosopher Christian von Wolff, contended that the foundation for international community should come as a world superstate (civitas maxima), having authority over the component member states. This view was rejected by the Swiss diplomat Emmerich de Vattel, who favoured a rationale of equality of states as articulated by 18th century natural law. Vattel suggested in his major work Le droit des gens that the law of nations was comprised of custom and law on the one hand, and natural law on the other.

Legal Positivism

The early positive school emphasized the importance of custom and treaties as sources of international law. Among the early positivists was Alberico Gentilis, a professor of civil law at Oxford who used historical examples to posit that positive law (jus voluntarium) was determined by general consent. Another professor at Oxford, Richard Zouche, published the first manual of international law in 1650.

In the 18th century legal positivism became popular and found its way into international legal philosophy. The principal figure among 18th century positivists was Cornelius van Bynkershoek, a celebrated Dutch jurist who asserted that the bases of international law were customs and treaties commonly consented to by various states. A second positivist, John Jacob Moser was a prolific German scholar who emphasized the importance of state practice in international law. A contemporary German scholar, Georg Friedrich von Martens, published the first systematic manual on positive international law, Precis du droit des gens moderne de l'Europe.

The growth of nationalism and Hegelian philosophy in the 19th century pushed natural law farther from the legal realm. Commercial law became nationalized into private international law, distinct from public international law. Positivism narrowed the range of international practice that might qualify as law, favouring rationality to morality and ethics. The Congress of Vienna in 1815 marked formal recognition of the political and international legal system based on the conditions of Europe.

BRANCHES OF INTERNATIONAL LAW

* International criminal law
* The law pertaining to use of force
* International human rights law
* International humanitarian law
* Law of the sea
* Diplomatic law
* Consular law
* Law of State Responsibility
* International environmental law
* International trade law.

The Bretton Woods Conference of 1944 proposed the creation of an International Trade Organization (ITO) to establish rules and regulations for trade between countries. The ITO would have complemented the other two Bretton Woods Institutions: The International Monetary Fund (IMF) and the World Bank.

The ITO charter was agreed at the UN Conference on Trade and Employment in Havana in March 1948, but was blocked by the U.S. Senate. As a result, the ITO never came into existence. It has been suggested that the failure may have resulted from fears within the American business community that the International Trade Organization could be used to regulate European cartels rather than to break them up.

Only one element of the ITO survived: the General Agreement on Tariffs and Trade (GATT). Seven rounds of negotiations occurred under GATT before the eighth round-the Uruguay Round-concluded in 1995 with the establishment of the World Trade Organisation (WTO) as the GATT's replacement. The GATT principles and agreements were adopted by the WTO, which was charged with administering and extending them.

NEW TRADE THEORY

New Trade Theory (NTT) is the economic critique of international free trade from the perspective of increasing returns to scale and the network effect. Beginning in the 1970s some economists asked whether it might be effective for a nation to shelter infant industries until they had grown to sufficient size to compete internationally.

The Theory

New Trade theorists challenge the assumption of diminishing returns to scale, and some argue that using protectionist measures to build up a huge industrial base in certain industries will then allow those sectors to dominate the world market (via a Network effect).

They wondered whether free trade would have prevented the development of the Japanese auto industries in the 1950s, when quotas and regulations prevented import competition. Japanese companies were encouraged to import foreign production technology but were required to produce 90 per cent of parts domestically within five years. It is said that the short-term hardship of Japanese consumers (who were unable to buy the superior vehicles produced by the world market) was more than compensated for by the long-term benefits to producers, who gained time to out-compete their international rivals.

Less quantitative forms of this "infant industry" argument against totally free trade have been advanced by trade theorists since at least 1848.

Impact of the Theory

Although there was nothing particularly 'new' about the idea of protecting 'infant industries' (an idea offered in theory since the 18th century, and in trade policy since the 1880s) what was new in "New Trade Theory" was the rigour of the mathematical economics used to model the increasing returns to scale, and especially the use of the network effect to argue that the formation of important industries was path dependent in a way which industrial planning and judicious tariffs might control.

The model they developed was highly technical, and predicted the possibilities of national specialization-by-industry observed in the industrial world (movies in Hollywood, watches in Switzerland, etc). The story of path-dependent industrial concentrations sometimes leads to monopolistic competition.

Econometric Testing

The econometric evidence for NTT was mixed, and again; highly technical. Due to the time-scales required and the particular nature of production in each 'monopolizable' sector, statistical judgements have been hard to make. In many ways, there is too limited a data-set to produce a reliable test of the hypothesis which doesn't require arbitrary judgements from the researchers.

Japan is cited as evidence of the benefits of "intelligent" protectionism, but critics of NTT have argued that the empirical support post-war Japan offers for beneficial protectionism is unusual, and that the NTT argument is based on a selective sample of historical cases. Although many examples (like Japanese cars) can be cited where a 'protected' industry subsequently grew to world status, regressions on the outcomes of such "industrial policies" (including the failures) have been less conclusive.

History of the Theory's Development

The theory was initially associated with Paul Krugman and the MIT economists of the early 1970s. Looking back in 1996 Krugman wrote that International economics a generation earlier had completely ignored returns to scale::"The idea that trade might reflect an overlay of increasing-returns specialization on comparative advantage was not there at all: instead, the ruling idea was that increasing returns would simply alter the pattern of comparative advantage."

OPEC

The Organization of the Petroleum Exporting Countries (OPEC) is made up of Algeria, Indonesia, Iran, Iraq, Kuwait, Libya, Nigeria, Qatar, Saudi

Arabia, the United Arab Emirates, and Venezuela; since 1965 its international headquarters have been in Vienna, Austria.

The principal aim of the Organization, according to its Statute, is "the coordination and unification of the petroleum policies of its member countries and the determination of the best means for safeguarding their interests, individually and collectively; devising ways and means of ensuring the stabilization of prices in international oil markets with a view to eliminating harmful and unnecessary fluctuations; giving due regard at all times to the interests of the producing nations and to the necessity of securing a steady income to the producing countries; an efficient, economic and regular supply of petroleum to consuming nations, and a fair return on their capital to those investing in the petroleum industry."

OPEC's influence on the market has not always been a stabilizing one, however. It alarmed the world and triggered high inflation across both the developing and developed world through its use of the oil weapon in the 1973 oil crisis. Its ability to control the price of oil has diminished greatly since its heyday, following the much-expanded development of the Gulf of Mexico, the North Sea, and the growing fluidity of the market. However, OPEC still has considerable impact on the price of oil. It is still commonly used as a textbook example of a cartel.

MEMBERSHIP

The Organization now has 11 member states. They are listed below with their affiliation dates.

Africa:

* (July 1969)

* (December 1962)

* (July 1971)

Middle East:

* (September 1960)

* (September 1960)

* (September, 1960)

* (December 1961)

* (September 1960)

* (November 1967)

South America:

* (September 1960)

Southeast Asia:

* (December 1962. Membership currently under review as Indonesia is no longer considered by OPEC as a net oil exporter. See also current acting OPEC secretaries general)

Former Members:

* (Full member from 1975 to 1995)

* (Full member from 1963 to 1993)

OPEC's official language is English, although the official language of a majority of OPEC member-states is Arabic, as seven current members are Arab states. Only one member nation (Nigeria) has English as an official language.

History

Venezuela was the first country to move towards the establishment of the Organization of the Petroleum Exporting Countries (OPEC) by approaching Iran, Iraq, Kuwait and Saudi Arabia, in 1949, and suggesting that they exchange views and explore avenues for regular and closer communications between them. In September 1960, government of Iraq invited Iran, Kuwait, Saudi Arabia and Venezuela to meet in Baghdad, to discuss the reduction in prices of crudes produced by their respective countries. As a result OPEC was founded to unify and coordinate members' petroleum policies. Original OPEC members include Iran, Iraq, Kuwait, Saudi Arabia, and Venezuela. Between 1960 and 1975, the organization expanded to include Qatar (1961), Indonesia (1962), Libya (1962), the United Arab Emirates (1967), Algeria (1969), and Nigeria (1971). Ecuador and Gabon were members of OPEC, but Ecuador withdrew in December 1992, and Gabon followed suit in January 1995. Although

Iraq remains a member of OPEC, Iraqi production has not been a part of any OPEC quota agreements since March 1998. EIA estimates that the current eleven OPEC members account for about 40% of world oil production, and about 2/3 of the world's proven oil reserves.

The Yom Kippur War

The persistence of the Arab-Israeli conflict finally triggered a response that transformed OPEC from a mere cartel into a formidable political force. After the Six Day War of 1967, the Arab members of OPEC formed a separate, overlapping group, the Organization of Arab Petroleum Exporting Countries, for the purpose of centering policy and exerting pressure on the West over its support of Israel. Egypt and Syria, though not major oil-exporting countries, joined the latter grouping to help articulate its objectives. Later, the Yom Kippur War of 1973 galvanized Arab opinion. Furious at the emergency re-supply effort that had enabled Israel to withstand Egyptian and Syrian forces, the Arab world imposed the 1973 oil embargo against the United States and Western Europe. In the 1970s, the great Western oil conglomerates suddenly faced a unified block of producers.

This Arab-Israeli conflict triggered a crisis already in the making. They consistently drew the oil away from non-Arab nations. The West could not continue to increase its energy use 5% annually, pay low oil prices, yet sell inflation-priced goods to the petroleum producers in the Third World. This was stressed by the Shah of Iran, whose nation was the world's second-largest exporter of oil, and the closest ally of the United States in the Middle East at the time. "Of course [the world price of oil] is going to rise," the Shah told the New York Times in 1973. "Certainly! And how...; You [Western nations] increased the price of wheat you sell us by 300%, and the same for sugar and cement...; You buy our crude oil and sell it back to us, redefined as petrochemicals, at a hundred times the price you've paid to us...; It's only fair that, from now on, you should pay more for oil. Let's say 10 times more." Quoted in Walter LaFeber, Russia, America, and the Cold War (New York, 2002), p. 292.

Operations

OPEC's member countries hold about two-thirds of the world's oil reserves. They supply 40% of the world's oil production and half of the exports.

Since worldwide oil sales are denominated in U.S. dollars, changes in the value of the dollar against other world currencies affect OPEC's decisions on how much oil to produce. For example, when the dollar falls relative to the other currencies, OPEC-member states receive smaller revenues in other currencies for their oil, causing substantial cuts in their purchasing power, because they continue to sell oil in the U.S. dollar. After the introduction of the euro, Iraq decided it wanted to be paid for its oil in euros instead of US dollars.

OPEC decisions have considerable influence on international oil prices. For example, in the 1973 energy crisis OPEC refused to ship oil to western countries that had supported Israel in the Yom Kippur War or October War, which they fought against Egypt and Syria. This refusal caused a fourfold increase in the price of oil, which lasted five months, starting on October 17, 1973, and ending on March 18, 1974. OPEC nations then agreed, on January 7, 1975, to raise crude oil prices by 10%.

At that time, OPEC nations-including many who had recently nationalized their oil industries-joined the call for a new international economic order to be initiated by coalitions of primary producers. Concluding the First OPEC Summit in Algiers they called for stable and just commodity prices, an international food and agriculture program, technology transfer from North to South, and the democratization of the economic system.

The policy has been successful, causing the price of crude oil to rise to levels that had, at one time, been reached only by refined products. However, OPEC's ability to raise prices does have some limits. An increase in oil price decreases consumption, and could cause a net decrease in revenue. Furthermore, an extended rise in price could encourage systematic behavior change, such as alternative energy utilization, or increased conservation.

Leading up to the 1990-91 Gulf War, Iraqi President Saddam Hussein advocated that OPEC push world oil prices up, thereby helping Iraq, and other member states, service debts. But the division of OPEC countries occasioned by the Iraq-Iran War and the Iraqi invasion of Kuwait marked a low point in the cohesion of OPEC. Once supply disruption fears that accompanied these conflicts dissipated, oil prices began to slide dramatically.

After oil prices slumped at around $10 a barrel, concerted diplomacy, sometimes attributed to Venezuela's president Hugo Chajvez, achieved a coordinated scaling back of oil production beginning in 1998. In 2000, Chajvez hosted the first summit of heads of state of OPEC in 25 years.

In August 2004, OPEC began communicating that its members had little excess pumping capacity, indicating that the cartel was losing influence over crude oil prices. Indonesia is reconsidering its membership having become a net importer and being unable to meet its production quota.

5

World Trade Organizations and Agreements

INTRODUCTION

After World War II, the world's leading nations wanted to create a permanent organization that would help foster world trade. Such an organization came into being in 1947 when representatives from the United States and twenty-three other nations signed the document creating the General Agreement on Tariffs and Trade (GATT), which now includes more than one hundred countries as signatories. The threefold purpose of GATT was to (1) foster equal, nondiscriminatory treatment for all member nations; (2) promote the reduction of tariffs by multilateral negotiations; and (3) foster the elimination of import quotas. GATT nations meet periodically to review progress toward established objectives and to set new goals that member countries want to achieve. The goals and objectives of GATT vary and change over time as trade issues evolve based on domestic and world economies.

Likewise, representatives from Belgium, Denmark, France, Germany, Greece, Ireland, Italy, Luxembourg, the Netherlands, Portugal, Spain, and the United Kingdom came together to form the European Economic Community (EEC)-sometimes called the Common Market-in 1958. The purpose of the EEC was to create equal and fair tariffs for all of the nations in the organization so that trade could flourish in Europe. The EEC has generally been regarded as successful.

The United States and Canada signed the U.S. Canadian Free Trade Agreement in 1989, which provided for the removal of all trade barriers between the two countries-such as tariffs, quotas, or other trade restrictions-within a ten-year period. This act helped promote even more trade between the two countries, thus further strengthening an already strong trade relationship.

The United States, Canada, and Mexico signed the North American Free Trade Agreement (NAFTA) in 1994 in order to create a free-trade zone among the three countries. Leaders of these three countries realized that a large North American free-trade zone could compete effectively against the EEC and other trading blocs that might develop in the future. This competitive factor was a driving force in the nations' signing of the agreement, each believing that, over the long run, all three would benefit from the agreement. In addition to feeling the impact of trade agreements and trade organizations per se, international trade is affected more indirectly by the financial stability and general economic well-being of all countries in our increasingly interconnected world. Thus two other international organizations ultimately affect the health of world trade.

To further promote trade among countries, the Allied nations of World War II met in 1944 in Bretton Woods, New Hampshire, to help set postwar global financial policies and thereby avoid future financial crises. The International Monetary Fund (IMF) was created as a result of that conference, its mission being to provide loans to countries that are in financial trouble. The IMF dictates the terms of the loans, which may include cutting domestic subsidies, privatizing government industries, and moderating trade policies. To fund these loans, IMF members make annual contributions, with each country's contribution determined by its size, national income, population, and volume of trade. Larger contributing countries, such as Britain and the United States, have more say as to what countries get loans and the terms of the loan.

The World Bank, with approximately 157 members, is another international organization to which the United States is a major contributor. The World Bank's mission is to help less developed countries achieve economic growth through improved trade. It does so by providing loans and guaranteeing or insuring private loans to nations in need of financial assistance. The World Bank has been characterized as (1) a last-resort lender, (2) a facilitator of development projects so as to encourage the inflow of private banking funds, and (3) a provider of technical assistance for fostering long-term economic growth.

The world has a long history of international trade. In fact, trading among nations can be traced back to the earliest civilizations. Trading activities are directly related to an improved quality of life for the citizens of nations involved in international trade. It is safe to say that nearly every person on earth has benefited from international trading activities.

INTERNATIONAL TRADE COMMISSION

The ITC is a quasi-judicial independent federal agency that provides objective trade expertise to both the legislative and executive branches of government. Tariff information, petitions, complaints, and reports are available here, along with the 1997 Harmonized Tariff Schedule and Federal Investigation Notices. Browse their Recent Petitions & Complaints Filed. Download their Monthly Calendar. They have also recently added a Tariff Database which allows the user to search for trade statistics based upon Tariff number.

Department of Commerce

- *Bureau of Export Administration:* The Bureau of Export Administration (BXA) plays an important role in export controls, guarding the national security, foreign policy and non-proliferation goals of the United States, and balancing them against the need of U.S. firms to be viable and competitive in the world marketplace. The BXA oversees the development, licensing and enforcement of export control laws. Their recently overhauled site now includes access to the Export Administration Regulations (by subscription), the List of Denied Parties, Fact Sheets on obtaining Export Licenses, descriptions of their programs, and office location and contact information.

International Trade Administration

As the DOC's international trade assistance program, the ITA is dedicated to helping U.S. businesses compete in the global marketplace. The site has a number of assistance related work-spaces and information resources, and includes the NAFTA Home Page, the Trade Information Centers, and the very helpful Export Assistance Center.

The U.S. & Foreign Commercial Service also prints (along with DOS) the extremely helpful Country Commercial Guides which include worldwide contacts, marketing info, best prospects and more. Their site has also recently added a Trade Compliance Center which helps U.S. exporters receive the fullest benefits from the more than 200 trade agreements the United States has concluded. Also, the OTEA has extensive trade statistics.

Import Administration

The Import Administration (IA) enforces laws and agreements to prevent unfairly traded imports and to safeguard jobs and the competitive strength of American industry.

Much information here related to imports including exchange rates, Federal Register notices and policy bulletins, and an extremely comprehensive Import Library with a large number of downloadable files including World Trade Organization Subsidies Notifications and AD and CVD Statistics and Information.

U.S. Census Bureau-International Trade

International trade related statistics, Export Declaration form, AES information and Schedule B, C, D, & K information. Items of special interest include 1997 Schedule B and Correct Way to Fill out a Shipper's Export Declaration, and Country by Commodity Trade Data.

Foreign Trade Zones Board

Foreign-trade zones are designated sites licensed by the Foreign-Trade Zones (FTZ) Board (the Secretary of Commerce is Chairman) at which special Customs procedures may be used. FTZ procedures allow domestic activity involving foreign items to take place as if it were outside U.S. Customs territory, thus offsetting Customs advantages available to overseas producers who export in competition with products made here. Subzones are special-purpose zones, usually at manufacturing plants.

STAT-USA

Daily economic news and statistics sponsored by the Dept. of Commerce. This subscription service also includes trade leads, research reports, country specific economic studies and more.

Patent and Trademark Office, Licensing and Review

Oversees patent filing data sent abroad.

Office of Industry and Trade

The Industry and Trade Office (ITO) is the National Marine Fisheries Services's (NMFS) principal contact for commercial industry issues. Domestic and international issues include, but are not limited to trade (access to markets), standards development and application, inspection of U.S. product imported to other countries, technological barriers to trade, traditional industry development, product utilization, and other issues related to industry competitiveness. Industry concerns over stakeholder and user conflicts may also be raised through the ITO. Although not up yet, this site promises seafood export opportunities, a basic guide to exporting seafood and more.

Department of the Treasury

- *Customs Service:* As the Nation's principal border agency, the mission of the United States Customs Service is to ensure that all goods entering and exiting the United States do so in accordance with all United States laws and regulations. Their Importing/Exporting section includes extensive resources regarding Quota and Entry information. Also, a very hot topic is their Informed Compliance information. Check out the Customs Valuation Encyclopedia, or Search CFR 19. Customs has also recently made their excellent Customs Electronic Bulletin Board available over the Web.
- *Bureau of Alcohol Tobacco and Firearms:* The BATF has information concerning the movement of these goods into and throughout the U.S.

ATF Forms

- *Office of Foreign Assets Control:* The Office of Foreign Assets Control of the U.S. Department of the Treasury administers and enforces economic and trade sanctions against targeted foreign countries, terrorism sponsoring organizations and international narcotics traffickers based on U.S. foreign policy and national security goals. FAC documents include "Foreign Assets Control Regulations for Exporters & Importers."

- *International Trade Data System:* ITDS is the National Performance Review (NPR) project A09 consisting of an interagency Board of Directors and a project office residing in the Department of Treasury. We are building a system to facilitate international trade. This system will provide a single entry point for the public to transmit information required by the U. S. government for international trade. The ITDS system is being developed to improve trade procedures, trade promotion, trade policy development, and trade statistics to benefit both the Public and the Government.

Department of State

- *America Desk:* The State Department's repository for commercial information. It includes Country Commercial Guides, business contact information, and security guidelines for Americans overseas.
- *Office of Defense Trade Controls (DTC):* This office controls the export and temporary import of defense articles and services by taking final action on license applications and other requests for approval for defense trade exports and retransfers, and handling matters related to defense trade compliance, enforcement and reporting. This is where you go for export license information on firearms and the like. Take a look at their Defense Trade News.

Department of Agriculture

- *Foreign Agricultural Service:* The FAS represents the diverse interests of U.S. farmers and the U.S. food and agricultural sector abroad. It also collects, analyzes, and disseminates information about global supply and demand, trade trends, and emerging market opportunities. An excellent international trade site, it provides foreign market research, trade leads, trade data, a wide variety of export assistance programs, detailed reports, foreign buyers lists, and even employment information.
- *Animal and Plant Health Inspection Service (APHIS):* APHIS ensures the health and care of animals and plants in the U.S. They also monitor

agricultural products and animals entering the U.S. Their Import/Export Directory has information on plant, animal and biotechnology import and export permits and procedures. Their Export Rules facilitates the movement of agricultural commodities to other countries. Plenty of forms available on their site.

APHIS Forms

- *Food Safety and Inspection Service:* The Food Safety and Inspection Service (FSIS), a public health agency in the U.S. Department of Agriculture, protects consumers by ensuring that meat and poultry products are safe, wholesome, and accurately labeled. FSIS inspects all meat and poultry sold in interstate and foreign commerce, including imported products. Their HAACP Implementation Page provides info and training programs for HAACP. Also valuable is their Export Library which contains information on the extra requirements (labelling, forms, etc.) required by other countries for U.S. agricultural products. The FSIS is also responsible for the U.S. involvement in the Codex Alimentarius Commission via the U.S. Codex Office.
- *Center for Food Safety and Applied Nutrition:* This agency component, the Center for Food Safety and Applied Nutrition (CFSAN), regulates $240 billion worth of domestic food, $15 billion worth of imported foods, and $15 billion worth of cosmetics sold across state lines. This regulation takes place from the products' point of U.S. entry or processing to their point of sale. Aside from their own HAACP site, CFSAN also has plenty of import and export information, including the very useful Import Alerts and Detentions.
- *The Center for Veterinary Medicine:* The CVM regulates the manufacture and distribution of drugs and feed additives intended for animals. This includes exported drugs and feed additives.
- *Agricultural Marketing Service:* In addition to FAS above, the USDA also runs this service. Although it mainly has information on domestic agricultural marketing, it also has some importer and exporter assistance.
- *Grain Inspection, Packers and Stockyards Administration:* This site includes information and procedures regarding the exports of grain and livestock.

- *USDA Economics and Statistics System:* This library has nearly 300 reports and datasets from the economics agencies of the U.S. Department of Agriculture. These materials cover U.S. and international agriculture and related topics.

Department of Transportation

- *Bureau of Transportation Statistics-BTS:* All types of transportation statistics and information are offered here. The BTS is an excellent jumping off point for packaging, HAZMAT and shipping information.
- *Federal Aviation Administration-FAA:* The FAA site has information and press releases related to airfreight and HAZMAT regulation.
- *Maritime Administration-MARAD:* Promoting the U.S. maritime industry and maintaining the U.S. Merchant Marine, MARAD's web site has all types of international shipping related information.
- *United States Coast Guard-USCG:* The USCG patrols the U.S. waterways. Their web site also has considerable documentation on vessel containers, hazardous materials and other maritime information.
- *St. Lawrence Seaway Development Corporation-SLSDC:* The St. Lawrence Seaway is a model of cooperation between the United States and Canada and is jointly managed by the U.S. Saint Lawrence Seaway Development Corporation (SLSDC) and the Canadian St. Lawrence Seaway Authority. The current toll schedule and management reports are available on their site.
- *National Highway Traffic Safety Administration:* NHTSA is responsible for reducing deaths, injuries and economic losses resulting from motor vehicle crashes. This is accomplished by setting and enforcing safety performance standards for motor vehicles and items of motor vehicle equipment, and through grants to state and local governments. If you are going to import an automobile, you will need to speak with these people. Especially helpful on their site are the Vehicle Importation Regulations.

Department of Health and Human Services

- *Food and Drug Administration Import Awareness Program:* The FDA Import Awareness Program informs import brokers, wholesalers, retailers and consumers about products that have been detained or would be detained without physical examination when presented for entry into the US via ORA/FDA Import Alerts. The FDA is in charge of monitoring food and drugs in the U.S, and their Office of Regulatory Affairs deals with imports.

Department of Energy

- *Office of Arms Controls and Nonproliferation:* The Export Control Operations Division licenses nuclear technology and technical data for nuclear power and special nuclear materials for export.
- *Office of Fossil Energy:* This office licenses natural gas and electric power for export.

Department of Defense

- *Defense Technology and Security Administration (DTSA):* The DTSA develops and implement DoD policy on international transfers of defense-related goods, services, and technologies to ensure such transfers are consistent with national security interests. They review certain dual use export license applications referred by Commerce. Their "ELISA Online" allows you to view the status of your Export License.

Department of the Interior

- *U.S. Fish and Wildlife Service, Chief Office of Management Authority:* Controls the export of endangered fish and wildlife species.

Department of Justice

- *Drug Enforcement Administration: International Drug Unit/International Chemical Control Unit:* Oversees the export of controlled substances and controlled chemicals with the Office of Diversion Control under the Controlled Substances Act.

U.S. Trade Representative

The Cabinet Office responsible for developing and coordinating U.S. trade, commodity, and direct investment policy. The site includes official press releases, reports, agreements, summary information, and more.

Federal Maritime Commission

The independent agency responsible for the regulation of shipping in the foreign trade of the U.S. Their site includes CFR, tariff filing, freight forwarding, NVOCC and investigation information. Especially interesting are their Docket Decisions.

FMC Forms

The Export Import Bank of the United States: The Ex-Im Bank is an independent U.S. Government agency that helps finance the overseas sales of U.S. goods and services.

U.S. Trade and Development Agency: The U.S. Trade and Development Agency assists in the creation of jobs for Americans by helping U.S. companies pursue overseas business opportunities. TDA trade briefs, press releases, feasibility studies, conference announcements are available here.

U.S. Arms Control and Disarmament Agency: The ACDA formulates, advocates, implements and verifies effective arms control, nonproliferation, and disarmament policies, strategies, and agreements. They also review certain dual use export license applications referred by Commerce.

Nuclear Regulatory Commission, Office of International Programs: NRC participates in a broad program of international cooperation related to nuclear safety and safeguards. Its role within the U.S. Government includes the licensing of exports and imports of nuclear facilities, equipment, material and related commodities. Summary status reports of applications received, cases completed, and cases pending, may be accessed on this site.

Environmental Protection Agency

- Office of Solid Waste and Emergency Response The International and Special Projects Branch regulates toxic waste exports.
- Office of Pesticide Program This office is responsible for pesticide regulation in the U.S.-including imports and exports.

EMPLOYMENT AND THE BALANCE OF TRADE

The mercantilist arguments for a favorable balance of trade so far considered all rest upon the desirability of more bullion. But there was one mercantilist argument which was not dependent upon the attachment of superior economic importance to the precious metals than to other commodities of equal exchange value, namely the "employment" argument. Exports were the product of English labor whereas imports, especially if they consisted of finished products and of commodities competitive with home products, displaced English labor. The greater, the exports, and the smaller the imports, the greater, therefore, was the employment of English labor. This argument was not, as is sometimes supposed, of late seventeenth-century origin. It is to be found in the very earliest mercantilist writings, and it persists without break throughout the literature of the seventeenth and eighteenth centuries. It is not even clear that it was more emphasized in the eighteenth-than in the seventeenth-century mercantilist literature, and it could even be argued that the sixteenth-century writers stressed it most of all. Of all the mercantilist reasoning, it withstood criticism most successfully, and persisted into the nineteenth and twentieth centuries as an important element in the protectionist doctrine.

The stress on employment led to an appraisal of exports not merely in terms of their value, or of their value relative to imports, but in terms of the amount of labor they represented. Exports of manufactured articles were rated more highly than exports to the same value of raw materials, because the former embodied a larger proportion of labor. The stress on employment sometimes took the form of measuring the gain from trade by the exports alone, and in a few cases the argument even went to the extreme of recommending production of goods simply to employ labor, even though the product of their labor were burnt upon their completion.

In the case of a few later writers, the employment argument gave rise to a new balance-of-trade concept, in which the amounts weighed against each other were not the values respectively of the exports and the imports, but the respective amounts of labor or employment they represented, i.e., the "balance of labor" or the "balance of employment." Barbon seems to have been the first to come close to this concept. The measure of benefit from different exports is the amount of employment they had given to English labor, and, similarly, the measure of benefit from imports is the amount of employment to which they will give rise in their further manufacture. His employment test leads him at times to liberal conclusions. Imports of raw silk are more profitable than imports of gold and silver, because more hands are employed in the manufacture of the first than in working the latter. If woolen goods are exported for Westphalian bacon and then the import of the latter is prohibited, England would lose even if the consumption of English bacon increased, because woolen cloth employs more hands in its production than does bacon.

Tucker stated the argument somewhat differently. The balance of trade for country A is the excess of the number of laborers working up manufactures for country B in A as compared to the number of laborers working up manufactures for A in B:

> When two countries are exchanging their produce or manufactures with each other, that nation which has thc greatest number employed in this reciprocal trade, is said to receive a balance from the other; because the price of the overplus labor must be paid in gold and silver.... This is the clearest and justest method of determining the balance between nation and nation: for though a difference in the value of the respective commodities may make some difference in the sum actually paid to balance accounts, yet the general principle, that labor (not money) is the riches of a people, will always prove, that the advantage is on the side of that nation which has most hands employed in labor.

A closely similar doctrine is presented also by Harris, Steuart, and Arthur Young: A nation that pays ultimately upon its trade a balance in bullion, is a loser of so much of its dead stock; and a loser also, if its exports maintained fewer of its own inhabitants, than its imports did of those foreign nations.

In all trade two things are to be considered in the commodity sold. The first is the matter; the second is the labor employed to render this matter useful. The matter exported from a country is what the country loses; the price of the labor exported is what it gains. If the value of the matter imported be greater than the value of what is exported the country gains. If a greater value of labor be imported, than exported, the country loses. Why? Because in the first case, strangers must have paid, in matter, the surplus of labor exported; and in the second case, because the country must have paid to strangers, in matter, the surplus of labor imported. It is therefore a general maxim, to discourage the importation of work, and to encourage the exportation of it.

A balance in our favor is a proof that foreigners take more products and fabrics from us than we do from them, which is an advantage of the highest consequence, because it suggests at least a strong probability that they employ more of our poor than we do of theirs.

These writers apparently would compare the amount of English labor embodied in the exports with the amount of foreign labor represented by the imports in computing the English "balance of labor." On this basis, a given trade balance measured in money would have to be regarded as more favorable the lower the prices at which English exports were sold and the lower the wages earned by English labor engaged in their production, although it is not evident that these writers saw this implication of their doctrine. The objective they had in mind, to the exclusion of other considerations, was employment of English labor, and in the case of Young the assumption is fairly clear that the labor engaged in the production of exported goods would in the absence of such exports remain idle. He states that "whatever is paid to other countries in bullion, as a balance upon the year's trade, is just so much loss to any nation that has unemployed poor or unpurchased commodities," but he concedes to Hume that the loss of the bullion is important only as it is a sign "that we do not export a due quantity of products and labor." The balance-of-labor doctrine is of course absurd and probably even more absurd than the earlier and at the time still dominant balance-of-trade doctrine. It nevertheless can be regarded as a stage of some importance in the evolution toward more sensible doctrine. In the first case, any criticism of or substitution for the dominant balance-of-trade doctrine helped to promote the disintegration of the mercantilist errors, and thus was a service even if it proposed an even less satisfactory alternative doctrine, provided the criticism survived and the proposed substitute did not survive. Secondly, the balance-of-labor doctrine reversed the roles of employment and foreign trade as compared to the conventional balance-of-trade doctrine.

In conventional mercantilism increased population, increased employment, improvement in the arts, in roads, canals, in the energy and skill of labor, were all welcomed because they would make possible increased production of goods for export or in lieu of imports from abroad, and would thus promote a favorable balance of trade. In the balance-of-labor doctrine the end was employment, and the favorable balance was the means, and even if its exponents did not themselves see clearly that income and consumption were in turn the rational ends of employment, and of economic activity in general, they at least made it easy for Adam Smith and later writers to take the next step and thus to bring about a revolutionary change in the orientation of economic thought.

One student of English mercantilism, E. A. Johnson, nothing the indisputable-and undisputed-fact that the mercantilists approved of a large working population, hard work on the part of laborers, the progress of skill in the application of labor, improvements in transportation and industry, and so forth, has concluded that serious injustice has been done to them by accounts such as presumably the present one of their doctrines: All of which should prove that the ultimate concern of the mercantilists was the creation of effective factors of production. Not ten per cent of English mercantilist literature is devoted to the ill-fated doctrine of the balance of trade. [Let anyone who doubts this assertion turn through the pages of the English mercantilist literature and be convinced!] Their ardent passion for productive efficiency is shown by their advocacy of improvement of lands, mines and fisheries, and by their encouragement of inland communication and canal building. Industry was to be encouraged, idleness to be repressed.

But evidence that the mercantilists desired efficient production, be it piled up mountain high, of itself proves nothing as to their "ultimate concern." They may have desired, and did desire, increased production, because they thought that it would promote a favorable balance of trade, even though they also desired it for other reasons. Such quantitative propositions have an unearned air of precision, but on the basis of my turning of the pages of English mercantilist literature I venture the conclusion that not ten per cent of it was free from concern, expressed or clearly implied, in the state of the balance of trade and in the means whereby it could be improved.

The labor doctrines of the English mercantilists need not be examined at length here, since they have been ably dealt with by other writers. On only one point, it seems to me, is critical comment on their exposition called for. The mercantilists, as they point out, were led by their obsession with the balance of trade and also, perhaps, by unconscious class sympathies, to deal with questions affecting labor as if laborers were a set of somewhat troublesome tools rather than human beings whose own comfort and happiness were a proper and primary object of concern for statesmen. The dominant doctrine, in consequence, advocated low wages, as a means of stimulating the worker to greater effort and of increasing England's competitive strength in foreign trade by lowering the money costs of English products. Sir James Steuart was merely expressing in blunter fashion than was common the position implicit in much of the mercantilist treatment of the labor question when he stated that "the lowest classes of a people, in a country of trade, must be restrained to their physical-necessary."

But Furniss and Gregory fail to do full justice to the size and importance of the dissenting group, who on grounds either of economic analysis or humanitarian sentiment opposed the dominant doctrine that low wages were desirable. Such important writers as Cary, Coke, Davenant, and Defoe belonged to this group, and in the latter part of the eighteenth century the growth of humanitarianism operated to give even stronger challenge to the prevailing views.

Representative of the opposition on humanitarian grounds was the complaint of an anonymous writer: "it is a great pity the laboring poor have not better encouragement, the cries of those unskillful men, who made a clamor of labor being too high, is a doctrine propagated more by theory than practice." Hume conceded that high wages resulted in some disadvantage in foreign trade, but insisted that "as foreign trade is not the most material circumstance, it is not to be put in competition with the happiness of so many millions." Since Hume was an enlightened critic of mercantilism, this is not of great significance, but Wallace, who was a mercantilist, agreed with Hume's doctrine, as "a maxim...suitable to a humane disposition. Agreeably to such a benevolent sentiment, we ought to extend our notions of trade, and consider not only how much money it gains to a nation, but how far it is conducive to the happiness of the people."

International trade allows us to expand our markets for both goods and services that otherwise may not have been available to us. It is the reason why you can pick between a Japanese, German and American car. As a result of international trade, the market contains greater competition and therefore more competitive prices, which bring a cheaper product home to the consumer.

INTERNATIONAL TRADE

International trade is the exchange of goods and services between countries. This type of trade gives rise to a world economy, in which prices, or supply and demand, affect and are affected by global events.

Political change in Asia, for example, could result in an increase in the cost of labor, thereby increasing the manufacturing costs for an American sneaker company based in Malaysia, which would then result in an increase in the price that you have to pay to buy the tennis shoes at your local mall. A decrease in the cost of labor, on the other hand, would result in you having to pay less for your new shoes.

Trading globally gives consumers and countries the opportunity to be exposed to goods and services not available in their own countries. Almost every kind of product can be found on the international market: food, clothes, spare parts, oil, jewelry, wine, stocks, currencies and water. Services are also traded: tourism, banking, consulting and transportation. A product that is sold to the global market is an export, and a product that is bought from the global market is an import. Imports and exports are accounted for in a country's current account in the balance of payments.

Increased Efficiency of Trading Globally

Global trade allows wealthy countries to use their resources-whether labor, technology or capital-more efficiently. Because countries are endowed with different assets and natural resources (land, labor, capital and technology), some countries may produce the same good more efficiently and therefore sell it more cheaply than other countries. If a country cannot efficiently produce an item, it can obtain the item by trading with another country that can. This is known as specialization in international trade.

Let's take a simple example. Country A and Country B both produce cotton sweaters and wine. Country A produces 10 sweaters and six bottles of wine a year while Country B produces six sweaters and 10 bottles of wine a year. Both can produce a total of 16 units. Country A, however, takes three hours to produce the 10 sweaters and two hours to produce the six bottles of wine (total of five hours). Country B, on the other hand, takes one hour to produce 10 sweaters and three hours to produce six bottles of wine (total of four hours).

But these two countries realize that they could produce more by focusing on those products with which they have a comparative advantage. Country A then begins to produce only wine and Country B produces only cotton sweaters. Each country can now create a specialized output of 20 units per year and trade equal proportions of both products. As such, each country now has access to 20 units of both products.

We can see then that for both countries, the opportunity cost of producing both products is greater than the cost of specializing. More specifically, for each country, the opportunity cost of producing 16 units of both sweaters and wine is 20 units of both products (after trading). Specialization reduces their opportunity cost and therefore maximizes their efficiency in acquiring the goods they need. With the greater supply, the price of each product would decrease, thus giving an advantage to the end consumer as well. Note that, in the example above, Country B could produce both wine and cotton more efficiently than Country A (less time). This is called an absolute advantage, and Country B may have it because of a higher level of technology. However, according to international trade theory, even if a country has an absolute advantage over another, it can still benefit from specialization.

Other Possible Benefits of Trading Globally

International trade not only results in increased efficiency but also allows countries to participate in a global economy, encouraging the opportunity of foreign direct investment (FDI), which is the amount of money that individuals invest into foreign companies and other assets. In theory, economies can therefore grow more efficiently and can more easily become competitive economic participants. For the receiving government, FDI is a means by which foreign currency and expertise can enter the country. These raise employment levels and, theoretically, lead to a growth in the gross domestic product. For the investor, FDI offers company expansion and growth, which means higher revenues.

Free Report: The Five Things That Move the Currency Market. Year after year, key players in the Forex market make a killing by picking the right currencies-now it's your turn. Access industry gurus Boris and Kathy's exclusive FREE report, The Five Things That Move the Currency Market-And How to Profit From Them, right now!

Free Trade vs. Protectionism

As with other theories, there are opposing views. International trade has two contrasting views regarding the level of control placed on trade: free trade and protectionism. Free trade is the simpler of the two theories: a laissez-faire approach, with no restrictions on trade. The main idea is that supply and demand factors, operating on a global scale, will ensure that production happens efficiently. Therefore, nothing needs to be done to protect or promote trade and growth because market forces will do so automatically. In contrast, protectionism holds that regulation of international trade is important to ensure that markets function properly. Advocates of this theory believe that market inefficiencies may hamper the benefits of international trade and they aim to guide the market accordingly. Protectionism exists in many different forms, but the most common are tariffs, subsidies and quotas. These strategies attempt to correct any inefficiency in the international market.

Conclusion

As it opens up the opportunity for specialization and therefore more efficient use of resources, international trade has potential to maximize a country's capacity to produce and acquire goods. Opponents of global free trade have argued, however, that international trade still allows for inefficiencies that leave developing nations compromised. What is certain is that the global economy is in a state of continual change and, as it develops, so too must all of its participants. The world has a long, rich history of international trade among nations that can be traced back to early Assyrian, Babylonian, Egyptian, and Phoenician civilizations. These and other early civilizations recognized that trade can be tied directly to an improved quality of life for the citizens of all the partners. Today, the practice of trade among nations is growing by leaps and bounds. There is hardly a person on earth who has not been influenced in some way by the growing trade among nations.

WHY INTERNATIONAL TRADE?

One of the most logical questions to ask is, why do modern countries trade with one another? There are numerous reasons that countries engage in international trade. Some countries are deficient in critical raw materials, such as lumber or oil. To make up for these various deficiencies, countries must engage in international trade to obtain the resources necessary to produce the goods and/or services desired by their citizens. In addition to trading for raw materials, nations also exchange a wide variety of processed foods and finished products. Each country has its own specialties that are based on its economy and the skills of its citizens. Three common specialty classifications are capital, labor, and land.

Capital-intensive products, such as cars and trucks, heavy construction equipment, and industrial machinery, are produced by nations that have a highly developed industrial base. Japan is an example of a highly developed industrial nation that produces large quantities of high-quality cars for export around the world. Another reason Japan has adapted to producing capital-intensive products is that it is an island nation; there is little land available for land-intensive product production. Labor-intensive commodities, such as clothing, shoes, or other consumer goods, are produced in countries that have relatively low labor costs and relatively modern production facilities. China, Indonesia, and the Philippines are examples of countries that produce many labor-intensive products. Products that require large tracts of land, such as cattle production and wheat farming, are examples of land-intensive commodities. Countries that do not have large tracts of land normally purchase land-intensive products from countries that do have vast amounts of suitable land. The United States, for example, is one of the leading exporters of wheat. The combination of advanced farming technology, skilled farmers, and large tracts of suitable farmland in the Midwest and the Great Plains makes the mass production of wheat possible.

Over time a nation's work force will change, and thus the goods and services that nation produces and exports will change. Nations that train their workers for future roles can minimize the difficulty of making a transition to a new, dominant market. The United States, for example, was the dominant world manufacturer from the end of World War II until the early 1970s. But, beginning in the 1970s, other countries started to produce finished products more cheaply and efficiently than the United States, causing U.S. manufacturing output and exports to drop significantly. However, rapid growth in computer technology began to provide a major export for the United States. Practically speaking, the United States has been slowly transformed from a manufacturing-based economy into a new Information Age-based economy that relies on exporting cutting-edge technology as high tech software and computer companies proliferate.

Political Environment

Each country varies regarding international trade and relocation of foreign plants on its native soil. Some countries openly court foreign companies and encourage them to invest in their country by offering reduced taxes or some other investment incentives. Other countries impose strict regulations that can cause large companies to leave and open a plant in a country that provides more favorable operating conditions. When a company decides to conduct business in another country, it should also consider the political stability of the host country's government. Unstable leadership can create significant problems in recouping profits if the government falls of the host country and/ or changes its policy towards foreign trade and investment. Political instability is often caused by severe economic conditions that result in civil unrest.

Another key aspect of international trade is paying for a product in a foreign currency. This practice can create potential problems for a company, since any currency is subject to price fluctuation. A company could lose money if the value of the foreign currency is reduced before it can be exchanged into the desired currency. Another issue regarding currency is that some nations do not have the necessary cash. Instead, they engage in counter trade, which involves the direct or indirect exchange of goods for other goods instead of for cash. Counter trade follows the same principles as bartering, a practice that stretches back into prehistory. A car company might trade new cars to a foreign government in exchange for high-quality steel that would be more costly to buy on the open market. The company can then use the steel to produce new cars for sale.

In a more extreme case, some countries do not want to engage in free trade with other nations, a choice known as self-sufficiency. There are many reasons for this choice, but the most important is the existence of strong political beliefs. For example, the former Soviet Union and its communist allies traded only with each other because the Soviet Union feared that Western countries would attempt to control their governments through trade. Self-sufficiency allowed the Soviet Union and its allies to avoid that possibility. However, these self-imposed trade restrictions created a shortage of products that could not be produced among the group, making the overall quality of life within the Soviet bloc substantially lower than in the West since consumer demand could not be met. When the Berlin Wall came down, trade with the West was resumed, and the shortage of products was reduced or eliminated.

Economic Environment

An important factor influencing international trade is taxes. Of the different taxes that can be applied to imported goods, the most common is a tariff, which is generally defined as an excise tax imposed on imported goods. A country can have several reasons for imposing a tariff. For example, a revenue tariff may be applied to an imported product that is also produced domestically. The primary reason for this type of tariff is to generate revenue that can be used later by the government for a variety of purposes. This tariff is normally set at a low level and is usually not considered a threat to international trade. When domestic manufacturers in a particular industry are at a disadvantage, vis-à-vis imports, the government can impose what is called a protective tariff. This type of tariff is designed to make foreign products more expensive than domestic products and, as a result, protect domestic companies. A protective tariff is normally very popular with the affected domestic companies and their workers because they benefit most directly from it.

In retaliation, a country that is affected by a protective tariff will frequently enact a tariff of its own on a product from the original tariff enacting country. In 1930, for example, the U.S. Congress passed the Smoot-Hawley Tariff Act, which provided the means for placing protective tariffs on imports. The United States imposed this protective tariff on a wide variety of products in an attempt to help protect domestic producers from foreign competition. This legislation was very popular in the United States, because the Great Depression had just begun, and the tariff was seen as helping U.S. workers. However, the tariff caused immediate retaliation by other countries, which immediately imposed protective tariffs of their own on U.S. products. As a result of these protective tariffs, world trade was severely reduced for nearly all countries, causing the wealth of each affected nation to drop, and increasing unemployment in most countries. Realizing that the 1930 tariffs were a mistake, Congress took corrective action by passing the Reciprocal Trade Agreements Act of 1934, which empowered the president to reduce tariffs by 50 percent on goods from any other country that would agree to similar tariff reductions. The goal was to promote more international trade and help establish more cooperation among exporting countries.

Another form of a trade barrier that a country can employ to protect domestic companies is an import quota, which strictly limits the amount of a particular product that a foreign country can export to the quota-enacting country. For example, the United States had threatened to limit the number of cars imported from Japan. However, Japan agreed to voluntary export quotas, formally known as "voluntary export restrictions," to avoid U.S. imposed import quotas. The power of import quotas has diminished because foreign manufacturers have started building plants in the countries to which they had previously exported in order to avoid such regulations.

A government can also use a no-ntariff barrier to help protect domestic companies. A nontariff barrier usually refers to government requirements for licenses, permits, or significant amounts of paperwork in order to allow imports into its country. This tactic often increases the price of the imported product, slows down delivery, and creates frustration for the exporting country. The end goal is that many foreign companies will not bother to export their products to those markets because of the added cost and aggravation. Japan and several European countries have frequently used this strategy to limit the number of imported products.

Cultural Environment

Before a corporation begins exporting products to other countries, it must first examine the norms, taboos, and values of those countries. This information can be critical to the successful introduction of a product into a particular country and will influence how it is sold and/or marketed. Such information can prevent cultural blunders, such as the one General Motors committed when trying to sell its Chevy Nova in Spanish-speaking countries. Nova, in Spanish, means "doesn't go"-and few people would purchase a car named "doesn't go." This marketing error-resulting simply from ignorance of the Spanish language-cost General Motors millions in initial sales-as well as considerable embarrassment.

Business professionals also need to be aware of foreign customs regarding standard business practices. For example, people from some countries like to sit or stand very close when conducting business. In contrast, people from other countries want to maintain a spatial distance between them and the people with whom they are conducting business. Thus, before business-people travel overseas, they must be given training on how to conduct business in the country to which they are traveling.

Business professionals also run into another practice that occurs in some countries-bribery. The practice of bribery is common in several countries and is considered a normal business practice. If the bribe is not paid to a business-person from a country where bribery is expected, a transaction is unlikely to occur. Laws in some countries prohibit businesspeople from paying or accepting bribes. As a result, navigating this legal and cultural thicket must be done very carefully in order to maintain full compliance with the law.

Physical Environment

Other factors that influence international trading activities are related to the physical environment. Natural physical features, such as mountains and rivers, and human-made structures, such as bridges and roads, can have an impact on international trading activities. For example, a large number of potential customers may live in a country where natural physical barriers, such as mountains and rivers, make getting the product to market nearly impossible.

6

Globalisation Trends of Banking

INTRODUCTION

Banking, the business of providing financial services to consumers and businesses. The basic services a bank provides are checking accounts, which can be used like money to make payments and purchase goods and services; savings accounts and time deposits that can be used to save money for future use; loans that consumers and businesses can use to purchase goods and services; and basic cash management services such as check cashing and foreign currency exchange. Four types of banks specialize in offering these basic banking services: commercial banks, savings and loan associations, savings banks, and credit unions.

A broader definition of a bank is any financial institution that receives, collects, transfers, pays, exchanges, lends, invests, or safeguards money for its customers. This broader definition includes many other financial institutions that are not usually thought of as banks but which nevertheless provide one or more of these broadly defined banking services. These institutions include finance companies, investment companies, investment banks, insurance companies, pension funds, security brokers and dealers, mortgage companies, and real estate investment trusts. This article, however, focuses on the narrower definition of a bank and the services provided by banks in Canada and the United States.

Banking services are extremely important in a free market economy such as that found in Canada and the United States. Banking services serve two primary purposes. First, by supplying customers with the basic mediums-of-exchange (cash, checking accounts, and credit cards), banks play a key role in the way goods and services are purchased. Without these familiar methods of payment, goods could only be exchanged by barter (trading one good for another), which is extremely time-consuming and inefficient. Second, by accepting money deposits from savers and then lending the money to borrowers, banks encourage the flow of money to productive use and investments. This in turn allows the economy to grow. Without this flow, savings would sit idle in someone's safe or pocket, money would not be available to borrow, people would not be able to purchase cars or houses, and businesses would not be able to build the new factories the economy needs to produce more goods and grow. Enabling the flow of money from savers to investors is called financial intermediation, and it is extremely important to a free market economy. It is the stated policy of most First World countries to eliminate protectionism through free trade policies enforced by international treaties and organizations such as the World Trade Organization. Despite this, many of these countries still place protective and/or revenue tariffs on foreign products to protect some favored or politically influential industries, or to reduce the taxation demands on their internal domestic manufacturing, making their products more competitive. The elimination of these tariffs remains a contentious peg their currencies to the dollar and, thus, set prices of their exports lower than they would be if the market determined the relative prices of each currency.

Protectionist quotas can cause foreign producers to become more profitable, mitigating their desired effect. This happens because quotas artificially restrict supply, so it is unable to meet demand; as a result the foreign producer can command a premium price for its products. These increased profits are known as quota rents.

For example, in the United States (1981-1994), Japanese automobile companies were held to voluntary export quotas. These quotas limited the supply of Japanese automobiles desired by consumers in the United States (1.68 million, raised to 1.85 million in 1984, and raised again to 2.30 million in 1985), increasing the profit margin on each automobile more than enough (14% or about $1200 in 1983 dollars, about $2300 in 2005 dollars) to cover the reduction in the number of automobiles that they sold, leading to greater overall profits for Japanese automobile manufacturers in the United States export market (Berry et al. 1999).

BANKING INSTITUTIONS

Banking institutions include commercial banks, savings and loan associations (SLAs), savings banks, and credit unions. The major differences between these types of banks involve how they are owned and how they manage their assets and liabilities. Assets of banks are typically cash, loans, securities (bonds, but not stocks), and property in which the bank has invested. Liabilities are primarily the deposits received from the bank's customers. They are known as liabilities because they are still owned by, and can be withdrawn by, the depositors of the financial institution.

Until the early 1980s, the assets and liabilities of banks were tightly regulated. As a result, clear distinctions existed between the activities and types of services offered by these different types of banks. Although subsequent deregulation in the 1990s blurred these distinctions, differences do remain.

Commercial Banks

Commercial banks are so named because they specialize in loans to commercial and industrial businesses. Commercial banks are owned by private investors, called stockholders, or by companies called bank holding companies. The vast majority of commercial banks are owned by bank holding companies. (A holding company is a corporation that exists only to hold shares in another company.) In 1984, 62 percent of banks were owned by holding companies. In 2000, 76 percent of banks were owned by holding companies. The bank holding company form of ownership became increasingly attractive for several reasons. First, holding companies could engage in activities not permitted in the bank itself-for example, offering investment advice, underwriting securities, and engaging in other investment banking activities. But these activities were permitted in the bank if the holding company owned separate companies that offer these services.

Using the holding company form of organization, bankers could then diversify their product lines and offer services requested by their customers and provided by their European counterparts. Second, many states had laws that restricted a bank from opening branches to within a certain number of miles from the bank's main branch. By setting up a holding company, a banking firm could locate new banks around the state and therefore put branches in locations not previously available.

Commercial banks are "for profit" organizations. Their objective is to make a profit. The profits either can be paid out to bank stockholders or to the holding company in the form of dividends, or the profits can be retained to build capital (net worth). Commercial banks traditionally have the broadest variety of assets and liabilities.

Their historical specialties have been commercial lending to businesses on the asset side and checking accounts for businesses and individuals on the liability side. However, commercial banks also make consumer loans for automobiles and other consumer goods as well as real estate (mortgage) loans for both consumers and businesses.

Savings and Loan Associations

Savings and loan associations (SLAs) are usually owned by stockholders, but they can be owned by depositors as well. (If owned by depositors, they are called "mutuals.") If stock owned, the goal is to earn a profit that can either be paid out as a dividend or retained to increase capital. If owned by depositors, the objective is to earn a profit that can be used either to build capital or lower future loan rates or to raise future deposit rates for the depositor-owners. Until the early 1980s, regulations restricted SLAs to investing in real estate mortgage loans and accepting savings accounts and time deposits (savings accounts that exist for a specified period of time). As a result, historically SLAs have specialized in savings deposits and mortgage lending.

Savings Banks

Traditional savings banks, also known as mutual savings banks (MSBs), have no stockholders, and their assets are administered for the sole benefit of depositors. Earnings are paid to depositors after expenses are met and reserves are set aside to insure the deposits. During the 1980s savings banks were in a great state of flux, and many began to provide the same kinds of services as commercial banks.

Since 1982 savings banks have been permitted to convert to SLAs. SLAs also may convert to savings banks. Both SLAs and MSBs can now offer a full range of financial services, including multiple savings instruments; checking accounts; consumer, commercial, and agricultural loans; and trust and credit card services.

Credit Unions

Credit unions are not-for-profit, cooperative organizations that are owned by their members. Their goal is to minimize the rate members pay on loans and maximize the rate paid to members on deposits. Whatever surplus is earned is retained to build the capital of the credit union. Members must share a common bond.

That bond is typically employment (members all work for the same employers) or geography (members all live in the same geographic area). Historically, credit unions specialized in providing automobile and other personal loans and savings deposits for their members. However, more recently credit unions have offered mortgage loans, credit card loans, and some commercial loans in addition to checking accounts and time deposits.

Credit unions, SLAs, and savings banks help encourage thriftiness by paying interest to consumers who put their money in savings deposits. Consequently, credit unions, SLAs, and savings banks are often referred to as thrift institutions.

Of the various types of banks in the United States, commercial banks account for the greatest single source of the financial industry's assets. In 2000 the 8,528 commercial banks in the United States controlled 24 percent of the financial industry's total assets. Commercial banks, however, have seen their share of financial-industry assets erode over time, as more money has shifted to money market and other mutual funds.

In the mid-1990s, for example, the approximately 11,000 commercial banks then in existence controlled 27 percent of assets. In 1950 they controlled nearly 50 percent of financial assets. Savings institutions' share of financial assets has also dropped from roughly 13 percent in 1950 to 5 percent in 2000. Credit unions' share has remained fairly constant at 2 percent.

BANKING SERVICES

Commercial banks and thrifts offer various services to their customers. These services fall into three major categories: deposits, loans, and cash management services.

Deposits

There are four major types of deposits: demand deposits, savings deposits, hybrid checking/savings deposits, and time deposits. What distinguishes one type from another are the conditions under which the deposited funds may be withdrawn.

A demand deposit is a deposit that can be withdrawn on demand at any time and in any amount up to the full amount of the deposit. The most common example of a demand deposit is a checking account. Money orders and traveler's checks are also technically demand deposits. Checking accounts are also considered transaction accounts in that payments can be made to third parties-that is, to someone other than the depositor or the bank itself-via check, telephone, or other authorized transfer instruction. Checking accounts are popular because as demand deposits they provide perfect liquidity (immediate access to cash) and as transaction accounts they can be transferred to a third party as payment for goods or services. As such, they function like money.

Savings accounts pay interest to the depositor, but have no specific maturity date on which the funds need to be withdrawn or reinvested. Any amount can be withdrawn from a savings account up to the amount deposited. Under normal circumstances, customers can withdraw their money from a savings account simply by presenting their "passbook" or by using their automated teller machine (ATM) card. Savings accounts are highly liquid. They are different from demand deposits, however, because depositors cannot write checks against regular savings accounts. Savings accounts cannot be used directly as money to purchase goods or services.

The hybrid savings and checking account allows customers to earn interest on the account and write checks against the account. These are called either negotiable order of withdrawal (NOW) accounts, or money market deposit accounts, which are savings accounts that allow a maximum of three third-party transfers each month.

Time deposits are deposits on which the depositor and the bank have agreed that the money will not be withdrawn without substantial penalty to the depositor before a specific date. These are frequently called certificates of deposits (CDs). Because of a substantial early withdrawal penalty, time deposits are not as liquid as demand or savings deposits nor can depositors write checks against them. Time deposits also typically require a minimum deposit amount.

Loans

Banks and thrifts make three types of loans: commercial and industrial loans, consumer loans, and mortgage loans. Commercial and industrial loans are loans to businesses or industrial firms. These are primarily short-term working capital loans (loans to finance the purchase of material or labor) or transaction or longer-term loans (loans to purchase machines and equipment). Most commercial banks offer a variable rate on these loans, which means that the interest rate can change over the course of the loan. Whether a bank will make a loan or not depends on the credit and loan history of the borrower, the borrower's ability to make scheduled loan payments, the amount of capital the borrower has invested in the business, the condition of the economy, and the value of the collateral the borrower pledges to give the bank if the loan payments are not made.

Consumer loans are loans for consumers to purchase goods or services. There are two types of consumer loans: closed-end credit and open-end credit.

Closed-end credit loans are loans for a fixed amount of money, for a fixed period of time (usually not more than five years), and for a fixed purpose (for example, to buy a car). Most closed-end loans are called installment loans because they must be repaid in equal monthly installments. The item purchased by the consumer serves as collateral for the loan. For example, if the consumer fails to make payments on an automobile, the bank can recoup the cost of its loan by taking ownership of the car.

Open-end credit loans are loans for variable amounts of money up to a set limit. Unlike closed-end loans, open-end credit does not require a borrower to specify the purpose of the loan and the lender cannot foreclose on the loan. Credit cards are an example of open-end credit. Most open-end loans carry fixed interest rates-that is, the rate does not vary over the term of the loan.

Open-end loans require no collateral, but interest rates or other penalties or fees may be charged-for example, if credit card charges are not paid in full, interest is charged, or if payment is late, a fee is charged to the borrower. Open-end credit interest rates usually exceed closed-end rates because open-end loans are not backed by collateral.

Mortgage loans or real estate loans are loans used to purchase land or buildings such as houses or factories. These are typically long-term loans and the interest rate charged can be either a variable or a fixed rate for the term of the loan, which often ranges from 15 to 30 years. The land and buildings purchased serve as the collateral for the loan.

Cash Management and Other Services

Although deposits and loans are the basic banking services provided by banks and thrifts, these institutions provide a wide variety of other services to customers. For consumers, these include check cashing, foreign currency exchange, safety deposit boxes in which consumers can store valuables, electronic wire transfer through which consumers can transfer money and securities from one financial institution to another, and credit life insurance which automatically pays off loans in the event of the borrower's death or disability.

In recent years, banks have made their services increasingly convenient through electronic banking. Electronic banking uses computers to carry out transfers of money. For example, automated teller machines (ATMs) enable bank customers to withdraw money from their checking or savings accounts by inserting an ATM card and a private electronic code into an ATM. The ATMs enable bank customers to access their money 24 hours a day and seven days a week wherever ATMs are located, including in foreign countries. Banks also offer debit cards that directly withdraw funds from a customer's account for the amount of a purchase, much like writing a check. Banks also use electronic transfers to deposit payroll checks directly into a customer's account and to automatically pay a customer's bills when they are due. Many banks also use the Internet to enable customers to pay bills, move money between accounts, and perform other banking functions.

For businesses, commercial banks also provide specialized cash management and credit enhancement services. Cash management services are designed to allow businesses to make efficient use of their cash. For example, under normal circumstances a business would sell its product to a customer and send the customer a bill. The customer would then send a check to the business, and the business would then deposit the check in the bank. The time between the date the business receives the check and deposits the check in the bank could be several days or a week. To eliminate this delay and allow the business to earn interest on its money sooner, commercial banks offer services to businesses whereby customers send checks directly to the bank, not the business. This practice is referred to as "lock box" services because the payments are mailed to a secure post office box where they are picked up by bank couriers for immediate deposit.

Another important business service performed by banks is a credit enhancement. Commercial banks back up the performance of businesses by promising to pay the debts of the business if the business itself cannot pay. This service substitutes the credit of the bank for the credit of the business. This is valuable, for example, in international trade where the exporting firm is unfamiliar with the importing firm in another country and is, therefore, reluctant to ship goods without knowing for certain that the importer will pay for them. By substituting the credit of a foreign bank known to the exporter's bank, the exporter knows payment will be made and will ship the goods. Credit enhancements are frequently called standby letters of credit or commercial letters of credit.

BENEFITS FOR THE ECONOMY

The deposit and loan services provided by banks benefit an economy in many ways. First, checking accounts, because they act like cash, make it much easier to buy goods and services and therefore help both consumers and businesses, who would find it inconvenient to carry or send through the mail huge amounts of cash. Second, loans enable consumers to improve their standard of living by borrowing money to purchase cars, houses, and other expensive consumer goods that they otherwise could not afford. Third, loans help businesses finance plant expansion and production of new goods, and therefore increase employment and economic growth. Finally, since banks want loans repaid, banks choose borrowers carefully and monitor performance of a company's managers very closely. This helps ensure that only the best projects get financed and that companies are run efficiently. This creates a healthy, efficient economy. In addition, since the owners (stockholders) of a company receiving a loan want their company to be profitable and managed efficiently, bankers act as surrogate monitors for stockholders who cannot be present on a regular basis to watch the company's managers.

The checking account services offered by banks provide an additional benefit to the economy. Because checks are widely accepted as payment for goods and services, the checking accounts offered by banks are functionally equivalent to real money-that is, currency and coin. When banks issue checking accounts they, in effect, create money without the federal government having to print more currency. Under government regulations in many countries, banks must hold a reserve of paper currency and coin equal to at least 10 percent of their checking account deposits. In the United States banks keep these reserves in their own vaults or on deposit with the U.S. government's central bank known as the Federal Reserve, or the Fed. If someone wants a $10 loan, the bank can give that person a $10 checking account with only $1 of currency in its vault. As a result U.S. banks can create at least $10 of checking account money for every $1 of real money (currency or coin) actually printed by the federal government. This arrangement, which allows extra deposit money to be created by banks, is referred to as a fractional reserve banking system. Because banks attract large amounts of savings from depositors, banks can make many loans to many different customers in various amounts and for various maturities (dates when loans are due). Banks can thereby diversify their loans, and this in turn means that a bank is at less risk if one of its customers fails to repay a loan. The lowering of risk makes bank deposits safer for depositors. Safety encourages even more bank deposits and therefore even more loans. This flow of money from savers through banks to the ultimate borrower is called financial intermediation because money flows through an intermediary-that is, the bank.

BANKING REGULATION

Banking is one of the most heavily regulated industries in the United States, and the regulatory structure is quite complex. This owes in part to the fact that the United States has a dual banking system. A dual banking system means that banks and thrifts can be chartered and therefore regulated either by the state in which they operate or by a national chartering agency.

The Office of the Comptroller of the Currency (OCC) in the U.S. Department of Treasury is the federal chartering agency for national banks. The Office of the Comptroller of the Currency provides general supervision of national banks, including periodic bank examinations to determine compliance with rules and regulations and the soundness of bank operations. The Office of Thrift Supervision (OTS) in the Treasury Department charters national savings and loans (SLAs) and savings banks.

The agencies that insure deposits in banks and thrifts also have a role in regulating them. Almost all banks and thrifts are federally insured by the Federal Deposit Insurance Corporation (FDIC). The FDIC insures each depositor (not each separate deposit) for up to $100,000 in each bank or thrift in which the depositor has deposits and up to $250,000 for individual retirement accounts (IRAs) held in a bank or savings association. The Bank Insurance Fund (BIF) in the FDIC insures commercial bank and savings bank deposits. The Savings Association Insurance Fund (SAIF) in the FDIC insures savings and loan deposits. The National Credit Union Share Insurance Fund (NCUSIF) in the National Credit Union Administration (NCUA) insures credit union deposits.

The Federal Reserve is also responsible for regulating commercial banks that are members of the Federal Reserve System and bank holding companies. As a result, a nationally chartered, federally insured, Federal Reserve member bank is subject to the regulations of the OCC, BIF, and the Federal Reserve.

The regulatory landscape is complicated further by the fact that state banking authorities regulate state-chartered banks and frequently conduct their own examinations of state banks. To help sort out the maze of potential regulators, banks are assigned one regulator with primary responsibility for examining the bank. The primary regulator of nationally chartered banks and thrifts is the OCC. The primary regulator of state-chartered banks that belong to the Federal Reserve is the Federal Reserve. The primary regulator of state-chartered banks that are not Fed members but are FDIC insured is the FDIC, while the primary regulator of state-chartered, non-insured banks is the state.

The regulatory agencies also enforce legislation passed by the U.S. Congress. Such legislation attempts to ensure that lending institutions act fairly and that bank customers are well informed about banking services and practices. For example, the Truth-in-Lending Act (1968) and the Fair Credit and Charge Card Disclosure Act (1988) require lenders to disclose the true interest rate on loans on a uniform basis so that borrowers know the true cost of credit.

The Fair Housing Act (1968) and the Equal Credit Opportunity Act (1976) prohibit discrimination against borrowers on the basis of race, color, religion, national origin, sex, marital status, age, or receipt of public assistance. The Community Reinvestment Act (1977) requires banks, savings and loans, and savings banks to meet the credit needs of their local communities. This act was intended to prevent banks located in low-income areas from refusing loans to local residents, who were often members of minority groups. The Truth-in-Savings Act (1991) mandates uniform disclosure of the terms and conditions that banking institutions impose on their deposit accounts so that depositors know the true interest rate they receive on their deposits.

CENTRAL BANKING

Governments create central banks to perform a variety of functions. The functions actually performed vary considerably from country to country. Broadly speaking, central banks serve as the government's banker, as the banker to the banking system, and as the policymaker for monetary and financial matters.

As the government's banker, the central bank can act as the repository for government receipts, as the collection agent for taxes, and as the auctioneer for government debt. It can also act as a lender to the government and as the government's advisor on financial matters. As the banker for the country's banks, the central bank can act as the repository for bank reserves, as the supervisor and regulator of banks, as the facilitator of interbank services such as check clearing and money transfers, and as a lender when banks need money to honor deposit withdrawals or other needs for liquidity.

As the country's monetary policymaker, the central bank controls the amount of credit and money available, the level of interest rates, and the exchange rate (the rate at which one nation's currency can be exchanged for another nation's). To achieve its monetary policy objectives, central bankers use a combination of policy tools. For example, the central bank may increase or decrease the amount of money (coin and currency) in circulation by buying or selling government debt instruments, such as bonds, on the open market. This policy tool is known as open market operations. Since interest rates are usually related to how much money and credit are available in the economy, the central bank can usually lower interest rates by buying bonds from the public with money. This increases the amount of money in the economy and lowers interest rates. To raise rates, the authority would sell bonds, thereby reducing the amount of money available to the public. The central bank could also cause a lowering or raising of interest rates by increasing or decreasing the amount of money banks must hold as a reserve against their deposits. By increasing reserves, the central bank forces banks to hold more money in their vaults, which means they can lend less money. Less money available for loans makes loans harder to get which, in turn, causes banks and other lenders to raise interest rates on loans.

Central banks can be either privately owned or owned by the government. In Europe, central banks are owned and operated by the government. In the United States, commercial banks own the central bank, which is called the Federal Reserve. The Federal Reserve, established in 1913, consists of a seven-person Board of Governors located in Washington, D.C., and the presidents of 12 regional Federal Reserve Banks. Each member of the Board of Governors is appointed by the U.S. president and confirmed by the U.S. Senate for staggered 14-year terms. From among the seven governors, the president also designates and the Senate confirms a chairman of the board for a four-year term. The Federal Reserve's primary policy group is called the Federal Open Market Committee (FOMC). It consists of the seven governors plus five regional Federal Reserve Bank presidents. The FOMC is responsible for controlling the money supply and interest rates in the United States.

Because central banks control the money supply, there is always the danger that central banks will simply create more money and then lend it to the government to finance its expenditures. This often leads to excessive money creation and inflation (a continuous increase in the prices of goods), which can be caused by having too much money available to purchase goods. Inflation occurred in the United States when the government printed Continental dollars to pay for the Revolutionary War. So many were printed that they became worthless, and a popular slogan of the day was "It's not worth a Continental."

The danger of inflation is particularly acute in countries where the government owns the central bank. Government ownership of the central bank is illegal in the United States, except in national emergencies. European countries agreed in the Maastricht Treaty of 1992 not to allow central banks to lend money to their governments.

BANKING IN OTHER COUNTRIES

Canada

Because of Canada's close historical relationship with the United States and the United Kingdom, development of the Canadian banking system has been influenced by both countries. Unlike the United States, however, Canada always had a branch-banking system. Until 1994 banks in the United States were restricted to opening branches only in the city or state where they were incorporated. One of the first laws passed by Canada's Parliament after confederation, in 1867, allowed any Canadian-chartered bank to operate in any part of the dominion. This law encouraged the growth of Canada's branch-banking system, in which a few large banks operate all the country's banking offices. In 2000 there were only 13 domestic banks in Canada, and the six largest controlled more than 90 percent of all bank assets in Canada. The remaining seven domestic banks accounted for about 2 percent of bank assets, and foreign banks accounted for about 7 percent of bank assets.

The largest commercial banks of Canada operate extensively in foreign countries, particularly in the West Indies, Asia, and the United States. In addition to the usual business of commercial loans, Canadian banks operating in foreign countries have specialized in investment banking and wealth-management activities. The regulator of federally chartered Canadian banks and financial institutions is the Office of the Superintendent of Financial Institutions (OSFI), which was established in 1987. Since 1967 deposit insurance has been provided by the Canada Deposit Insurance Corporation (CBIC), which insures up to $60,000 Canadian per depositor per institution. Both the OSFI and the CBIC are Crown Corporations owned by the government.

The central bank of Canada is the Bank of Canada. Created in 1935, it is owned by the Ministry of Finance and is responsible for Canadian monetary policy. Unlike the U.S. Federal Reserve, the Bank of Canada is also responsible for issuing and managing the national debt. In the United States, this function is performed by the Department of the Treasury. The primary policy group of the Bank of Canada is called the Governing Council. This group consists of the governor of the Bank of Canada, the senior deputy governor, and four deputy governors. The Bank of Canada is less independent of the government than is the U.S. Federal Reserve because it must consult with the minister of finance on policy matters.

The European Continent

Until recently, European banking was very different from banking in the United States. European banks were frequently owned by the government and could engage in activities that were prohibited to banks in the United States. Most of these prohibited activities involved investment banking such as security underwriting (selling a firm's stock or bonds at a guaranteed price) or security placement (finding buyers for a firm's stock or bonds). These services are important to businesses and being able to provide them gave European banks an advantage over U.S. banks. These differences are rapidly disappearing. Most European banks are now privately owned and recent U.S. legislation has allowed U.S. banks to engage in investment-banking activities through the bank holding company form of organization.

Two differences remain between U.S. and European banking. The first is that many European banks can own nonbank commercial and industrial businesses. Such ownership is still prohibited, for the most part, for U.S. banks and holding companies. As a result, banks in Europe tend to be more business oriented and much more involved with corporate governance (corporate decision-making) than their U.S. counterparts. This also explains why most European companies rely more heavily on bank loans to finance their activities than do U.S. companies which rely more on funds raised by selling stocks and bonds in financial markets.

The second difference is that banking is much more concentrated in Europe. In other words, banking markets are dominated by a few large banks whereas in the United States many banks compete for a customer's deposits and loans. This stems from the fact that European countries have had very liberal branching laws allowing banks to have extensive deposit-gathering networks in their home country and also from the fact that most European countries are not as concerned about monopolies as are U.S. regulators. It is not clear how long this difference will last, however, as legislation in the United States in 1994 allowed banks to establish banks and branches in other states.

The establishment of the Economic and Monetary Union (EMU) in 1992 created a new banking system in Europe that parallels that of the United States in many ways. The EMU created a new European Central Bank (ECB) that will coordinate monetary policy throughout most of continental Europe. It also established a uniform currency in Europe called the euro that beginning in 2002 was the currency used throughout Western Europe, except in Denmark, Sweden, and the United Kingdom. The EMU also allowed banks to branch throughout Europe and not just in their home country.

United Kingdom

Since the 17th century Britain has been known for its prominence in banking. The capital, London, still remains a major financial center, and virtually all the world's leading commercial banks are represented there.

Aside from the central Bank of England, which was incorporated, early English banks were privately owned rather than stock-issuing firms. Bank failures were common; so in the early 19th century, stock-issuing banks, with a larger capital base, were encouraged as a means of stabilizing the industry.

By 1833 these corporate banks were permitted to accept and transfer deposits in London, although they were prohibited from issuing money, a prerogative monopolized by the Bank of England. Corporate banking flourished after legislation in 1858 approved limited liability for stock-issuing banks. The banking system, however, failed to preserve the large number of institutions typical of U.S. banking. At the turn of the 20th century, a wave of bank mergers reduced both the number of private and stock-issuing banks.

The present structure of British commercial banking was substantially in place by the 1930s, with the Bank of England, then privately owned, at the apex, and 11 London clearing banks ranked below the Bank of England. Clearing banks sort and then forward checks to the bank from which they were originally drawn for payment. Two changes have occurred since then: The Bank of England was nationalized (became government-owned) in 1946 by the postwar Labour government; and in 1968 a merger among the largest five clearing banks left the industry in the hands of four: Barclays, Lloyds (now Lloyds TSB Group), Midland (now part of HSBC Holdings), and National Westminster (taken over by the Royal Bank of Scotland in 2000).

The larger clearing banks, with their national branch networks, dominate British banking. They are the key links in the transfer of business payments through the checking system, as well as the primary source of short-term business finance.

Moreover, through their ownership and control over subsidiaries, the big British banks influence other financial markets such as consumer and housing finance and merchant banking. The dominance of the clearing banks was challenged in recent years by the rise of "parallel markets," encompassing financial activities by smaller banking houses, building societies (banking institutions similar to SLAs in the United States), and other financial concerns, as well as local government authorities. The major banks responded to this competition by offering new services and competitive terms.

A restructuring in the banking industry took place in the late 1970s. The Banking Act of 1979 formalized Bank of England control over the British banking system, which was previously supervised on an informal basis. Only institutions approved by the Bank of England as "recognized banks" or "licensed deposit-taking institutions" are permitted to accept deposits from the public. The act also extended Bank of England control over the new financial intermediaries that have flourished since 1960.

Developing Countries

The type of national economic system that characterizes developing countries plays a crucial role in determining the nature of the banking system in those countries. In capitalist countries a system of private enterprise in banking prevails.

In state-managed economies, banks have been nationalized. Other countries have patterned themselves after the social-democracies of Europe; in Egypt, Peru, and Kenya, for instance, government-owned and privately owned banks coexist. In many countries, the banking system developed under colonialism, with banks owned by institutions in the parent country. In some, such as

Zambia and Cameroon, this heritage continued, although modified, after decolonization.

In other nations, such as Nigeria and Saudi Arabia, the rise of nationalism led to mandates for majority ownership by the indigenous population. Banks in developing countries are similar to their counterparts in developed nations. Commercial banks accept and transfer deposits and are active lenders, especially for short-term purposes.

Other financial intermediaries, particularly government-owned development banks, arrange long-term loans. Banks are often used to finance government expenditures. The banking system may also play a major role in financing exports.

7

Types of Banking Activity and Issuing Fiduciary Money

INTRODUCTION

Modern banks, beside their banking activities proper, carry on various other more or less closely related branches of business. There is, for example, the business of exchanging money, on the basis of which the beginnings of the banking system in the Middle Ages were developed, and to which the bill of exchange, one of the most important instruments of banking activity, owes its origin. Banks still carry on this business nowadays, but so do exchange bureaus, which perform no banking functions; and these also devote themselves to such business as the purchase and sale of securities. The banks have also taken over a number of functions connected with the general management of the property of their customers. They accept and look after securities as "open" deposits, detach interest and dividend coupons as they fall due, and receive the sums concerned. They superintend the allotment of shares, attend to the renewal of coupon sheets, and see to other similar matters. The business of banking falls into two distinct branches: the negotiation of credit through the loan of other people's money and the granting of credit through the issue of fiduciary media, that is, notes and bank balances that are not covered by money. Both branches of business have always been closely connected.

They have grown up on a common historical soil, and nowadays are still often carried on together by the same firm. This connection cannot be ascribed to merely external and accidental factors; it is founded on the peculiar nature of fiduciary media, and on the historical development of the business of banking. Nevertheless, the two kinds of activity must be kept strictly apart in economic theory; for only by considering each of them separately is it possible to understand their nature and functions. The unsatisfactory results of previous investigations into the theory of banking are primarily attributable to inadequate consideration of the fundamental difference between them. They carry out stock exchange dealings for their customers and also the purchase and sale of securities that are not quoted on the exchange. They let out strong rooms which are used for the secure disposal of articles of value under the customer's seal. All of these activities, whatever their bearing in individual cases upon the profitability of the whole undertaking, and however great their economic significance for the community as a whole, yet have no inherent connection with banking proper as we have defined it above.

The connection between banking proper and the business of speculation and flotation is similarly loose and superficial. This is the branch of their activities on which the general economic importance of the banks nowadays depends, and by means of which on the continent of Europe and in the United States they secured control of production, no less than of the provision of credit. It would not be easy to overestimate the influence on the organization of economic life that has been exerted by the change in the relation of the banks to industry and commerce; perhaps it would not be an exaggeration to describe it as the most important event in modern economic history. But in connection with the influence of banking on the exchange ratio between money and other economic goods, which alone concerns us here, it has no significance at all.

BANKS AS CREDIT NEGOTIATORS

The activity of the banks as negotiators of credit is characterized by the lending of other people's, that is, of borrowed, money. Banks borrow money in order to lend it; the difference between the rate of interest that is paid to them and the rate that they pay, less their working expenses, constitutes their profit on this kind of transaction. Banking is negotiation between granters of credit and grantees of credit. Only those who lend the money of others are bankers; those who merely lend their own capital are capitalists, but not bankers. Our use of this definition of the Classical School should not furnish any ground for terminological controversy. The expression banking may be extended or contracted as one likes, although there seems little reason for departing from a terminology that has been usual since Smith and Ricardo. But one thing is essential: that activity of the banks that consists in lending other people's money must be sharply distinguished from all other branches of their business and subjected to separate consideration.

For the activity of the banks as negotiators of credit the golden rule holds, that an organic connection must be created between the credit transactions and the debit transactions. The credit that the bank grants must correspond quantitatively and qualitatively to the credit that it takes up. More exactly expressed, "The date on which the bank's obligations fall due must not precede the date on which its corresponding claims can be realized." Only thus can the danger of insolvency be avoided. It is true that a risk remains. Imprudent granting of credit is bound to prove just as ruinous to a bank as to any other merchant. That follows from the legal structure of their business; there is no legal connection between their credit transactions and their debit transactions, and their obligation to pay back the money they have borrowed is not affected by the fate of their investments; the obligation continues even if the investments prove dead losses. But it is just the existence of this risk which makes it worthwhile for the bank to play the part of an intermediary between the granter of credit and the grantee of it. It is from the acceptance of this risk that the bank derives its profits and incurs its losses. That is all that needs to be said here about this branch of the business of banking. For as far as money and monetary theory are concerned, even the function of the banks as negotiators of credit is of significance only so far as it is able to influence the issue of fiduciary media, which alone will be discussed in the rest of the present work.

BANKS AS ISSUERS OF FIDUCIARY MEDIA

To comprehend the significance of fiduciary media, it is necessary to examine the nature of credit transactions.

Acts of exchange, whether direct or indirect, can be performed either in such a way that both parties fulfill their parts of the contract at the same time, or in such a way that they fulfill them at different times. In the first case we speak of cash transactions; in the second, of credit transactions. A credit transaction is an exchange of present goods for future goods.

Credit transactions fall into two groups, the separation of which must form the starting point for every theory of credit and especially for every investigation into the connection between money and credit and into the influence of credit on the money prices of goods. On the one hand are those credit transactions which are characterized by the fact that they impose a sacrifice on that party who performs his part of the bargain before the other does-the forgoing of immediate power of disposal over the exchanged good, or, if this version is preferred, the forgoing of power of disposal over the surrendered good until the receipt of that for which it is exchanged. This sacrifice is balanced by a corresponding gain on the part of the other party to the contract-the advantage of obtaining earlier disposal over the good acquired in exchange, or, what is the same thing, of not having to fulfill his part of the bargain immediately. In their respective valuations both parties take account of the advantages and disadvantages that arise from the difference between the times at which they have to fulfill the bargain. The exchange ratio embodied in the contract contains an expression of the value of time in the opinions of the individuals concerned.

The second group of credit transactions is characterized by the fact that in them the gain of the party who receives before he pays is balanced by no sacrifice on the part of the other party. Thus the difference in time between fulfillment and counterfulfillment, which is just as much the essence of this kind of transaction as of the other, has an influence merely on the valuations of the one party, while the other is able to treat it as insignificant. This fact at first seems puzzling, even inexplicable; it constitutes a rock on which many economic theories have come to grief. Nevertheless, the explanation is not very difficult if we take into account the peculiarity of the goods involved in the transaction. In the first kind of credit transactions, what is surrendered consists of money or goods, disposal over which is a source of satisfaction and renunciation of which a source of dissatisfaction. In the credit transactions of the second group, the granter of the credit renounces for the time being the ownership of a sum of money, but this renunciation (given certain assumptions that in this case are justifiable) results for him in no reduction of satisfaction. If a creditor is able to confer a loan by issuing claims which are payable on demand, then the granting of the credit is bound up with no economic sacrifice for him. He could confer credit in this form free of charge, if we disregard the technical costs that may be involved in the issue of notes and the like. Whether he is paid immediately in money or only receives claims at first, which do not fall due until later, remains a matter of indifference to him.

It seems desirable to choose special names for the two groups of credit transactions in order to avoid any possible confusion of the concepts. For the first group the name commodity credit (Sachkredit) is suggested, for the second the name circulation credit (Zirkulationskredit). It must be admitted that these expressions do not fully indicate the essence of the distinction that they are intended to characterize. This objection, however, which can in some degree be urged against all technical terms, is not of very great importance. A sufficient reply to it is contained in the fact that there are no better and more apt expressions in use to convey the distinction intended, which, generally speaking, has not received the consideration it merits. In any case the expression circulation credit gives occasion for fewer errors than the expression emission credit (Emissionskredit), which is sometimes used and has been chosen merely with regard to the issue of notes. Besides, what applies to all such differences of opinion is also true of this particular terminological controversy-the words used do not matter; what does matter is what the words are intended to mean.

Naturally, the peculiarities of circulation credit have not escaped the attention of economists. It is hardly possible to find a single theorist who has devoted serious consideration to the fundamental problems of the value of money and credit without having referred to the peculiar circumstances in which notes and checks are used. That this recognition of the individuality of certain kinds of credit transactions has not led to the distinction of commodity credit and circulation credit is probably to be ascribed to certain accidents in the history of our science. The criticism of isolated dogmatic and economico-political errors of the Currency principle that constituted the essence of most nineteenth-century investigation into the theory of banking and credit led to an emphasis being placed on all the factors that could be used to demonstrate the essential similarity of notes and other media of bank credit, and to the oversight of the important differences that exist between the two groups of credit characterized above, the discovery of which constitutes one of the permanent contributions of the Classical School and its successors, the Currency theorists.

The peculiar attitude of individuals toward transactions involving circulation credit is explained by the circumstance that the claims in which it is expressed can be used in every connection instead of money. He who requires money, in order to lend it, or to buy something, or to liquidate debts, or to pay taxes, is not first obliged to convert the claims to money (notes or bank balances) into money; he can also use the claims themselves directly as means of payment. For everybody they therefore are really money substitutes; they perform the monetary function in the same way as money; they are "ready money" to him, that is, present, not future, money. The practice of the merchant who includes under cash not merely the notes and token coinage which he possesses but also any bank balances which he has constantly at his immediate disposal by means of checks or otherwise is just as correct as that of the legislator who endows these fiduciary media with the legal power of settling all obligations contracted in terms of money-in doing which he only confirms a usage that has been established by commerce.

In all of this there is nothing special or peculiar to money. The objective exchange value of an indubitably secure and mature claim, which embodies a right to receive a definite individual thing or a definite quantity of fungible things, does not differ in the least from the objective exchange value of the thing or quantity of things to which the claim refers. What is significant for us lies in the fact that such claims to money, if there is no doubt whatever concerning either their security or their liquidity, are, simply on account of their equality in objective exchange value to the sums of money to which they refer, commercially competent to take the place of money entirely. Anyone who wishes to acquire bread can achieve his aim by obtaining in the first place a mature and secure claim to bread.

If he only wishes to acquire the bread in order to give it up again in exchange for something else, he can give this claim up instead and is not obliged to liquidate it. But if he wishes to consume the bread, then he has no alternative but to procure it by liquidation of the claim. With the exception of money, all the economic goods that enter into the process of exchange necessarily reach an individual who wishes to consume them; all claims which embody a right to the receipt of such goods will therefore sooner or later have to be realized. A person who takes upon himself the obligation to deliver on demand a particular individual good, or a particular quantity of fungible goods (with the exception of money), must reckon with the fact that he will be held to its fulfillment, and probably in a very short time.

Therefore he dare not promise more than he can be constantly ready to perform. A person who has a thousand loaves of bread at his immediate disposal will not dare to issue more than a thousand tickets each of which gives its holder the right to demand at any time the delivery of a loaf of bread. It is otherwise with money. Since nobody wants money except in order to get rid of it again, since it never finds a consumer except on ceasing to be a common medium of exchange, it is quite possible for claims to be employed in its stead, embodying a right to the receipt on demand of a certain sum of money and unimpugnable both as to their convertibility in general and as to whether they really would be converted on the demand of the holder; and it is quite possible for these claims to pass from hand to hand without any attempt being made to enforce the right that they embody. The obligee can expect that these claims will remain in circulation for so long as their holders do not lose confidence in their prompt convertibility or transfer them to persons who have not this confidence. He is therefore in a position to undertake greater obligations than he would ever be able to fulfill; it is enough if he takes sufficient precautions to ensure his ability to satisfy promptly that proportion of the claims that is actually enforced against him.

The fact that is peculiar to money alone is not that mature and secure claims to money are as highly valued in commerce as the sums of money to which they refer, but rather that such claims are complete substitutes for money, and, as such, are able to fulfill all the functions of money in those markets in which their essential characteristics of maturity and security are recognized. It is this circumstance that makes it possible to issue more of this sort of substitute than the issuer is always in a position to convert. And so the fiduciary medium comes into being in addition to the money certificate.

Fiduciary media increase the supply of money in the broader sense of the word; they are consequently able to influence the objective exchange value of money. To the investigation of this influence the following chapters are devoted.

DEPOSITS AS THE CIRCULATION CREDIT ORIGIN

Fiduciary media have grown up on the soil of the deposit system; deposits have been the basis upon which notes have been issued and accounts opened that could be drawn upon by checks. Independently of this, coins, at first the smaller and then the mediumsized, have developed into fiduciary media. It is usual to reckon the acceptance of a deposit which can be drawn upon at any time by means of notes or checks as a type of credit transaction and juristically this view is, of course, justified; but economically, the case is not one of a credit transaction. If credit in the economic sense means the exchange of a present good or a present service against a future good or a future service, then it is hardly possible to include the transactions in question under the conception of credit. A depositor of a sum of money who acquires in exchange for it a claim convertible into money at any time which will perform exactly the same service for him as the sum it refers to, has exchanged no present good for a future good. The claim that he has acquired by his deposit is also a present good for him. The depositing of the money in no way means that he has renounced immediate disposal over the utility that it commands.

Therefore the claim obtained in exchange for the sum of money is equally valuable to him whether he converts it sooner or later, or even not at all; and because of this it is possible for him, without damaging his economic interests, to acquire such claims in return for the surrender of money without demanding compensation for any difference in value arising from the difference in time between payment and repayment, such, of course, as does not in fact exist. That this could be so repeatedly overlooked is to be ascribed to the long accepted and widely accepted view that the essence of credit consists in the confidence which the lender reposes in the borrower The fact that anybody hands money over to a bank in exchange for a claim to repayment on demand certainly shows that he has confidence in the bank's constant readiness to pay.

But this is not a credit transaction, because the essential element, the exchange of present goods for future goods, is absent. But another circumstance that has helped to bring about the mistaken opinion referred to is the fact that the business performed by banks in exchanging money for claims to money payable on demand which can be transferred in the place of money, is very closely and intimately connected with that particular branch of their credit business that has most influenced the volume of money and entirely transformed the whole monetary system of the present day, namely, the provision of circulation credit. It is with this sort of banking business alone, the issue of notes and the opening of accounts that are not covered by money, that we are concerned. For this sort of business alone is of significance in connection with the function and value of money; the volume of money is affected by no other credit transactions than these.

While all other credit transactions may occur singly and be per formed on both sides by persons who do not regularly occupy themselves with such transactions, the provision of credit through the issue of fiduciary media is only possible on the part of an undertaking which conducts credit transactions as a matter of regular business. Deposits must be accepted and loans granted on a fairly considerable scale before the necessary conditions for the issue of fiduciary media are fulfilled. Notes cannot circulate unless the person who issues them is known and trustworthy. Moreover, payment by transfer from one account to another presupposes either a large circle of customers of the same bank or such a union of several banking undertakings that the total number of participants in the system is large. Fiduciary media can therefore be created only by banks and bankers; but this is not the only business that can be carried on by banks and bankers.

One branch of banking business deserves particular mention because, although closely related to that circle of banking activities with which we have to deal, it is quite without influence on the volume of money. This is that deposit business which does not serve the bank as a basis for the issue of fiduciary media. The activity carried on here by the bank is merely that of an intermediary, concerning which the English definition of a banker as a man who lends other people's money is perfectly apt. The sums of money handed over to the bank by its customers in this branch of business are not a part of their reserves, but investments of money which are not necessary for day-to-day transactions. As a rule the two groups of deposits are distinguished even by the form they have in banking technique.

The current accounts can be withdrawn on demand, that is to say, without previous notice. Often no interest at all is paid upon them, but when interest is paid, it is lower than that on the investment deposits. On the other hand, the investment deposits always bear interest and are usually repayable only on notice being given in advance. In the course of time, the differences in banking technique between the two kinds of deposit have been largely obliterated. The development of the savings-deposit system has made it possible for the banks to undertake the obligation to pay out small amounts of savings deposits at any time without notice. The larger the sums which are brought to the banks in the investment-deposit business, the greater, according to the law of large numbers, is the probability that the sums paid in on any particular day will balance those whose repayment is demanded, and the smaller is the reserve which will guarantee the bank the possibility of not having to break any of its promises. Such a reserve is all the easier to maintain inasmuch as it is combined with the reserve of the current-account business. Small business people or not very well-to-do private individuals, whose monetary affairs are too insignificant to be transferred as a whole to a bank, now make use of this development by trusting part of their reserve to the banks in the form of savings deposits. On the other hand, the circumstance that competition among banks has gradually raised the rate of interest on current accounts causes sums of money that are not needed for current-account purposes, and therefore might be invested, to be left on current account as a temporary investment. Nevertheless, these practices do not alter the principle of the matter; it is not the formal technical aspect of a transaction but its economic character that determines its significance for us.

From the point of view of the banks there does exist a connection between the two kinds of deposit business inasmuch as the possibility of uniting the two reserves permits of their being maintained at a lower level than their sum would have to be if they were completely independent. This is extremely important from the point of view of banking technique, and explains to some degree the advantage of the deposit banks, which carry on both branches of business, over the savings banks, which only accept savings deposits (the savings banks being consequently driven to take up current account business also). For the organization of the banking system this circumstance is of importance; for the theoretical investigation of its problems it is negligible.

The essential thing about that branch of banking business which alone needs to be taken into consideration in connection with the volume of money is this: the banks that undertake current-account business for their customers are, for the reasons referred to above, in a position to lend out part of the deposited sums of money. It is a matter of indifference how they do this, whether they actually lend out a portion of the deposited money or issue notes to those who want credit or open a current account for them. The only circumstance that is of importance here is that the loans are granted out of a fund that did not exist before the loans were granted. In all other circumstances, whenever loans are granted they are granted out of existing and available funds of wealth. A bank which neither possesses the right of note issue nor carries on current-account business for its customers can never lend out more money than the sum of its own resources and the resources that other persons have entrusted to it. It is otherwise with those banks that issue notes or open current accounts. They have a fund from which to grant loans, over and above their own resources and those resources of other people that are at their disposal.

GRANTING OF CIRCULATION CREDIT

According to the prevailing opinion, a bank which grants a loan in its own notes plays the part of a credit negotiator between the borrowers and those in whose hands the notes happen to be at any time. Thus in the last resort bank credit is not granted by the banks but by the holders of the notes. The intervention of the banks is said to have the single object of permitting the substitution of its well-known and indubitable credit for that of an unknown and perhaps less trustworthy debtor and so of making it easier for a borrower to get a loan taken up by "the public." It is asserted, for example, that if bills are discounted by the bank and the discounted equivalent paid out in notes, these notes only circulate in place of the bills, which would otherwise be passed directly from hand to hand in lieu of cash. It is thought that this can also be proved historically by reference to the fact that before the development of the bank-of-issue system, especially in England, bills circulated to a greater extent than afterward; that in Lancashire, for example, until the opening of a branch of the Bank of England in Manchester, nine-tenths of the total payments were made in bills and only one-tenth in money or banknotes.

Now this view by no means describes the essence of the matter A person who accepts and holds notes, grants no credit; he exchanges no present good for a future good. The immediately convertible note of a solvent bank is employable everywhere as a fiduciary medium instead of money in commercial transactions, and nobody draws a distinction between the money and the notes which he holds as cash. The note is a present good just as much as the money.

Notes might be issued by banks in either of two ways. One way is to exchange them for money. According to accounting principles, the bank here enters into a debit transaction and a credit transaction; but the transaction is actually a matter of indifference, since the new liability is balanced by an exactly corresponding asset. The bank cannot make a profit out of such a transaction. In fact such a transaction involves it in a loss, since it brings in nothing to balance the expense of manufacturing the notes and storing the stocks of money. The issue of fully backed notes can therefore only be carried on in conjunction with the issue of fiduciary media. This is the second possible way of issuing notes, to issue them as loans to persons in search of credit. According to the books, this, like the other, is a case of a credit and a debit transaction only. It is true that this is not shown by the bank's balance sheet. On the credit side of the balance sheet are entered the loans granted and the state of the till, and on the debit side, the notes. We approach a better understanding of the true nature of the whole process if we go instead to the profit-and-loss account. In this account there is recorded a profit whose origin is suggestive-"profit on loans." When the bank lends other people's money as well as its own resources, part of this profit arises from the difference between the rates of interest that it pays its depositors and the rates that it charges its borrowers. The other part arises from the granting of circulation credit. It is the bank that makes this profit, not the holders of the notes. It is possible that the bank may retain the whole of it; but sometimes it shares it, either with the holders of the notes or, more probably, with the depositors. But in either case there is a profit.

Let us imagine a country whose monetary circulation consists in 100 million ducats. In this country a bank-of-issue is established. For the sake of simplicity, let us assume that the bank's own capital is invested as a reserve outside the banking business, and that it has to pay the annual interest on this capital to the state in return for the concession of the right of note issue-an assumption that does correspond closely with the actual situation of some banks-of-issue. Now let the bank have fifty million ducats paid into it and issue fifty million ducats' worth of one-ducat notes against this sum. But we must suppose that the bank does not allow the whole sum of fifty million ducats to remain in its vaults; it lends out forty million on interest to foreign businessmen. The interest on these loans constitutes its gross profit which is reduced only by the cost of manufacture of the notes, by administrative expenses, and the like. Is it possible in this case to say that the holders of the notes have granted credit to the foreign debtors of the bank, or to the bank itself?

Let us alter our example in a nonessential point. Let the bank lend the forty million not to foreigners but to persons within the country. One of these, A, is indebted to B for a certain sum, say the cost of goods which he has bought from him. A has no money at his disposal, but is ready to cede to B a claim maturing in three months, which he himself holds against P. Can B agree to this? Obviously only if he himself does not need for the next three months the sum of money which he could demand immediately, or if he has a prospect of finding somebody who can do without a corresponding sum of money for three months and is therefore ready to take over the claim against P. Or the situation might arise in which B wished to buy goods immediately from C, who was willing to permit postponement of payment for three months. In such a case, if C was really in agreement with the postponement, this could only be for one of the three reasons that might also cause B to be content with payment after the lapse of three months instead of immediate payment. All these, in fact, are cases of genuine credit transactions, of the exchange of present goods for future goods. Now the number and extent of these transactions is dependent on the quantity of present goods available; the total of the possible loans is limited by the total quantity of money and other goods available for this purpose. Loans can be granted only by those who have disposal over money or other economic goods which they can do without for a period. Now when the bank enters the arena by offering forty million ducats on the loan market, the fund available for lending pur poses is increased by exactly this sum; what immediate influence this must have on the rate of interest, should not need further explanation. Is it then correct to say that when the bank discounts bills it does nothing but substitute a convenient note currency for an inconvenient bill currency? Is the banknote really nothing but a handier sort of bill of exchange? By no means. The note that embodies the promise of a solvent bank to pay a sum to the bearer on demand at any time, that is, immediately if desired, differs in an important point from the bill that contains the promise to pay a sum of money after the passage of a period of time. The sight bill, which as is well known) plays no part in the credit system, is comparable with the note; but not the time bill, which is the form regularly assumed by the bills that are usual in credit transactions. A person who pays the price of a purchased commodity in money, in notes, or by the transfer of any other claim payable on demand, has carried through a cash transaction; a person who pays the purchase price by the acceptance of a three-month bill has carried through a credit transaction.

Let us introduce a further unessential variation into our example, which will perhaps help to make the matter clearer. Let us assume that the bank has first issued notes to the value of fifty million ducats and received for them fifty million ducats in money; and now let us suppose it to place a further forty million ducats in its own notes on the loan market. This case is in every way identical with the two considered above.

The activity of note issue cannot in any way be described as increasing the demand for credit in the same sense as, say, an increase in the number of bills current. Quite the contrary. The bank-of-issue does not demand credit; it grants it. When an additional quantity of bills comes on to the market, this increases the demand for credit, and therefore raises the rate of interest. The placing of an additional quantity of notes on the loan market at first has the opposite effect; it constitutes an increase in the supply of credit and has therefore an immediate tendency to diminish the rate of interest.

It is one of the most remarkable phenomena in the history of political economy that this fundamental distinction between notes and bills could have passed unnoticed. It raises an important problem for investigators into the history of economic theory. And in solving this problem it will be their principal task to show how the beginnings of a recognition of the true state of affairs that are to be found even in the writings of the Classical School and were further developed by the Currency School, were destroyed instead of being continued by the work of those who came after.

FIDUCIARY MONEY AND THE NATURE OF INDIRECT EXCHANGE

It should be sufficiently clear from what has been said that the traditional way of looking at the matter is but little in harmony with the peculiarities of fiduciary media. To regard notes and current accounts, whether they are covered by money or not, as constituting the same phenomenon, is to bar the way to an adequate conception of the nature of these peculiarities. To regard noteholders or owners of current accounts as granters of credit is to fail to recognize the meaning of a credit transaction. To treat both notes and bills of exchange in general (that is, not merely sight bills) as "credit instruments" alike is to renounce all hope of getting to the heart of the matter.

On the other hand, it is a complete mistake to assert that the nature of an act of exchange is altered by the employment of fiduciary media. Not only those exchanges that are carried through by the cession of notes or current-account balances covered by money, but also those exchanges that are carried through by the employment of fiduciary media, are indirect exchanges involving the use of money. Although from the juristic point of view it may be significant whether a liability incurred in an act of exchange is discharged by physical transference of pieces of money or by cession of a claim to the immediate delivery of pieces of money, that is, by cession of a money substitute, this has no bearing upon the economic nature of the act of exchange.

It would be incorrect to assert, for instance, that when payment is made by check, commodities are really exchanged against commodities, only without any of the crude clumsiness of primitive barter. Here, just as in every other indirect exchange made possible by money, and in contrast to direct exchange, money plays the part of an intermediary between commodity and commodity. But money is an economic good with its own fluctuations in value. A person who acquires money or money substitutes will be affected by all the variations in their objective exchange value. This is just as true of payment by notes or checks as of the physical transference of pieces of money. But this is the only point that matters, and not the accidental circumstance whether money physically "enters into" the transaction as a whole. Anybody who sells commodities and is paid by means of a check and then immediately uses either the check itself or the balance that it puts at his disposal to pay for commodities that he has purchased in another transaction, has by no means exchanged commodities directly for commodities. He has undertaken two independent acts of exchange, which are connected no more intimately than any other two purchases.

It is possible that the terminology proposed is not the most suitable that could be found. This must be freely admitted. But it may at least be claimed for it that it opens the way to a better comprehension of the nature of the phenomena under discussion than those that have been previously employed. For if it is not quite true to say that inexact and superficial terminology has been chiefly responsible for the frequently unsatisfactory nature of the results of investigations into the theory of banking, still a good deal of the ill success of such investigations is to be laid to that account.

That economic theory puts questions of law and banking technique in the background and draws its boundaries differently from those drawn by jurisprudence or business administration is or should be self-evident. Reference to discrepancies between the above theory and the legal or technical nature of particular procedures is therefore no more relevant as an argument against the theory than economic considerations would be in the settlement of controversial juristic questions.

EVOLUTION OF FIDUCIARY MONEY

Thus fiduciary media are claims to the payment of a given sum on demand, which are not covered by a fund of money and whose legal and technical characteristics make them suitable for tender and acceptance instead of money in fulfillment of obligations that are in terms of money. As has already been suggested, it is not the dead letter of the law so much as actual business practice that counts, so that some things function as fiduciary media, although they cannot be regarded as promises to pay money from the juristic point of view, because they nevertheless are in fact honored as such by somebody or other.

We were able to show that, so far as they are not money certificates, even modern token coins and such kinds of money as the German thaler during the period from the establishment of the gold standard until its abolition, constitute fiduciary media and not money.

Fiduciary media may be issued in two ways: by banks, and otherwise. Bank fiduciary media are characterized by being dealt with as constituting a debt of the issuing body. They are entered as liabilities, and the issuing body does not regard the sum issued as an increase of its income or capital, but as an increase on the debit side of its account, which must be balanced by a corresponding increase on the credit side if the whole transaction is not to figure as a loss. This way of dealing with fiduciary media makes it necessary for the issuing body to regard them as part of its trading capital and never to spend them on consumption but always to invest them in business. These investments need not always be loans; the issuer may himself carry on a productive enterprise with the working capital that is put into his hands by the issue of fiduciary media. It is known that some deposit banks sometimes open deposit accounts without a money cover not only for the purpose of granting loans, but also for the purpose of directly procuring resources for production on their own behalf. More than one of the modern credit and commercial banks has invested a part of its capital in this manner, and the question of the right attitude in this case of the holders of the money substitutes, and of the state legislature that feels itself called upon to protect them, remains an open one. In earlier times there was a similar problem concerning banks issuing notes until banking practice or the law prescribed short-term loans as "cover."

The issuer of fiduciary media may, however, regard the value of the fiduciary media put into circulation as an addition to his income or capital. If he does this, he will not take the trouble to cover the increase in his obligations due to the issue by setting aside a special credit fund out of his capital. He will pocket the profits of the issue, which in the case of token coinage is called seigniorage, as composedly as any other sort of income.

The only difference between the two ways of putting fiduciary media into circulation lies in the attitude of the issuer. Naturally, this cannot have any significance for the determination of the value of the fiduciary media. The difference between the methods of issue is a result of historical factors. Fiduciary media have sprung from two different roots: from the activities of the deposit and giro banks on the one hand, and from the state prerogative of minting on the other hand.

The former is the source of notes and current accounts; the latter, that of convertible Treasury notes, token coins, and that current money of which the coinage is restricted, but which can be regarded neither as credit money nor as fiat money because it is actually convertible into money on demand to its full amount. Today the difference between the two methods of issuing is gradually disappearing, all the more as the state endeavors to act in the same way as the banks in issuing fiduciary media. Some states are already in the habit of devoting the profits of their coinage to special purposes and of refusing to treat them in any way as an increase of wealth.

Of the two types of money substitutes issued by the banks, the current account is the older. The banknote, in fact, is only a development of it. It is true that the two are different in the eyes of the law and the banker, but they do not differ at all in the eyes of the economist.

The only distinctions between them are in those legal or banking or commercial peculiarities of the banknote which give it a special capacity of circulation. It is easily transferable and very like money in the way in which it is transferred. Banknotes were therefore able to outstrip the older money substitute, the current account, and penetrate into commerce with extraordinary rapidity. For medium and small payments they offer such great advantages that the current account was hardly able to maintain its ground beside them. It was not until the second half of the nineteenth century that the current account once more became important along with the banknote.

In large transactions, check and clearing payments are often superior to notes. But the chief reason why the current account was able in part to expel the banknote must by no means be sought in any inherent requirements of business. The current account is not, as it is sometimes the fashion to assert without any reason or proof, a "higher" form of money substitute than the banknote.

The banknote has been supplanted by the current account in many countries because its development was artificially hindered and that of the current account artificially encouraged, the reason for this being that acceptance of the doctrines of the Currency principle led people to see danger for the stability of the exchange ratio between money and other economic goods only in the overissue of notes, and not in the excessive increase of bank deposits.

For the study of the credit system from the economic point of view, the contrast between notes and deposits is of minor importance. There are payments for which one or other form is the more suitable, and payments for which both forms are suitable. If their development had been allowed to take its own course, this fact would undoubtedly have been more evident than it is today when the attempt is sometimes made to bring about the employment of one or other kind of fiduciary medium by artificial means in circumstances where it appears the less appropriate technically.

FIDUCIARY MONEY AND THE CLEARING SYSTEM

That want of clarity concerning the nature of fiduciary media which constitutes the chief characteristic of the writings of the banking theorists and their epigoni, the modern writers on problems of banking theory, leads to a perpetual confusion between money substitutes and a series of institutions which reduce the demand for money in the narrower sense, and also to relative neglect of the differences that exist between money certificates and fiduciary media within the group of money substitutes proper.

The economic effect of an exchange that is carried out with the help of a certain quantity of a fungible good, can sometimes, if several persons have to transact business at the same time, be attained more indirectly in ways which, while they are formally of a more complicated legal structure, nevertheless fundamentally simplify the technical transaction and make it possible to dispense in particular instances with the physical presence of pieces of the medium of exchange. If A has to deliver a piece of cloth to B and receive a sheep from him for it, and if A at the same time has to give a sheep to C and receive from him a horse, these two exchanges can also be transacted if B gives a sheep to C on behalf and on account of A, so freeing himself from the obligation that he is under to give A a sheep in return for the cloth and A from the obligation that he is under to give C a sheep in return for the horse. Whereas the direct transaction of these two exchanges would have necessitated four transfers, this procedure necessitates only three.

The possibility of facilitating exchanges in this way is extraordinarily increased by extension of the custom of using certain goods as common media of exchange. For the number of cases in which anybody simultaneously owes and has a claim to a certain fungible good will increase with the number of cases in which one and the same fungible good-the common medium of exchange-is the object of exchange in individual transactions. Full development of the use of money leads at first to a splitting up into two acts of indirect exchange even of such transactions as could in any case have been carried through by direct exchange. The butcher and the baker, who could also exchange their products directly, often prefer to have their mutual relations take the form of an exchange carried through with the help of money which their other transactions assume also. The butcher sells meat to the baker for money and the baker sells bread to the butcher for money. This gives rise to reciprocal money claims and money obligations. But it is clear that a settlement can be arrived at here, not only by each party actually handing money over to the other, but also by means of offsetting, in which merely the balance remaining over is settled by payment of money. To complete the transaction in this way by full or partial cancellation of counterclaims offers important advantages in comparison with direct exchange: all the freedom connected with the use of money is combined with the technical simplicity that characterizes direct exchange transactions.

This method of carrying through indirect exchanges by cancellation of counterclaims is very greatly stimulated at the time when the cases where its employment is possible are increased by the fact that credit transactions, or the exchange of present goods for future goods, are becoming customary. When all exchanges have to be settled in ready cash, then the possibility of performing them by means of cancellation is limited to the case exemplified by the butcher and baker and only then on the assumption, which of course only occasionally holds good, that the demands of both parties are simultaneous. At the most, it is possible to imagine that several other persons might join in and so a small circle be built up within which drafts could be used for the settlement of transactions without the actual use of money. But even in this case simultaneity would still be necessary, and, several persons being involved, would be still seldomer achieved.

These difficulties could not be overcome until credit set business free from dependence on the simultaneous occurrence of demand and supply. This, in fact, is where the importance of credit for the monetary system lies. But this could not have its full effect so long as all exchange was still direct exchange, so long even as money had not established itself as a common medium of exchange. The instrumentality of credit permits transactions between two persons to be treated as simultaneous for purposes of settlement even if they actually take place at different times. If the baker sells bread to the cobbler daily throughout the year and buys from him a pair of shoes on one occasion only, say at the end of the year, then the payment on the part of the baker, and naturally on that of the cobbler also, would have to be made in cash, if credit did not provide a means first for delaying the one party's liability and then for settling it by cancellation instead of by cash payment.

Exchanges made with the help of money can also be settled in part by offsetting if claims are transferred within a group until claims and counterclaims come into being between the same persons, these being then canceled against each other, or until the claims are acquired by the debtors themselves and so extinguished. In interlocal and international dealing in bills, which has been developed in recent years by the addition of the use of checks and in other ways which have not fundamentally changed its nature, the same sort of thing is carried out on an enormous scale. And here again credit increases in a quite extraordinary fashion the number of cases in which such offsetting is feasible. In all these cases we have an exchange made with the help of money which is nevertheless transacted without the actual use of money or money substitutes simply by means of a process of offsetting between the parties. Money in these cases is still a medium of exchange, but its employment in this capacity is independent of its physical existence. Use is made of money, but not physical use of actually existing money or money substitutes. Money which is not present performs an economic function; it has its effect solely by reason of the possibility of its being able to be present.

The reduction of the demand for money in the broader sense which is brought about by the use of offsetting processes for settling exchanges made with the help of money, without affecting the function performed by money as a medium of exchange, is based upon the reciprocal cancellation of claims to money. The use of money is avoided because claims to money are transferred instead of actual money. This process is continued until claim and debt come together, until creditor and debtor are united in the same person. Then the claim to money is extinguished, since nobody can be his own creditor or his own debtor. The same result may be reached at an earlier stage by reciprocal cancellation, that is by the liquidation of counterclaims by a process of offsetting. In either case the claim to money ceases to exist, and then, and not until then, is the act of exchange which gave birth to the claim finally completed.

Any transfer of a claim which does not bring it nearer to being extinguished by cancellation or offsetting cannot decrease the demand for money. In fact, if the transfer of the claim is not instead of payment in money, then it is on the contrary the source of a fresh demand for money. Now cession of claims instead of payment in money has, apart from the use of money substitutes, never been of very great commercial importance. As far as claims that are already due are concerned, the holder will as a rule prefer to call in the outstanding sums of money, because he will invariably find it easier to buy (and carry through other transactions in the market) with money or money substitutes than with claims whose goodness has not been indisputably established. But if the holder does in exceptional cases transfer such a claim by way of payment, then the new holder will be in the same position. A further hindrance to the transfer of claims to money that are not yet due instead of payment in money is the fact that such claims can be accepted only by such persons as are able to agree to postponement of payment; to rest content with a claim that is not yet due, when immediate payment could be enforced, is to grant credit.

Commercial requirements had previously made use of the legal institution of the bill in a way that caused it to circulate in a manner fairly similar to that of fiduciary media. Toward the end of the eighteenth and at the beginning of the nineteenth century bills were current in the European commercial centers which were endorsed by the merchants in place of payment in money. Since it was the general custom to make payments in this way, anybody could accept a bill that still had some time to run even when he wanted cash immediately; for it was possible to reckon with a fair amount of certainty that those to whom payments had to be made would also accept a bill not yet mature in place of ready money. It is perhaps hardly necessary to add that in all such transactions the element of time was of course taken into consideration, and discount consequently allowed for. Now it is true that this might increase the technical difficulties in handling the circulatory apparatus, which was already not an easy matter to deal with for other reasons, such, for example, as the different amounts of the bills. But, on the other hand, it offered a profit to any holder who did not pass the bill on immediately but kept it for a while, even if only for a very short while, in his portfolio. Used in this way, the bill was able to make up to a certain extent for the lack of fiduciary media. Even though it might not be due for a long time ahead, the holder could regard it as liquid, because he could pass it on at any time.

Despite this, bills of this sort were not fiduciary media in the sense in which notes or deposits are. They lack the characteristic features and properties which enabled the fiduciary medium, the indefinitely augmentable product of the arbitrary issuing activity of the banks, to become a complete substitute for money for business purposes. It is true that the cooperation of issuers and acceptors can give the circulation of bills the capacity of unlimited augmentation and unlimited lease of life through the agency of bill jobbing and regular prolongation, even if technical difficulties alone are sufficient to prevent the bills from ever being used in business to the same extent as money substitutes.

But every increase in the amount of bills in circulation makes negotiation of individual bills more difficult. It reduces the resources of the market. In fact, the holder of a bill, as distinct from the holder of a note or of a current account, is a creditor A person who accepts a bill must examine the standing of the previous endorser, and also that of the issuer and the others who are liable for the bill, but in particular the primary acceptor Whoever passes a bill on, in endorsing it undertakes responsibility for the payment of the amount of the bill. The endorsement of the bill is in fact not a final payment; it liberates the debtor to a limited degree only. If the bill is not paid then his liability is revived in a greater degree than before. But the peculiar rigor of the law relating to its enforcement and the responsibility of its signatories could not be eliminated, for it was these very characteristics alone that had made the bill a suitable instrument for the cession, in place of money payment, of unmatured claims for which the common-law provisions regarding indebtedness are little suited. To whatever extent the custom of issuing or endorsing bills in place of payment in money may have established itself, every single payment that was made in this way nevertheless retained the character of a credit transaction.

It was necessary in each individual case for the parties to the transaction to begin by coming to a special agreement as to the present price to be paid for the claim that would not fall due until some future time; if the amount of bills in circulation increased greatly, or if doubts happened to arise concerning the solidity of the position of any of the signatories, then it became more difficult to place the bill even on fairly tolerable terms. Issuer and acceptor had then in addition to make arrangements for covering the bill before it fell due, even if only by negotiating a prolongation bill. There is none of this in the case of fiduciary media, which pass like money from hand to hand without any sort of friction.

The modern organization of the payment system makes use of institutions for systematically arranging the settlement of claims by offsetting processes. There were beginnings of this as early as the Middle Ages, but the enormous development of the clearinghouse belongs to the last century. In the clearinghouse, the claims continuously arising between members are subtracted from one another and only the balances remain for settlement by the transfer of money or fiduciary media. The clearing system is the most important institution for diminishing the demand for money in the broader sense.

In the literature of the banking system it is not as a rule customary to draw a sufficient distinction between the diminution of the demand for money in the broader sense which is due to the operations of the clearinghouses and the diminution of the demand for money in the narrower sense which is due to the extension of the use of fiduciary media. This is the cause of much obscurity.

FIDUCIARY MONEY IN DOMESTIC TRADE

In the domestic trade of most civilized countries, the actual use of money for transacting exchanges made with the help of money has been very largely superseded by the use of money substitutes. And among the money substitutes, fiduciary media play a constantly increasing part. At the same time, the number of exchanges made with the help of money which are settled by the offsetting of counterclaims is growing also. There are countries in which nearly all the internal payments that are not settled by the clearing process are made without the use of money merely with the aid of banknotes and deposits that are not covered by money, of token coins in the proper sense of the word, and of other coins convertible on demand into money.

In other countries, again, the fiduciary medium has not yet been developed to a like extent; but if we disregard those countries in which the insecurity of the law hinders the birth of that confidence in the soundness of the issuer which is the sine qua non for the circulation of money substitutes, then we shall find no part of the world in which a large proportion of the internal payments are not made by means of the use of fiduciary media alone, without the actual transference of money. It is only in medium-sized transactions that there is still room for the transference of actual money. In Germany and England before the war it was usual to make payments of twenty to one hundred marks and £1 and £5 by the transference of gold coins. Smaller and larger payments were made almost exclusively by the cession of token coins or notes or deposits which were only partly covered by money. It was the same in other countries.

The fact that money continued to be in actual circulation at all in a series of states, like Germany and England, and was not entirely superseded by fiduciary media and money certificates, was due solely to legislative intervention. For reasons which were connected with certain views on the nature of notes, it was thought that the circulation of notes of small denominations ought to be opposed. The battle against the one-pound note in England ended with the complete victory of the sovereign, and this victory had a significance outside England, too, for the disfavor in which small banknotes were held for decades on the continent of Europe was based upon English opinion. It is certain that in those states which have a sound administration of justice and a developed banking system, the employment of actual money in commerce could be replaced without difficulty by the issue of a corresponding quantity of small notes.

In some countries in which the actual transfer of money has been completely superseded by fiduciary media and money certificates, this end has been systematically sought and attained in a peculiar fashion and under very peculiar conditions. The silver-standard countries-India, primarily, but the situation was similar in other Asiatic states-after the great controversy about the standards had been decided in favor of monometallism, were forced to accept the world gold standard. But there were extraordinary difficulties in the way of the transition to a monetary system in imitation of English of German institutions.

To introduce gold money in the circulation of these countries would have necessitated the conveyance of enormous quantities of gold to them, which would not have been practicable without serious convulsion of the European money market and would have meant great sacrifice. The governments of these countries, however, had to endeavor at all costs on the one hand not to raise the value of gold (so as not to disturb the European markets), and on the other hand not to reduce the value of silver any more than was necessary. The English government in India did not dare to undertake anything which might have had an unfavorable influence on the London money market; but, having regard to India's Asiatic competitors, which presumably would remain on the silver standard, neither did it dare to take any steps which would expedite the fall in the price of silver and consequently weaken for a time, even if only in appearance, the ability of India to compete with China, Japan, the Straits Settlements, and the other silver countries. It therefore had the task of conducting India's transition to the gold standard without buying gold in considerable quantities or selling silver.

The problem was not insoluble. Within limits, the circumstances were similar to those of the bimetallic countries which had discontinued the free coinage of silver at the end of the seventies. And besides, careful scientific consideration of the problem showed that it was possible to create a gold standard without a gold currency; that it was enough to discontinue the free coinage of silver and to announce its convertibility into gold at a specific rate, making this effective by establishing a suitable conversion fund, in order to give the country a gold standard which would differ from that of England only in the lower level of the stock of gold.

It was only necessary to go back to the writings of Ricardo in order to find the plan for such a currency system already worked out in detail. Lindsay and Probyn followed this path and, building upon Ricardo, worked out plans for this kind of currency regulation. Both wanted to close the mints to silver and to make the rupee convertible into gold at a fixed ratio. For the future, only the rupee was to be legal tender. The two proposals differed on some minor points, of which the most important was that while Probyn held it necessary that the rupee should be convertible into gold in India itself, Lindsay was of the opinion that it would suffice if the conversion were to be in London from a gold reserve to be established there. Both proposals were rejected, by the Indian government and by the commissions appointed to inquire into the Indian monetary system. The opinion was expressed that a normal gold standard necessitates an actual gold currency, and that the lack of such a currency would awaken mistrust.

The report of the commission of 1898 was signed by the most eminent experts of the day; its comments on the recommendations of Probyn and Lindsay were supported on the decisive point by the expert opinions of the biggest bankers in the British Empire. The course of events vindicated the theorists, however, not the statesmen and great financiers who had regarded them with amused commiseration. What was ultimately done in India corresponded roughly and on the whole to the recommendations of Probyn and Lindsay, even if there were variations in detail. And the monetary systems of other countries that had previously been on a silver standard were organized in a precisely similar manner The present currency system of India, of the Straits Settlements, of the Philippines, and of the other Asiatic countries which have followed their example, is superficially characterized by the fact that in domestic trade, payments in money, that is, in gold, do not occur at all or at least are far rarer than in the gold-standard countries of Europe and America, and even in these the actual circulation of gold is only quite small in proportion to the total of all the payments made with the help of money. Under the system in India, payments are made, along with notes, checks, and giro transfers, chiefly in silver coins, which are partly relics of the time of the silver standard, and partly minted by the government for the account of the state and to the benefit of the Treasury, which receives the considerable profits of the coinage. A conversion fund, which is set up and administered by the government, exchanges these silver coins at a fixed ratio for gold, gold securities, or other claims to money, payable on demand, while, on the other hand, it issues such silver coins in exchange for gold in unlimited quantities at the same rate, allowance being made for the expenses of storage, transportation, etc.

The minor details of this arrangement differ in different countries; but the differences in its legal or banking technique are insignificant as far as its nature is concerned. It is, for example, of no further significance, whether or not the silver coins are converted on the basis of a legal obligation. All that matters is whether the conversion actually does take place on demand.

There exists no fundamental difference at all between the currency system of these Asiatic and American countries and that that the European gold-standard countries once had. Under both systems, payments are made without the actual transference of money by the aid of the surrender of fiduciary media.

The fact that in England and Germany the actual transference of money also played a certain part for medium-sized payments, whereas in India and in the Philippines the number of actual transfers of money is scarcely worth mentioning, or that in the former countries the proportion of the circulation that was not covered by money was smaller than in the latter, is quite inessential; it is a difference that is merely quantitative, not qualitative. Of no great relevance is the circumstance that the fiduciary media were in the one case predominantly banknotes and checks and are in the other case predominantly silver coins. The silver rupee is in truth nothing but a metallic note, for the conversion of which its issuer, the state, is responsible.

Following up a train of thought of Ricardo's, who was the first to develop the plan of this monetary system more than a hundred years ago, it is customary to speak of it as the gold-exchange standard. The aptness of this designation can only be conceded if it is intended to stress the peculiarities in banking and currency technique that characterize the system. But it is a name that must be rejected if it is intended to indicate the existence of a fundamental difference from what used to be the English and German type of gold standard.

It is not correct to assert that in these countries gold functions merely as a measure of prices while the silver coins are used as a common medium of exchange. We know what little justification there is for speaking of a price-measuring function of money. In Ricardo's sense, it was possible to speak of measurement and measures of value; from the point of view of the subjective theory of value these and similar concepts are untenable. In India and Austria-Hungary and in all other countries with similar currency and banking systems, gold is or was just as much a common medium of exchange as in prewar England or Germany; the difference between the two systems is only one of degree, not one of kind.

FIDUCIARY MONEY IN INTERNATIONAL TRADE

The practice of making payments by the writing off or reciprocal balancing of claims is not restricted by the boundaries of states or countries. It was in fact in trade between different areas that the need for it was earliest and most strongly felt. The transportation of money always involves not inconsiderable cost, loss of interest, and risk. If the claims arising out of various transactions are liquidated not by the actual transference of money, but by balancing or offsetting, then all these expenses and dangers can be avoided. This provided an extraordinarily effective motive for developing those methods of making payments over long distances which saved the transference of sums of money. Quite early we find the use of bills established for interlocal payments; then in addition we later find checks, and ordinary and cable transfers, all forming the basis of an interlocal clearing system which worked through the ordinary free play of the market without the help of a special clearinghouse.

When making payments within a given locality the advantages for the individual of the method of settling transactions by the clearing process and therefore without the use of cash are smaller than those when making payments between localities, and therefore it was a longer time before the system of reciprocal cancellation came into full operation with the establishment of clearinghouses.

If the clearing system has without difficulty transcursed political boundaries and created for itself a world-embracing organization in the international bill and check system, the validity of the fiduciary media, like that of all money substitutes, is nationally limited. There are no money substitutes, and so no fiduciary media, that are recognized internationally and consequently able to take the place of money in international trade for settling the balances that remain over after the clearing process.

That is often overlooked in discussions of the present position of the international system of payments and the possibilities of its future development. Here again, in fact, the confusion creeps in, that has already been criticized adversely, between the system of reciprocal cancellation and the circulation of fiduciary media. This is most clear in the usual arguments about international giro transactions. In domestic giro transactions, payments are effected by the transfer of money substitutes, which are often fiduciary media, namely, the balances of the members at the giro bank. In international transactions, the money substitute is lacking, and even the international clearing system that is recommended in various quarters is not intended to introduce one. Rather it should be pointed out that this so-called international giro system-which incidentally was done away with again by the inflation during the war-while it may have changed the external form of the traditional manner of settling international monetary claims, has not changed in nature. When banks of various countries agree to give their clients the right to undertake direct transference from their balances to the balances of the clients of foreign banks, this may quite well constitute a new and additional method of international settlement of accounts. A Viennese desirous of paying a sum of money to somebody in Berlin was previously able either to use an international money order or to go to the exchange and buy a bill on Berlin and send it to his creditor As a rule he would have made use of the intermediate services of a bank, which for its part would perform the transaction through the purchase of a foreign bill or a check.

Later, if he was a member of the check system of the Austrian Post Office Savings Bank and his creditor belonged to that of the German post office, he would have been able to make the transfer more simply by sending the appropriate order on the Vienna office of the Post Office Savings Bank. This might well be more convenient and better suited to the demands of business than the only method that was once usual; but, however excellent a method, it was not a new method of international monetary intercourse. For the balances of this international giro system, if they could not be paid by bills, had to be paid by the actual transference of money. It is not true that the international giro system has decreased the international transportation of money. Even before its introduction, the Viennese who wanted to pay money to somebody in Berlin did not buy twenty-mark pieces and send them to Berlin in a parcel.

The only thing calculated to create international money substitutes and subsequently international fiduciary media would be the establishment of an international giro bank or bank-of-issue. When it became possible to use the notes issued by the world bank and the accounts opened by it for the settlement of money claims of all kinds, there would no longer be any need to settle the national balances of payments by transportation of money. The actual transference of money could be superseded by the transference of the notes issued by the world bank or of checks giving disposal over the issuer's account with the world bank, or even by simple entries in the books of the world bank. The balances of the international "clearinghouse," which already exists today although it is not concentrated in any one locality and has not the rigid organization of the national clearinghouses, would then be paid off in the same way as those of the national clearinghouses are at present.

Proposals have been made again and again for the creation of international fiduciary media through the establishment of an interstate bank. It is true that this must not be taken to include every project for extending the international giro system in the sense in which this word is commonly used. Nevertheless, in certain writings which demand the foundation of a world bank, or at least of an interstate banking organization, there gleams the idea of an international fiduciary medium.

The problems of organization raised by the establishment of such an international institution could be solved in various ways. The establishment of the world bank as a special form of organization and as an independent legal body would probably be the simplest form for the new creation. It would, however, also be possible, apart from this, to establish a special central authority for administering and investing the sums of money paid in to open the accounts, and for issuing the money substitutes. An attempt could be made to avoid the obstructions which the susceptibilities of national vanity would probably oppose to the local concentration of the business of the bank by leaving the reserves of the world giro authority and the world issuing authority in the keeping of the separate national banks.

In the reserves of every central bank a distinction would then have to be made between two sums: one, which would have to serve as a basis for the world organization of the system of payments, and over which only the authorities of the latter would have power of disposal; and a second, which would continue to be at the service of the national monetary system. It would even be possible to go still further and leave the issue of international notes and other money substitutes to the individual banks, which would only be required in doing this to follow the instructions given by the authorities of the world organization. It is not our task to investigate which of the various possibilities is the most practical; it is its nature alone that interests us, not the actual form it might take.

Special reference must nevertheless be made to one point. If the balances in the books of the world bank are to be acquired only by cash payment of the full sum in money, or by transfer from some other account that has been acquired by cash payment of the full sum in money, and if the world bank is to issue notes only in exchange for money, then its establishment may certainly render unnecessary the transportation of quantities of money (which still plays a large part nowadays in the international payments system), but it would not have the effect of economizing money payments.

It is true that it would be able to reduce the demand for money, because transferences would perhaps be completed more quickly and with less friction. But, as before, the payments that were made through the bank would involve the actual use of money. Of course, the money would remain in the vaults of the world bank and only the right to demand its surrender would be transferred. But the amount of the payments would be arithmetically limited by the amount of the money deposits in the bank. The possibility of trans ferring sums of money would be bound up with the existence of these sums of money in actual monetary shape. In order to free the international monetary system from these fetters the world bank would have to be granted the right of issuing notes as loans also and of opening accounts on credit; that is to say, the right of partly lending out its reserves of money. Then, and not until then, would the interstate system of payments be given a fiduciary medium such as is already possessed by the domestic system; it would become independent of the quantity of money in existence.

The realization of a world-bank project developed in this way is opposed by tremendous obstacles which it would hardly be possible to surmount in the near future. The least of these obstacles is constituted by the variety of the kinds of money that are in use in the individual states. Nevertheless, in spite of the inflation that was created by the world war and its consequences, we are every day approaching nearer and nearer to the situation of having a world monetary unit based on the metallic money gold. More important are the difficulties due to political considerations. The establishment of a world bank might come to grief owing to the uncertainty of its position in international law. No state would wish to incur the danger of the accounts of its citizens being impounded by the world bank in case of war. This involves questions of primary importance and therefore no provisions of international law, however surrounded with precautions they might be, could satisfy the individual states so far as to overcome their opposition to membership in such an organization.

Nevertheless, the biggest difficulty in the way of issuing international credit instruments lies in the circumstance that it would scarcely be possible for the states that had joined the world-banking system to come to an agreement concerning the policy to be followed by the bank in issuing the credit instruments. Even the question of determining the quantity of them to be issued would disclose irreconcilable antagonisms. Under present conditions, therefore, proposals for the establishment of a world bank with power of issuing fiduciary media attract hardly any notice.

FIDUCIARY MONEY AND THE DEMAND FOR MONEY

Influence of Fiduciary Money on Demand for Money in the Narrower Sense

The development of the clearing system, especially the extension of the clearinghouse proper, reduces the demand for money in the broader sense: part of the exchanges made with the help of money can be carried through without the actual physical circulation of money or money substitutes. Thus a tendency has arisen toward the reduction of the objective exchange value of money, which has counteracted the tendency for it to rise which was bound to result from the enormous increase in the demand for money in consequence of the progressive extension of the exchange economy. The development of fiduciary media has the same sort of effect; fiduciary media, which can, as money substitutes, take the place of money in commerce, reduce the demand for money in the narrower sense. This constitutes the great significance of fiduciary media, in this their effect on the exchange ratio between money and other economic goods is to be sought.

The development of fiduciary media, the most important institution for reducing the need for money in the narrower sense, equally with the establishment and development of clearinghouses, the most important institution for reducing the need for money in the broader sense, has not been merely left to the free play of economic forces. The demand for credit on the part of merchants and manufacturers and princes and states, and the endeavor to make a profit on the part of the bankers, were not the sole forces affecting its development. Intervention took place with the object of furthering and expediting the process. As the naive Midas-like trust in the usefulness of a large stock of precious metals disappeared and was replaced by sober consideration of the monetary problem, so the opinion gained strength that a reduction of the national demand for money in the narrower sense constituted an outstanding economic interest.

Adam Smith suggested that the expulsion of gold and silver by paper, that is to say notes, would substitute for an expensive means of exchange a less expensive, which, however, would perform the same service. He compares gold and silver which is circulating in a country with a road over which all the corn has to be brought to market but on which nevertheless nothing grows.

The issue of notes, he says, creates, as it were, a path through the air and makes it possible to turn a large part of the roads into fields and meadows and in this way considerably to increase the annual yield of land and labor. Similar views are entertained by Ricardo.

He also sees the most fundamental advantage of the use of notes in the diminution of the cost to the community of the apparatus of circulation. His ideal monetary system is one which would ensure to the community with the minimum cost the use of a money of invariable value. Starting from this point of view, he formulates his recommendations, which aim at expelling money composed of the precious metal from actual domestic circulation.

The views on the nature of methods of payment which diminish the demand for money, which were developed by the Classical economists, were already known in the eighteenth century. Their acceptance in the writings of the Classical economists and the brilliant way in which they were expounded, ensured general recognition for them in the nineteenth and twentieth centuries also. The opposition which they occasionally called forth, has now sunk into silence. In all countries the aim of banking policy is to secure the greatest possible extension of money-economizing means of payment.

If metallic money is employed, then the advantages of a diminution of the demand for money due to the extension of such other means of payment are obvious. In fact, the development of the clearing system and of fiduciary media has at least kept pace with the potential increase of the demand for money brought about by the extension of the money economy, so that the tremendous increase in the exchange value of money, which otherwise would have occurred as a consequence of the extension of the use of money, has been completely avoided, together with its undesirable consequences.

If it had not been for this the increase in the exchange value of money, and so also of the monetary metal, would have given an increased impetus to the production of the metal. Capital and labor would have been diverted from other branches of production to the production of the monetary metal. This would undoubtedly have meant increased returns to certain individual undertakings; but the welfare of the community would have suffered.

The increase in the stock of precious metals which serve monetary purposes would not have improved the position of the individual members of the community, would not have increased the satisfaction of their wants; for the monetary function could also have been fulfilled by a smaller stock. And, on the other hand, a smaller quantity of economic goods would have been available for the direct satisfaction of human wants if a part of the capital and labor power that otherwise would have been used for their production had been diverted to mining precious metals. Even apart from the diversion of production, a decrease of prosperity would result from the fact that as a consequence of the rise in value of the precious metals caused by the use for monetary purposes the stock available for industrial employment would decrease, since certain quantities would be transferred from the latter employment to the former This all becomes particularly clear if we think of an economic community which does not itself produce the precious metals, but imports them. Here the amount of their cost is expressed by the quantity of commodities that must be surrendered to foreign countries in order to obtain the supplementary quantity of monetary metal in exchange.

In a country that itself produces the precious metals, the matter is the same in principle; all that is different is the way of reckoning the loss of welfare through the sacrifice of the other branches of production and the preference for mining the precious metals; it is perhaps less perceptible, but it is just as comprehensible in theory. The measure of the additional harm done by the diversion of metal to monetary uses is always given by the quantity of metal that is withdrawn from other uses in favor of the monetary use.

Where fiat or credit money is employed, these reasons in favor of the extension of clearing methods of payment and of the use of fiduciary media do not arise. The only thing in their favor is that they would avoid an increase in the value of money; although this consideration is decisive. Where they are employed, the principle of establishing the national monetary apparatus and maintaining it in working order with the minimum cost must be attained in another way. It must be an object of policy, for example, to manufacture the paper notes with the minimum cost of production. It is immediately obvious that nothing like the same quantitative significance can be attributed to this problem as to that of decreasing the monetary demand for precious metals. However great the care taken in producing the notes, their cost of production could never be anything near so great as that of the precious metals. If we take into further consideration the fact that the artistic production of the notes also constitutes a precautionary measure against counterfeiting, so that merely on this ground, economizing in this sphere is not worth considering, it follows that the problem of diminishing the cost of the circulatory apparatus when fiat or credit money is employed must be of an entirely different nature from what it is when commodity money is employed.

FLUCTUATIONS IN THE MONEY DEMAND

In order to be able to make an accurate estimate of the bearing of clearing methods of payment and of fiduciary media on the development of the demand for money, it is necessary to be clear about the nature of variations in the demand for money.

Fluctuations in the demand for money, insofar as the objective conditions of its development are concerned, are governed in all communities by the same law. An extension of the procedure of exchange mediated by money increases the demand for money; a decrease of indirect exchange, a return to exchange in natura, decreases it. But even apart from variations in the extent of indirect exchange which are insignificant nowadays, large variations in the demand for money occur which are determined by factors of general economic development.

Increase of population, and progress in division of labor, together with the extension of exchange which goes hand in hand with it, increase the demand for money of individuals, and also therefore the demand for money of the community, which consists merely in the sum of the demands for money of individuals. Decrease of population and retrogression of the exchange economy, bring about a contraction in it. These are the determinants of the big changes in the demand for money. Within these large variations, it is possible to observe smaller periodical movements. Such are in the first place brought about by commercial and industrial fluctuations, by the alternation of boom and depression peculiar to modern economic life, by good and bad business.

The crest and the trough of the wave always cover a period of several years. But also within single years, quarters, months, and weeks, even within single days, there are considerable fluctuations in the level of the demand for money. The transactions involving the use of money are concentrated together at particular points of time; and even where this is not the case, the demand for money is differentiated by the practice on the part of buyers of settling their share of transactions on particular dates. On the daily markets it may perhaps seldom happen that the demand for money during the hours of the market is greater than before or after The periodical rise and fall of the demand for money can be seen much more clearly where transactions are concentrated in weekly, monthly and annual markets. A similar effect results from the custom of not paying wages and salaries daily, but weekly, monthly, or quarterly. Rents, interest, and repayment installments, are as a rule paid on particular days.

The accounts of the tailor, the shoemaker, the butcher, the baker, the bookseller, the doctor, and so forth, are often settled not daily but periodically. The tendency in all these arrangements is enormously strengthened by the mercantile practice of establishing certain days as days of settlement, or paydays. The middle and last days of the month have gained a special significance in this connection, and among the last days of the month, particularly the last day of the quarters. But, above all, the payments that have to be made in a community during the year are concentrated in the autumn, the decisive circumstance being that agriculture, for natural reasons, has its chief business period in the autumn. All of these facts have been repeatedly and exhaustively illustrated by statistics; nowadays they are the common property of all discussions on the nature of banks and money.

ELASTICITY OF THE RECIPROCAL CANCELLATION SYSTEM

It is usual to ascribe to the payment system elasticity that is said to be attained by means of the credit system and the continual improvements in banking organization and technique, the capacity of adjusting the available stock of money to the level of the demand for money at any time without exerting any influence on the exchange ratio between money and other economic goods. Between the volume of fiduciary media and the bank transactions or private arrangements that can take the place of a transfer of money, on the one hand, and the quantity of money, on the other hand, there is said to be no fixed relationship which could make the former rigidly dependent upon the latter. Instead of there being a fixed quantitative relationship between money and its substitutes, that is to say, between the stock of money and the various exchange and payment transactions, it is said that the organization of banking institutions and the credit system has made commerce in the highest degree independent of the quantity of money available.

The present-day organization of the money, clearing, and credit system is said to have the tendency to balance out variations in the quantity of money and render them ineffective, and so to make prices as far as possible independent of the stock of money. By others, this adjusting capacity is ascribed only to fiduciary media, uncovered banknotes, or unbacked deposits.

Before the soundness of these assertions can be tested, they must be brought out of the obscurity that is due to a confusion between the effects of the clearing system and those of the issue of fiduciary media. The two must be considered separately.

The reduction in the demand for money in the broader sense that results from the practice of settling counterclaims by balancing them against each other is limited in the first place by the number and amount of the claims and counterclaims falling due on the same date. No greater number or amount of claims can be reciprocally canceled between two parties than exist between them at the given moment. If, instead of payment in money, claims on third persons are transferred which are canceled by the transferee and the debtor by means of claims held by the latter against the former, the sphere of the offsetting process can be extended. The clearinghouses which nowadays exist in all important commercial centers are able to avoid the technical and legal difficulties in the way of such transfers, and have thus performed a quite extraordinary service in the extension of the system of reciprocal cancellation. Nevertheless, the clearing system is still capable of further improvement. Very many payments that could be settled by way of cancellation are still made by the actual transfer of money.

If we imagine the clearing system fully developed, so that all payments are first attempted to be settled by balancing, even those in everyday retail trade (which, for practical reasons, would not appear to be easy of accomplishment), then we are faced with a second limit to the extension of the clearing system, although this, unlike the first, is not surmountable. Even if the community were in a stable condition in which there were no variations in the relative incomes and wealth of individuals and in the sizes of their reserves, complete reciprocal cancellation of all the transfers of money that have to be made at a given moment would be possible, only if the money received by individuals was spent again immediately and nobody wanted to hold a sum of money in reserve against unforeseen and indefinite expenditure. But since these assumptions do not hold good, and in fact never could hold good, so long as money is in demand at all as a common medium of exchange, it follows that there is a rigid maximum limit to the transactions that can be settled through the clearing system. A community's demand for money in the broader sense, even with the fullest possible development of the system of reciprocal cancellation, cannot be forced below a minimum which will be determined according to circumstances.

Now the degree in which a clearing system is actually developed within the limits which the circumstances of the time allow for it, is in no way dependent upon the ratio between the demand for money and the stock of money. A relative decline in the one or the other can of itself exercise neither a direct nor an indirect influence on the development of the clearing system. Such development is invariably due to special causes. It is no more justifiable to assume that progressive extension of settlement on the clearing principle reduces the demand for money precisely in the degree in which the increasing development of commerce augments it, than to suppose that the growth of the clearing system can never outstrip the increase in the demand for money. The truth is rather that the two lines of development are completely independent of one another. There is a connection between them only insofar as deliberate attempts to counteract an increase in the exchange value of money by reducing the demand of money through a better development of the clearing system may be made with greater vigor during a period of rising prices; assuming, of course, that the aim of currency policy is to prevent an increase in the purchasing power of money. But this is no longer a case of an automatic adjustment of the forces acting upon the objective exchange value of money, but one of political experiments in influencing it, and the extent to which these measures are accompanied by success remains a matter of doubt.

Thus it is easy to see what little justification there is for ascribing to the clearing system the property, without affecting the objective exchange value of money, of correcting the disparities that may arise between the stock of money and the demand for it, and which could otherwise be eliminated only by suitable automatic variations in the exchange ratio between money and other economic goods. The development of the clearing system is independent of the other factors that determine the ratio between the supply of money and the demand for it. The effect on the demand for money of an expansion or contraction of the system of reciprocal cancellation thus constitutes an independent phenomenon which is just as likely to strengthen as to weaken the tendencies which for other reasons have an influence in the market on the exchange ratio between money and commodities. It seems self-evident that an increase in the number and size of payments cannot be the sole determinant of the demand for money. Part of the new payments will be settled by the clearing system; for this, too, ceteris paribus, will be extended in such a way as thenceforward to be responsible for the settlement of the same proportion of all payments as before. The rest of the payments could only be settled by clearing processes if there was an extension of the clearing system beyond the customary degree; but such an extension can never be called forth automatically by an increase in the demand for money.

ELASTICITY OF A CREDIT CIRCULATION BASED ON BILLS

The doctrine of the elasticity of fiduciary media, or more correctly expressed, of their automatic adjustment at any given time to the demand for money in the broader sense, stands in the very center of modern discussions of banking theory. We have to show that this doctrine does not correspond to the facts, or at least not in the form in which it is generally expounded and understood; and the proof of this will at the same time refute one of the most important arguments of the opponents of the quantity theory.

Tooke, Fullarton, Wilson, and their earlier English and German disciples, teach that it does not lie in the power of the banks-of-issue to increase or diminish their note circulation. They say that the quantity of notes in circulation is settled by the demand within the community for media of payment. It the number and amount of the payments are increasing, then, they say, the media of payment must also increase in number and amount; if the number and amount of the payments are diminishing, then, they say, the number and amount of the media of payment must also diminish. Expansion and contraction of the quantity of notes in circulation are said to be never the cause, always only the effect, of fluctuations in business life. It therefore follows that the behavior of the banks is merely passive; they do not influence the circumstances which determine the amount of the total circulation, but are influenced by them. Every attempt to extend the issue of notes beyond the limits set by the general conditions of production and prices is immediately frustrated by the reflux of the surplus notes, because they are not needed for making payments. Conversely, it is said, the only result of any attempt at an arbitrary reduction of the note circulation of a bank is the immediate filling of the gap by a competing bank; or, if this is not possible, as for instance because the issue of notes is legally restricted, then commerce will create for itself other media or circulation, such as bills, which will take the place of the notes.

It is in harmony with the views expounded by the Banking theorists on the essential similarity of deposits and notes to apply what they say on this point about notes to deposits also. It is in this sense that the doctrine of the elasticity of fiduciary media is generally understood today; it is in this sense alone that it is possible to defend it even with only an appearance of justification. We may further suppose, as being generally admitted, that it is not because of lack of public confidence in the issuing bank that the fiduciary media are returned to it, whether in the form of notes presented for conversion into cash or as demands for the withdrawal of deposits. This assumption also agrees with the teachings of Tooke and his followers.

The fundamental error of the Banking School lies in its failure to understand the nature of the issue of fiduciary media. When the bank discounts a bill or grants a loan in some other way, it exchanges a present good for a future good. Since the issuer creates the present good that it surrenders in the exchange-the fiduciary media-practically out of nothing, it would only be possible to speak of a natural limitation of the quantity of fiduciary media if the quantity of future goods that are exchanged in the loan market against present goods was limited to a fixed amount. But this is by no means the case. The quantity of future goods is indeed limited by external circumstances, but not that of the future goods that are offered on the market in the form of money. The issuers of the fiduciary media are able to induce an extension of the demand for them by reducing the interest demanded to a rate below the natural rate of interest, that is below that rate of interest that would be established by supply and demand if the real capital were lent in natura without the mediation of money, whereas on the other hand the demand for fiduciary media would be bound to cease entirely as soon as the rate asked by the bank was raised above the natural rate. The demand for money and money substitutes that is expressed on the loan market is in the last resort a demand for capital goods or, when consumption credit is involved, for consumption goods. He who tries to borrow "money" needs it solely for procuring other economic goods. Even if he only wishes to supplement his reserve, he has no other object in this than to secure the possibility of acquiring other goods in exchange at the given moment. The same is true if he needs the money for making payments that have fallen due; in this case it is the person receiving the payment who intends to purchase other economic goods with the money received.

That demand for money and money substitutes which determines the exchange ratio between money and other economic goods achieves expression only in the behavior of individuals when buying and selling other economic goods. Only when, say, money is being exchanged for bread is the position of the economic goods, money and commodity, in the value scales of the individual parties to the transaction worked out and used as a basis of action; and from this the precise arithmetical exchange ratio is determined. But when what is demanded is a money loan that is to be paid back in money again, then such considerations do not enter into the matter. Then only the difference in value between present goods and future goods is taken into account, and this alone has an influence on the determination of the exchange ratio, that is, on the determination of the level of the rate of interest.

For this reason the Banking principle is unable to prove that no more fiduciary media can be put into circulation than an amount determined by fixed circumstances not dependent on the will of the issuer. It has therefore directed its chief attention to the proof of the assertion that any superfluous quantity of fiduciary media will be driven out of circulation back to the issuing body. Unlike money, fiduciary media do not come on to the market as payments, but as loans, Fullarton teaches; they must therefore automatically flow back to the bank when the loan is repaid. This is true. But Fullarton overlooks the possibility that the debtor may procure the necessary quantity of fiduciary media for the repayment by taking up a new loan.

Following up trains of thought that are already to be found in Fullarton and the other writers of his circle, and in support of certain institutions of the English and Continental banking system, which, it must be said, have quite a different significance in practice than that which is erroneously ascribed to them, the more recent literature of banking theory has laid stress upon the significance of the short-term commodity bill for the establishment of an elastic credit system. The system by which payments are made could, it is said, be made capable of the most perfect adjustment to the changing demands upon it, if it were brought into immediate causal connection with the demand for media of payment.

According to Schumacher, that can only be done through banknotes, and has been done in Germany by basing the banknotes on the commodity bills, the quantity of which increases and decreases with the intensity of economic life. Through the channel of the discounting business, in place of interest-bearing commodity bills (which have only a limited capacity of circulation because their amounts are always different, their validity of restricted duration, and their soundness dependent on the credit of numerous private persons), banknotes are issued (which are put into circulation in large quantifies by a well-known semipublic institution and always refer to the same sums without limitation as to time, and therefore possess a much wider capacity of circulation, comparable to that of metallic money). Then on the redemption of the discounted bill an exchange in the contrary direction is said to take place: the banknotes, or instead of them metallic money, flow back to the bank, diminishing the quantity of media of payment in circulation. It is argued that if money is correctly defined as a draft on a consideration for services rendered, then a banknote based on an accepted commodity bill corresponds to this idea to the fullest extent, since it closely unites the service and the consideration for it and regularly disappears again out of circulation after it has negotiated the latter. It is claimed that through such an organic connection between the issue of banknotes and economic life, created by means of the commodity bill, the quantity of the means of payment in circulation is automatically adjusted to variations in the need for means for payment. And that the more completely this is attained, the more out of the question is it that the money itself will experience the variations in value affecting prices, and the more will the determination of prices be subject to the supply and demand on the commodity market.

In the face of this, we must first of all ask how it is possible to justify the drawing of a fundamental distinction between banknotes and other money substitutes, between banknotes not covered by money and other fiduciary media. Deposits which can be drawn upon at any time by check, apart from certain minor technical and juristic details which make them unusable in retail trade and for certain other payments, are just as good a money substitute as the banknote. It is a matter of indifference from the economic point of view whether the bank discounts a bill by paying out currency in notes or by a credit on a giro account. From the point of view of banking technique there may be certain differences of importance to the bank official; but whether the bank issues credit in the business of discounting only or whether it also grants other short-term loans cannot be a very fundamental issue. A bill is only a form of promissory note with a special legal and commercial qualification. No economic difference can be found between a claim in the form of a bill and any other claim of equal goodness and identical time of maturity. And the commodity bill, again, differs only juristically from an open book debt that has come into being through a credit-purchase transaction. Thus it comes to the same thing in the end whether we talk of the elasticity of the note circulation based on commodity bills or of the elasticity of a circulation of fiduciary media resulting from the cession of short-term claims arising out of credit sales.

Now the number and extent of purchases and sales on credit are by no means independent of the credit policy followed by the banks, the issuers of fiduciary media. If the conditions under which credit is granted are made more difficult, their number must decrease; if the conditions are made easier, their number must increase. When there is a delay in the payment of the purchase price, only those can sell who do not need money immediately; but in this case bank credit would not be requisitioned at all. Those, however, who want money immediately can only make sales on credit if they have a prospect of immediately being able to turn into money the claims which the transaction yields them. Other granters of credit can only place just so many present goods at the disposal of the loan market as they possess; but it is otherwise with the banks, which are able to procure additional present goods by the issue of fiduciary media. They are in a position to satisfy all the requests for credit that are made to them. But the extent of these requests depends merely upon the price that they demand for granting the credit. If they demand less than the natural rate of interest-and they must do this if they wish to do any business at all with the new issue of fiduciary media; it must not be forgotten that they are offering an additional supply of credit to the market-then these requests will increase.

When the loans granted by the bank through the issue of fiduciary media fall due for repayment, then it is true that a corresponding sum of fiduciary media returns to the bank, and the quantity in circulation is diminished. But fresh loans are issued by the bank at the same time and new fiduciary media flow into circulation. Of course, those who hold the commodity-bill theory will object that a further issue of fiduciary media can take place only if new commodity bills come into existence and are presented for discounting. This is quite true. But whether new commodity bills come into existence depends upon the credit policy of the banks.

Let us just picture to ourselves the life history of a commodity bill, or, more correctly, of a chain of commodity bills. A cotton dealer has sold raw cotton to a spinner. He draws on the spinner and has the three-month bill discounted that the latter has accepted. After three months have passed, the bill will be presented by the bank to the spinner and redeemed by him. The spinner provides himself with the necessary sum of cash, having meanwhile spun the cotton and sold the yarn to a weaver, by negotiating a bill drawn on the weaver and accepted by him. Whether these two sale-and-purchase transactions come to pass depends now chiefly upon the level of the bank discount rate. The seller, in the one case the cotton dealer, in the second case the spinner, needs the money immediately; he can only make the sale with a delay in the payment of the purchase price if the sum due in three months less discount at least equals the sum under which he is not inclined to sell his commodity. It is unnecessary to give any further explanation of the significance attaching to the level of the bank discount rate in this calculation. Our example proves our point just as well even if we assume that the commodity that is sold reaches the consumers in the course of the three months during which the bill circulates and is paid for by them without direct requisitioning of credit. For the sums which the consumers use for this purpose have come to them as wages or profits out of transactions that were only made possible through the granting of credit on the part of the banks.

When we see that the quantity of the commodity bills presented for discount increases at certain times and decreases again at other times, we must not conclude that these fluctuations are to be explained by variations in the demands for money of individuals. The only admissible conclusion is that under the conditions made by the banks at the time there is no greater number of people seeking credit. If the banks-of-issue bring the rate of interest they charge in their creditor transactions near to the natural rate of interest, then the demands upon them decrease; if they reduce their rate of interest so that it falls lower than the natural rate of interest, then these demands increase. The cause of fluctuations in the demand for the credit of the banks-of-issue is to be sought nowhere else than in the credit policy they follow.

By virtue of the power at their disposal of granting bank credit through the issue of fiduciary media the banks are able to increase indefinitely the total quantity of money and money substitutes in circulation. By issuing fiduciary media, they can increase the stock of money in the broader sense in such a way that an increase in the demand for money which otherwise would lead to an increase in the objective value of money would have its effects on the determination of the value of money nullified. They can, by limiting the granting of loans, so reduce the quantity of money in the broader sense in circulation as to avoid a diminution of the objective exchange value of money which would otherwise occur for some reason or other In certain circumstances, as has been said, this may occur. But in all the mechanism of the granting of bank credit and in the whole manner in which fiduciary media are created and return again to the place whence they were issued, there is nothing which must necessarily lead to such a result. It may quite as well happen, for instance, that the banks increase the issue of fiduciary media at the very moment when a reduction in the demand for money in the broader sense or an increase in the stock of money in the narrower sense is leading to a reduction of the objective exchange value of money; and their intervention will strengthen the existing tendency to a variation in the value of money. The circulation of fiduciary media is in fact not elastic in the sense that it automatically accommodates the demand for money to the stock of money without influencing the objective exchange value of money, as is erroneously asserted. It is only elastic in the sense that it allows of any sort of extension of the circulation, even completely unlimited extension, just as it allows of any sort of restriction. The quantity of fiduciary media in circulation has no natural limits. If for any reason it is desired that it should be limited, then it must be limited by some sort of deliberate human intervention-that is by banking policy.

Of course, all of this is true only under the assumption that all banks issue fiduciary media according to uniform principles, or that there is only one bank that issues fiduciary media. A single bank carrying on its business in competition with numerous others is not in a position to enter upon an independent discount policy. If regard to the behavior of its competitors prevents it from further reducing the rate of interest in bank-credit transactions, then-apart from an extension of its clientele-it will be able to circulate more fiduciary media only if there is a demand for them even when the rate of interest charged is not lower than that charged by the banks competing with it. Thus the banks may be seen to pay a certain amount of regard to the periodical fluctuations in the demand for money. They increase and decrease their circulation pari passu with the variations in the demand for money, so far as the lack of a uniform procedure makes it impossible for them to follow an independent interest policy. But in doing so, they help to stabilize the objective exchange value of money. To this extent, therefore, the theory of the elasticity of the circulation of fiduciary media is correct; it has rightly apprehended one of the phenomena of the market, even if it has also completely misapprehended its cause. And just because it has employed a false principle for explaining the phenomenon that it has observed, it has also completely closed the way to understanding of a second tendency of the market, that emanates from the circulation of fiduciary media. It was possible for it to overlook the tact that so far as the banks proceed uniformly, there must be a continual augmentation of the circulation of fiduciary media, and consequently a fall of the objective exchange value of money.

EXCLUSIVE EMPLOYMENT OF BILLS AS COVER FOR FIDUCIARY MONEY

The German Bank Act of March 14, 1875, required that the notes issued in excess of the gold cover should be covered by bills of exchange; but in practice this provision has been understood to refer only to commodity bills. The significance of this prescription differs from that popularly attributed to it. It does not make the note issue elastic; it does not even bring it, as is erroneously believed, into an organic connection with the conditions of demand for money; these are all illusions, which should long ago have been destroyed. Neither has it the significance for maintaining the possibility of conversion of the notes that is ascribed to it; this will have to be referred to in greater detail later.

The limitation of the note issue not covered by metal, that is of fiduciary media in the form of banknotes, is the fundamental principle of the German act, which is based upon Peel's Act. And among the numerous and multiform obstacles that have been set up with this aim, the strict provision concerning the investment of the assets backing the note issue takes a not altogether unimportant place. That these must consist not merely in claims, but in claims in the form of bills; that the bills must have at the most three months to run; that they should bear the names, preferably of three, but at least of two, parties known to be solvent-all these conditions limit the note issue. At the very beginning, a considerable part of the national credit is kept away from the banks. A similar effect results from the further limitation of the note cover merely to commodity bills, as was undoubtedly intended by the legislature even though express provision for it was omitted from the Bank Act, probably because of the impossibility of giving a legal definition of the concept of a commodity bill. That this limitation did in fact amount to a restriction of the issue of fiduciary media is best shown by the fact that when the Bank Act was passed the number of commodity bills was already limited, and that since then, in spite of a considerable increase in the demand for credit, their number has decreased to such an extent that the Reichsbank meets with difficulties when it attempts to select such bills only for purposes of investing without decreasing the amount of credit granted.

THE PERIODICAL RISE AND FALL IN THE EXTENT TO WHICH BANK CREDIT IS REQUISITIONED

The requests made to the banks are requests, not for the transfer of money, but for the transfer of other economic goods. Would-be borrowers are in search of capital, not money. They are in search of capital in the form of money, because nothing other than power of disposal over money can offer them the possibility of being able to acquire in the market the real capital which is what they really want. Now the peculiar thing, which has been the source of one of the most difficult puzzles in economics for more than a hundred years, is that the would-be borrower's demand for capital is satisfied by the banks through the issue of money substitutes. It is clear that this can only provide a provisional satisfaction of the demands for capital. The banks cannot evoke capital out of nothing. If the fiduciary media satisfy the desire for capital, that is if they really procure disposition over capital goods for the borrowers, then we must first seek the source from which this supply of capital comes. It will not be particularly difficult to discover it. If the fiduciary media are perfect substitutes for money and do all that money could do, if they add to the social stock of money in the broader sense, then their issue must be accompanied by appropriate effects on the exchange ratio between money and other economic goods. The cost of creating capital for borrowers of loans granted in fiduciary media is borne by those who are injured by the consequent variation in the objective exchange value of money; but the profit of the whole transaction goes not only to the borrowers, but also to those who issue the fiduciary media, although these admittedly have sometimes to share their gains with other economic agents, as when they hold interest-bearing deposits, or the state shares in their profits.

The entrepreneurs who approach banks for loans are suffering from shortage of capital; it is never shortage of money in the proper sense of the word that drives them to present their bills for discounting. In some circumstances this shortage of capital may be only temporary; in other circumstances it may be permanent. In the case of the many undertakings which constantly draw upon short-term bank credit, year in, year out, the shortage of capital is a permanent one.

For the problem with which we are concerned, the circumstances causing the shortage of capital on the part of entrepreneurs do not matter. We may even provisionally disregard, as of minor importance, the question whether the shortage is one of investment capital or working capital. Sometimes the view is propounded that it is unjustified to procure investment capital partly by way of bank credit although this is less undesirable as a way of procuring working capital. Such arguments as these have played an important part in recent discussions of banking policy. The banks have been adversely criticized on the ground of their having used a considerable part of the credit issued by them for granting loans to industrial enterprises in search not of fixed but of working capital and of having thus endangered their liquidity. Legislation has been demanded to limit to liquid investments only the assets backing the liabilities arising from the issue of fiduciary media. Provisions of this sort are designed to deal with fiduciary media in the form of deposits in the same way as the note issue has been dealt with under the influence of the doctrines of the Currency School. We have already commented on their significance and have shown, as further discussion will remind us, that the only practical value of these, as of all similar restrictions, lies in the obstacles they oppose to unlimited expansion of credit.

The cash reserve which is maintained by every business enterprise also is a part of its working capital. If an enterprise feels for any reason obliged to increase its reserve this must be regarded as an increase of its capital. If it requisitions credit for this purpose, its action cannot be regarded as any different from a demand for credit that arises from any other cause-say, on account of an extension of plant or the like.

But attention must now be drawn to a phenomenon which, even if it adds nothing new to what has been said already, may serve to set some important processes of the money-and-capital market in a clearer light. It has been repeatedly mentioned already that commercial practice concentrates all kinds of settlements on particular days of the year so that there is bound to be a bigger demand for money on these days than on others. The concentration of days of settlement at the end of the week, the fortnight, the month, and the quarter, is a factor which considerably increases the demand for money, and so of course the demand for capital, on the part of undertakings. Even though an entrepreneur could reckon safely on sufficient receipts on a given day to meet the obligations falling due on that or the following day, still it would only be in the rarest cases that he could use the former directly for paying the latter. The technique of payment is not so far developed that it would always be possible to fulfill obligations punctually without having secured some days beforehand free disposal over the necessary means. A person who has to redeem a bill that falls due at his bank on September 30 will usually have to take steps, before that date, for covering it; sums which do not reach him until the very day of maturity of the bill will mostly prove useless for this purpose. In any case it is completely impracticable to use the receipts on any given day for making payments that fall due on the same day at distant places. On the days of settlement there must therefore necessarily be an increased demand for money on the part of the individual undertaking, and this will disappear again just as quickly as it arose. Of course, this demand for money too is a demand for capital. Hypercritical theorists, following Mercantile usage, are accustomed to draw a subtle distinction between the demand for money and the demand for capital; they contrast the demand for short-term credit, as a demand for money, with the demand for long-term credit, as a demand for capital. There is little reason for retaining this terminology, which has been responsible for much confusion. What is here called the demand for money is nothing but a real demand for capital; this must never be forgotten. If the undertaking takes up a short-term loan to supplement its cash reserve, then the case is one of a genuine credit transaction, of an exchange of future goods for present goods.

The increased demand of the entrepreneur for money and consequently for capital which occurs on these days of settlement, expresses itself in an increase of the requests for loans that are made to credit-issuing banks. In those countries where notes and not deposits are the chief kind of fiduciary media, this is perceptible in an increase in the quantity of bills handed in at the banks-of-issue for discounting and, if these bills are actually discounted, in the quantity of notes in circulation. Now this regular rise and fall of the level of the note circulation round about the days of settlement can in no way be explained by an increase in the total quantity of bills in existence in the community. No new bills, particularly no new short-term bills, are drawn and handed in to the banks to be discounted. It is bills that have the normal period to run, that are negotiated shortly before maturity. Until then they are retained in the portfolios either of nonbankers or of banks whose issue of fiduciary media is limited, whether because they have a small clientele or because of legal obstacles. It is not until the demand for money increases that the bills reach the large banks-of-issue. It is clear how little justification there is for the assertion that the amount of the note issue of central European banks-of-issue is organically connected with the quantity of bills drawn in the community. Only some of the bills are discounted at the banks by the issue of fiduciary media; the others complete their term without calling bank credit into use. But the proportion between the two amounts depends entirely on the credit policy that the credit-issuing banks follow.

Bank legislation has taken particular account of the extraordinary increase in the demand for money round about quarter-day. Article two of the German Bank (Amendment) Act of June 1, 1909, extends the usual tax-free quota of notes of 550 million marks to 750 million marks for the tax accounts based on information concerning the last days of March, June, September, and December in each year, thus sanctioning a procedure that the banks had been in the habit of following for decades. On every day of settlement, the entrepreneur's demand for credit increases, and therefore the natural rate of interest also. But the credit-issuing banks have endeavored to counteract the increase in interest on loans either by not raising the rate of discount at all, or by not raising it to an extent corresponding to the increase in the natural rate of interest. Of course, the consequence of this has necessarily been to swell their circulation of fiduciary media. State banking policy has in general put no obstacles in the way of this practice of the banks, which undoubtedly helps to stabilize the objective exchange value of money. The German Bank Act of 1909 was the first which took steps to give it direct support.

INFLUENCE OF FIDUCIARY MONEY ON FLUCTUATIONS IN THE OBJECTIVE EXCHANGE VALUE OF MONEY

Thus there is no such thing as an automatic adjustment of the quantity of fiduciary media in circulation to fluctuations in the demand for money without an effect on the objective exchange value of money. Consequently all those arguments are ill founded which seek to deny practical significance to the quantity theory by reference to the alleged elasticity of the circulation of money. The increase and decrease of the stock of fiduciary media in a free banking system have no greater natural connection, direct or indirect, with the rise and fall of the demand for money in the broader sense, than the increase and decrease of the stock of money have with the rise and fall of the demand for money in the narrower sense. Such a connection exists only insofar as the credit banks deliberately try to bring it about. Apart from this, the only connection that can be established between the two sets of variations, which are in themselves independent of each other, is like that of the policy which, say, in a period of increasing demand for money in the broader sense aims at an increase of fiduciary media in order to counteract the rise in the objective exchange value of money which might otherwise be expected. Since it is impossible to measure fluctuations in the objective exchange value of money, even only approximately, we are not able to judge whether the increase of fiduciary media that has occurred during the last century in nearly all the countries of the world has together with the increase in the quantity of money kept pace with the increase in the demand for money in the broader sense, or fallen behind it, or outstripped it. All that we can be sure of is that at least a part of the increase in the demand for money in the broader sense has been robbed of its influence on the purchasing power of money by the increase in the quantity of money and fiduciary media in circulation.

8

Intellectual Property

INTRODUCTION

Historically, the free trade movement was skeptical and even hostile to the notion of intellectual property, regarding it as monopolistic and harmful to a free, competitive economy. Indeed, during the late 19th century, free trade advocates succeeded in reducing the length of the patents available in many European countries. The Netherlands, remarked for its laissez-faire policies in the 19th century, even abolished its patent system (mostly used by foreign companies) in 1867. Under the stipulations of the Convention of Paris however did the Netherlands have to re-introduce the patent system (made law in 1910), and was the last European country to do so (after Switzerland).

The 19th century anti-patent cause failed largely because the recession of 1874 weakened the free trade movement of the time Fritz Machlup & Edith Penrose, "The Patent Controversy in the 19th Century", Journal of Economic History, 10 (1) pp. 1-29, 1950]]. (and also because patent advocates used a public relations campaign which was remarkably sophisticated for its time).

It is thus remarkable (maybe even ironic) that corporations lobbying for expanded intellectual property rights have succeeded in including Agreement on Trade-Related Aspects of Intellectual Property Rights (TRIPS), a very strong treaty on intellectual property rights, as a membership requirement for the World Trade Organization, the international organization dedicated to furthering the cause of free trade (although some modern free traders would argue that markets are impossible without property protections, and that incentives to produce highly capitalized intellectual property would be diminished if inventors could not profit from inventions).

CRITICISM OF FREE TRADE

Free trade is one of the most debated topics of the 20th and 21st century. Different arguments are used by those who favour and by those who oppose free trade, or feel that more constraints are needed. These arguments can be divided in economic, moral and socio-political arguments.

ALTERNATIVES TO FREE TRADE

Tobin Tax: A Tobin tax is the suggested tax on all trade of currency across borders. This is supposed to put a penalty on short-term speculation in currencies.

Fair Trade: The fair trade movement, also known as the trade justice movement, promotes international labor, environment and social standards for the production of traded goods and services. The movement focuses in particular on exports from the Third and Second Worlds to the First World.

Balanced Trade: Balanced trade is an alternative economic model to free trade. Under balanced trade, nations are required to provide a fairly even reciprocal trade pattern; they cannot run large trade deficits. If deficits appear, the surplus nation must find a way to balance out trade or risk sanctions, fees, or quotas. Critics say this may discourage innovation as one country may reduce its efforts to produce products needed by the other.

International Barter

Some nations have prohibited trade under monetary terms of trade. For example, Hjalmar Schacht arranged barter for Nazi Germany to bypass the free market which he thought was rigged by Anglo-American capitalists. Officially, the 1933 bilateral-barter policy was designed to ensure that foreign countries bought as much from industrial Germany as she bought from them. However, Milton Friedman has argued that Hjalmar Schacht's exchange controls were primarily designed to restrict capital flight. The former Soviet Union occasionally arranged bilateral barter within its sphere of influence. See

Comprehensive Program for Socialist Economic Integration or Comecon. Arab League nations have also occasionally replaced monetary trade with barter.

Increase the Credit Risk to International Loans

George Soros and others argue that some of the most destructive free trade, such as developing world agricultural monoculture, is driven by export-oriented production targets set by the International Monetary Fund (IMF) and the governments it supports. He suggests that the volume of this trade would be lower if the lending banks were liable for credit default instead of receiving IMF bail-outs. If banks were responsible for default, the levels of lending would be lower and lead to more sustainable export programs due to the discipline of the free market, he believes.

International Price Floors

Some argue that free trade is responsible for the decline in international commodity prices. One reason for these low prices is the over-production of subsidized commodities in the developed world. Rather than removing the production subsidy for farmers in the rich world some suggest extending them to farmers in the developing world. For instance, producers in Poland lobbied to be included in the Common Agriculture Policy. The reason that rich-country farmers need subsidies to thrive is the comparative advantage of cheap land and labour enjoyed by their poor-country competitors.

Separating World Prices from Domestic Prices

Foreign trade of Communist Czechoslovakia was conducted at "free trade" import prices, with the Ministry of Foreign Trade selling the goods on, into the internal market, at pre-determined prices for each good. In this way, Czechoslovakian consumers were insulated from shifts in world prices whilst having some access to foreign products.

It is difficult for governments to sustain different internal prices over the long term. If the internal price is set below world prices, smugglers try to profit from the differential by illegally exporting the product to nations where they can sell it at a higher price. To the extent smugglers succeed, the domestic government is indirectly subsidizing foreign consumers. This problem has been vividly illustrated in nations where fuel prices are subsidized below world prices; domestic shortages frequently occur as a significant portion of the good is illegally smuggled out of the country. Rationing and black markets are stimulated by artificially low prices; in Iraq the famously long petrol pump queues for petrol at 50 dinars/litre can be bypassed by buying on the black market at 250 dinars/litre. Unofficial markets are a common problem wherever the "official" price is below the free trade price.

Despite the difficulties of maintaining fixed commodity prices, many Governments that attempt it claim that doing so "immunizes" their economies against destabilizing price shocks. It is sometimes argued that the social and economic benefits alone, outweigh the disadvantages (of import-price stability).

On the other hand, international prices tell the costs of producing certain products and the benefits of consuming them.

By separating the prices this flow of information is halted and therefore the local decisions are decoupled from the global needs and possibilities, thus hindering the producers in the country to produce the products where they have a comparative advantage and the consumers to consume the products that can elsewhere be produced so cheaply that they would like to consume them at those prices instead of consuming some other kind of products or less products (or services).

Several different models have been proposed to predict patterns of trade and to analyze the effects of trade policies such as tariffs.

COMPARATIVE ADVANTAGE

In economics, the theory of comparative advantage explains why it can be beneficial for two parties (usually countries) to trade, even though one of them may be able to produce every kind of item more cheaply than the other. What matters is not the absolute cost of production, but rather the ratio between how easily the two countries can produce different kinds of things. The concept is highly important in modern international trade theory.

Comparative advantage may be compared to absolute advantage. When one entity (be it a company or a country) is able to produce more efficiently than another entity it has an absolute advantage: that is, assuming equal inputs, the entity with an absolute advantage will have a greater output.

ORIGIN OF THE THEORY

Comparative advantage was first described by Robert Torrens in 1815 in an essay on the corn trade. He concluded that it was to England's advantage to trade various goods with Poland in return for corn, even though it might be possible to produce that corn more cheaply in England than Poland.

However, the theory is usually attributed to David Ricardo who created a systematic explanation in his 1817 book The Principles of Political Economy and Taxation using an example involving England and Portugal. In Portugal it is possible to produce both wine and cloth with less work than it takes in England. However, the relative costs of producing those two goods are different in the two countries.

In England it is very hard to produce wine, and only moderately difficult to produce cloth. In Portugal both are easy to produce. Therefore, while it is cheaper to produce cloth in Portugal than England, it is cheaper still for Portugal to produce excess wine, and trade that for English cloth. Conversely, England benefits from this trade because its cost for producing cloth has not changed but it can now get wine at closer to the cost of cloth.

Stanislaw Ulam once challenged Nobel laureate Paul Samuelson to name one theory in all of the social sciences which is both true and nontrivial. Several years later, Samuelson responded with David Ricardo's theory of comparative advantage:

> *"That it is logically true need not be argued before a mathematician; that it is not trivial is attested by the thousands of important and intelligent men who have never been able to grasp the doctrine for themselves or to believe it after it was explained to them."*
> *—Paul Samuelson.*

CRITICAL ANALYSIS OF RICARDO'S THEORY

Ricardo's principle relies on a variety of implicit assumptions that are debatable, such as that there is no (or a low) cost for transportation, and that the advantages of increased production outweigh externalities such as environmental contamination or social inequities. It is also necessary that there be restrictions on the flow of capital-otherwise, there would be no incentive to invest in the manufacture of either wine or cloth in England, since both are more costly to produce there.

Opponents of free trade often point out that globalized communications and transportation unavailable in Ricardo's time invalidate the assumption of capital immobility and cause capital to gravitate toward absolute advantage. Another concern is that comparative advantage only works when competition is absolutely perfect. It has also been argued that comparative advantage may reduce economic diversity to risky levels.

Free trade advocates would dissent, however, and say that modernization has decreased transportation and logistics costs through inventions such as the airplane and internet unavailable in Ricardo's time making his theory ever more sound with time, furthermore, despite the increased movement of capital, differences in capacities of production are still wide, in fact, free trade creates a wider gap of production in many areas despite the larger increases it makes in absolute wealth. In theory, as long a country has one more worker, one more machine, or one extra source of natural resources comparative advantage will still apply. As to perfect competition, supporters of free trade claim that perfect competition is the result of universal free trade, not its precondition. For free trade advocates, comparative advantage is what a capitalist country must embrace to gain an advantage in an existing mercantalist world.

On a final note, Gottfried Haberler showed in the 1930s that Ricardo's thinking on comparative advantage could also be expressed in neoclassical terms of opportunity cost.

FREE TRADE

In international trade, free trade is an idealized market model, often stated as a political objective, wherein trade of goods and services between countries flows unhindered by government-imposed artificial costs. Intellectually, this arrangement is supported by followers of the neoclassical and microeconomic schools of thought. It is opposed by anti-globalization and labor due to shown tendencies for abuse by wealthier states.

The term is given to economic policies, as well as political parties that support increases in such trade.

Free trade is a concept in economics and government, encompassing:

* International trade of goods without tariffs (taxes on imports) or other trade barriers (e.g., quotas on imports)

* International trade in services without tariffs or other trade barriers
* The free movement of labour between countries
* The free movement of capital between countries
* The absence of trade-distorting policies (such as taxes, subsidies, regulations or laws) that give domestic firms, households or factors of production an advantage over foreign ones
* Trade-distorting policies to enforce property rights so as to ensure the above conditions

The relative costs, benefits and beneficiaries of free trade are debated by academics, economists, governments and interest groups. Aspects of the ongoing debate are addressed below.

WIDER MEANING

Depending on the specific context, use of the term free trade can signify one or more of the above conditions. However, it is fundamental that only governments can restrict trade: they have the legal monopoly over the use of physical force in a geographical area. The term free trade has become very politically based, and it is not uncommon for so-called "free trade agreements" to impose additional trade restrictions. Such restrictions on trade are often due to domestic political pressure by powerful corporate, environmental or labor interest groups seeking special protections of their perceived interests.

Free trade agreements are a key element of customs unions and free trade areas. The details and differences of these agreements are covered in their respective articles.

HISTORY OF FREE TRADE

The history of free trade is a history of international trade focusing on the developments of open markets.

It is known that various prosperous world cultures throughout history have engaged in trade. Based on this, theoretical rationalizations as to why a policy of free trade would be beneficial to nations developed over time. These theories were developed in its academic modern sense from the commercial culture of England, and more broadly Europe, in the past five centuries. In opposition to free trade, a policy of mercantilism was developed in Europe in the 1500s and persists in various forms to this day. Early free trade theorists who were opposed to mercantilism were David Ricardo and Adam Smith. Free trade theorists offered trade as the reason why certain cultures prospered economically. Adam Smith, for example, pointed to increased trading as being the reason for the flourishing of not just Mediterranean cultures such as Egypt, Greece, and Rome, but also of Bengal (East Indies) and China.

Free trade policies have battled with mercantilist, protectionist, isolationist, communist, and other policies over the centuries. Wars, such as the Opium Wars, have been fought primarily over trade.

All developed countries have used protectionism, but usually reduced it as they gained more wealth. Some critics say that having more wealth guarantees that the country would benefit from free trade, although the majority of scientists think that also poor countries would benefit from free trade.

Ricardian Model

The Ricardian model focuses on comparative advantage and is perhaps the most important concept in international trade theory. In a Ricardian model, countries specialize in producing what they produce best. Unlike other models, the Ricardian framework predicts that countries will fully specialize instead of producing a broad array of goods. Also, the Ricardian model does not directly consider factor endowments, such as the relative amounts of labor and capital within a country.

Heckscher-Ohlin Model

The Heckscher-Ohlin model was produced as an alternative to the Ricardian model of basic comparative advantage. Despite its greater complexity it did not prove much more accurate in its predictions. However from a theoretical point of view it did provide an elegant solution by incorporating the neoclassical price mechanism into international trade theory.

The theory argues that the pattern of international trade is determined by differences in factor endowments. It predicts that countries will export those goods that make intensive use of locally abundant factors and will import goods that make intensive use of factors that are locally scarce. Empirical problems with the H-O model, known as the Leontief paradox, were exposed in empirical tests by Wassily Leontief who found that the United States tended to export labor intensive goods despite having a capital abundance.

Specific Factors

While labor can move freely between sectors, there are other factors specific to sectors, there are other factors specific to particular industries. This model is ideal for particular industries. This model is ideal forunderstanding income distribution but awkward for discussion the pattern of trade.

Gravity Model

The Gravity model of trade presents a more empirical analysis of trading patterns rather than the more theoretical models. The gravity model, in its basic form, predicts trade based on the distance between countries and the interaction of the countries' economic sizes. The model mimics the Newtonian law of gravity which also considers distance and physical size between two objects. The model has been proven to be empirically strong through econometric analysis. Other factors such as income level, diplomatic relationships between countries, and trade policies are also included in expanded versions of the model.

REGULATION OF INTERNATIONAL TRADE

Traditionally trade was regulated through bilateral treaties between two nations. For centuries under the belief in Mercantilism most nations had high tariffs and many restrictions on international trade. In the 19th century, especially in Britain, a belief in free trade became paramount and this view has dominated thinking among western nations for most of the time since then. In the years since the Second World War multilateral treaties like the GATT and World Trade Organization have attempted to create a globally regulated trade structure.

Free trade is usually most strongly supported by the most economically powerful nations in the world, though they often engage in selective protectionism for those industries which are politically important domestically, such as the protective tariffs applied to agriculture and textiles by the United States and Europe. The Netherlands and the United Kingdom were both strong advocates of free trade when they were economically dominant, today the United States, the United Kingdom and Japan are its greatest proponents. However, many other countries (such as India, China and Russia) are increasingly becoming advocates of free trade as they become more economically powerful themselves. As tariff levels fall there is also an increasing willingness to negotiate non tariff measures, including foreign direct investment, procurement and trade facilitation. The latter looks at the transaction cost associated with meeting trade and customs procedures.

Traditionally agricultural interests are usually in favour of free trade while manufacturing sectors often support protectionism. This has changed somewhat in recent years, however. In fact, agricultural lobbies, particularly in the United States, Europe and Japan, are chiefly responsible for particular rules in the major international trade treaties which allow for more protectionist measures in agriculture than for most other goods and services.

During recessions there is often strong domestic pressure to increase tariffs to protect domestic industries. This occurred around the world during the Great Depression leading to a collapse in world trade that many believe seriously deepened the depression. The regulation of international trade is done through the World Trade Organization at the global level, and through several other regional arrangements such as MERCOSUR in South America, NAFTA between the United States, Canada and Mexico, and the European Union between 25 independent states. The 2005 Buenos Aires talks on the planned establishment of the Free Trade Area of the Americas (FTAA) failed largely due to opposition from the populations of Latin American nations. Similar agreements such as the MAI (Multilateral Agreement on Investment) have also failed in recent years.

RISKS INVOLVED

The risks that exist in international trade can be divided into two major groups:

Economic Risks

* Risk of insolvency of the buyer,
* Risk of protracted default-the failure of the buyer to pay the amount due within six months after the due date, and

* Risk of non-acceptance
* Surrendering economic sovereignty

Political Risks

* Risk of cancellation or non-renewal of export or import licences
* War risks
* Risk of expropriation or confiscation of the importer's company
* Risk of the imposition of an import ban after the shipment of the goods
* Transfer risk-imposition of exchange controls by the importer's country or foreign currency shortages
* Surrendering political sovereignty.

Customs Union

A customs union is a free trade area with a Common External Tariff. The participant countries set up common external trade policy, but in some cases they use different import quotas. Common competition policy is also helpful to avoid competition deficiency.

Purposes for establishing a customs union normally include increasing economic efficiency and establishing closer political and cultural ties between the member countries.

It is the third stage of economic integration.

Customs union is established through trade pact.

Agreement for the creation of the International Monetary Fund came at the United Nations Monetary and Financial Conference. The United Nations was at the time only a wartime alliance, not yet an international organization in Bretton Woods, New Hampshire, United States, on July 22, 1944. The principal architects of the IMF at the conference were British economist John Maynard Keynes and the chief international economist at the US Treasury Department, Harry Dexter White.

The Articles of Agreement: Articles of Agreement of the International Monetary Fund came into force on December 27, 1945, the organization came into existence on May 1, 1946, as part of a post-WWII reconstruction plan, and it began financial operations on March 1, 1947.

It is sometimes referred to as a Bretton Woods institution, along with the International Bank for Reconstruction and Development (now part of the larger World Bank Group).

The IMF is the referee and, when the need arises, rescuer of the world's financial system. It was set up to supervise the newly established fixed exchange rate system. After this fell apart in 1971-73, the IMF became more involved with its member countries' economic policies, doling out advice on fiscal policy and monetary policy as well as microeconomic changes such as privatisation, of which it became a forceful advocate. In the 1980s, it played a leading part in sorting out the problems of developing countries' mounting debt. More recently, it has several times co-ordinated and helped to finance assistance to countries with a currency crisis.

The Fund has been criticised for the conditionality of its support, which is usually given only if the recipient country promises to implement IMF-approved economic reforms. Unfortunately, the IMF has often approved "one size fits all" policies that, not much later, turned out to be inappropriate. It has also been accused of creating moral hazard, in effect encouraging governments (and firms, banks and other investors) to behave recklessly by giving them reason to expect that if things go badly the IMF will organise a bail-out. Indeed, some financiers have described an investment in a financially shaky country as a "moral-hazard play" because they were so confident that the IMF would ensure the safety of their money, one way or another. Following the economic crisis in Asia during the late 1990s, and again after the crisis in Argentina early in this decade, some policymakers argued (to no avail) for the IMF to be abolished, as the absence of its safety net would encourage more prudent behaviour all round. More sympathetic folk argued that the IMF should evolve into a global lender of last resort.

A bank is an institution that provides financial service, particularly taking deposits and extending credit.

Currently the term bank is generally understood as an institution that holds a banking license. Banking licenses are granted by bank regulatory authorities and provide rights to conduct the most fundamental banking services such as accepting deposits and making loans. There are also financial institutions that provide certain banking services without meeting the legal definition of a bank, a so called non-banking financial company. Banks have a long history, and have influenced economies and politics for centuries. The word bank is derived from the Italian banca, which is derived from German language and means bench. The terms bankrupt and broke are similarly derived from banca rotta, which refers to an out-of-business bank, having its bench physically broken. Money lenders in Northern Italy originally did business in open areas, or big open rooms, with each lender working from his own bench or table. Traditionally, a bank generates profits from transaction fees on financial services and from the interest it charges for lending. In recent history, with historically low interest rates limiting banks' ability to earn money by lending deposited funds, much of a bank's income is provided by overdraft fees and riskier investments.

INTERNATIONAL MONETARY FUND

The International Monetary Fund (IMF) is an international organization that oversees the global financial system by monitoring exchange rates and balance of payments, as well as offering technical and financial assistance when asked. Its headquarters are in Washington, D.C.

ORGANIZATION AND PURPOSE

The IMF describes itself as "an organization of 184 countries, working to foster global monetary cooperation, secure financial stability, facilitate international trade, promote high employment and sustainable economic growth, and reduce poverty". With the exception of North Korea, Cuba, Liechtenstein, Andorra, Monaco, Tuvalu and Nauru, all UN member states either participate directly in the IMF or are represented by other member states.

In the 1930s, as economic activity in the major industrial countries dwindled, countries started adopting mercantilist practices, attempting to defend their economies by increasing restrictions on imports. To conserve dwindling reserves of gold and foreign exchange, some countries curtailed foreign imports, some devalued their currencies, and some introduced complicated restrictions on foreign exchange accounts held by their citizens. These measures were arguably detrimental to the countries themselves as the Ricardian comparative advantage states that everyone gains from trade without restrictions. It is noteworthy to mention that, although the "size of the pie" is enhanced according to this theory of free trade, when distributional concerns are taken into account, there are always industries that lose out even as others benefit. World trade declined sharply, as did employment and living standards in many countries.

As World War II came to a close, the leading allied countries considered various plans to restore order to international monetary relations, and at the Bretton Woods conference the IMF emerged. The founding members drafted a charter (or Articles of Agreement) of an international institution to oversee the international monetary system and to promote both the elimination of exchange restrictions relating to trade in goods and services, and the stability of exchange rates.

The IMF came into existence in December 1945, when the first 29 countries signed its Articles of Agreement. The statutory purposes of the IMF today are the same as when they were formulated in 1944. From the end of World War II until the late-1970s, the capitalist world experienced unprecedented growth in real incomes. (Since then, China's integration into the capitalist system has added substantially to the growth of the system.) Within the capitalist system, the benefits of growth have not flowed equally to all (either within or among nations) but most capitalist countries have seen recent increases in prosperity that contrast starkly with the conditions within capitalist countries during the interwar period. The lack of a recurring global depression is likely due to improvements in the conduct of international economic policies that have encouraged the growth of international trade and helped smooth the economic cycle of boom and bust.

In the decades since World War II, apart from rising prosperity, the world economy and monetary system have undergone other major changes that have increased the importance and relevance of the purposes served by the IMF, but that has also required the IMF to adapt and reform. Rapid advances in technology and communications have contributed to the increasing international integration of markets and to closer linkages among national economies. As a result, financial crises, when they erupt, now tend to spread more rapidly among countries.

The IMF's influence in the global economy steadily increased as it accumulated more members. The number of IMF member countries has more than quadrupled from the 44 states involved in its establishment, reflecting in particular the attainment of political independence by many developing countries and more recently the collapse of the Soviet bloc. The expansion of the IMF's membership, together with the changes in the world economy, have required the IMF to adapt in a variety of ways to continue serving its purposes effectively.

MEMBERSHIP QUALIFICATIONS

Any country may apply for membership of the IMF. The application will be considered, first, by the IMF's Executive Board. After its consideration, the Executive Board will submit a report to the Board of Governors of the IMF with recommendations in the form of a "Membership Resolution." These recommendations cover the amount of quota in the IMF, the form of payment of the subscription, and other customary terms and conditions of membership. After the Board of Governors has adopted the "Membership Resolution," the applicant state needs to take the legal steps required under its own law to enable it to sign the IMF's Articles of Agreement and to fulfill the obligations of IMF membership.

A member's quota in the IMF determines the amount of its subscription, its voting weight, its access to IMF financing, and its allocation of SDRs.

As of 2006, participating nations were discussing changes to the voting formula, to increase equity.

ASSISTANCE AND REFORMS

The primary mission of the IMF is to provide financial assistance to countries that experience serious financial difficulties. Member states with balance of payments problems may request loans and/or organizational management of their national economies. In return, the countries are usually required to launch certain reforms, an example of which is the "Washington Consensus". These reforms are generally required because countries with fixed exchange rate policies can engage in fiscal, monetary, and political practices which may lead to the crisis itself. For example, nations with severe budget deficits, rampant inflation, strict price controls, or significantly over-valued or under-valued currencies run the risk of facing balance of payment crises in their future. Thus, the structural adjustment programs are at least ostensibly intended to ensure that the IMF is actually helping to prevent financial crises rather than merely funding financial recklessness.

However, this approach is not without its critics, as described below. Many proponents of the IMF contend that some criticisms are the result of the fact that many people are not familiar with the operations and objectives of the IMF, and blame a lack of transparency within the IMF for this, as well as the dense nature of international finance in general. Suggestions for improving these understandings have included greater community outreach efforts, tighter accounting standards, possible regulatory oversight, and changes in the organizational structure of the IMF to include fewer economists, whom many fear are attempting to use developing countries as nothing more than lab raccoons. Some fear, however, that some of these reforms to the IMF itself introduce political considerations rather than economic considerations, many of which may have resulted in the financial crises in the first place.

CRITICISM

The role of the two Bretton Woods institutions has been controversial to many since the late Cold War period. Critics claim that IMF policy makers deliberately supported capitalistic military dictatorships friendly to American and European corporations. Critics also claim that the IMF is generally apathetic or hostile to their views of democracy, human rights, and labor rights. These criticisms generated a controversy that helped spark the anti-globalization movement. Others claim the IMF has little power to democratize sovereign states, nor is that its stated objective: to advise and promote financial stability. Arguments in favor of the IMF say that economic stability is a precursor to democracy.

Two criticisms from economists have been that financial aid is always bound to so-called "Conditionalities", including Structural Adjustment Programs. Conditionalities, it is claimed, retard social stability and hence inhibit the stated goals of the IMF.

Typically the IMF and its supporters advocate a Keynesian approach. As such, adherents of supply-side economics generally find themselves in open disagreement with the IMF. The IMF frequently advocates currency devaluation, criticized by proponents of supply-side economics as inflationary. Secondly they link higher taxes under "austerity programmes" with economic contraction.

Currency devaluation is recommended by the IMF to the governments of poor nations with struggling economies. Supply-side economists claim these Keynesian IMF policies are destructive to economic prosperity, although many other economists disagree.

Complaints are also directed toward International Monetary Fund gold reserve being undervalued. At its inception in 1945, the IMF pegged gold at 35 dollars per Troy ounce of gold. In 1973 the Nixon administration lifted the fixed asset value of gold in favour of a world market price. Hence the fixed exchange rates of currencies tied to gold were switched to a floating rate, also based on market price and exchange. This largely came about because Petrodollars outside the United States were more than could be backed by the gold at Fort Knox under the fixed exchange rate system. The fixed rate system only served to limit the amount of assistance the organization could use to help debt-ridden countries.

That said, the IMF sometimes advocates "austerity programmes," increasing even when the economy is weak, in order to generate government revenue and balance budget deficits, which is the opposite of Keynesian policy. These policies were criticised by Joseph E. Stiglitz, former chief economist at the World Bank, in his book Globalization and Its Discontents. He argued that by converting to a more Monetarist approach, the fund no longer had a valid purpose, as it was designed to provide funds for countries to carry out Keynesian reflations.

Most altermondialists, like ATTAC, believe that IMF interventions aggravate the poverty and debt of Third World and developing countries. According to the analysis by Yves Engler, the IMF is considered to be responsible for worsening or actually creating famine in Malawi (2002), Ethiopia (2003) and Niger (2005).

Opposition to the IMF is often fragmented. For instance, advocates of supply-side economics would generally regard the policies advocated by ATTAC to be little different in form to the ideas peddled by the IMF. In other words, they would see ATTAC tax-and-spend policies and the IMF's austerity policies as being fundamentally similar.

Argentina, which had been considered by the IMF to be a model country in its compliance to policy proposals by the Bretton Woods institutions, experienced a catastrophic economic crisis in 2001, generally believed to have been caused by IMF-induced budget restrictions-which undercut the government's ability to sustain national infrastructure even in crucial areas such as health, education, and security-and privatization of strategically vital national resources. The crisis added to widespread hatred of this institution in Argentina and other South American countries, with many blaming the IMF for the region's economic problems. The current-as of early 2006-trend towards moderate left-wing governments in the region and a growing concern with the development of a regional economic policy largely independent of big business pressures has been ascribed to this crisis.

Another example of where IMF Structural Adjustment Programmes aggravated the problem was in Kenya. Before IMF got involved in the country, the Kenya central bank oversaw all currency movement in and out of the country. IMF mandated that Kenya central bank had to allow easier currency movement. However, the adjustment resulted in very little foreign investment, but allowed Kamlesh Manusuklal Damji Pattni, with the help of corrupt government officials, to siphon out billions of Kenya shillings in what came to be known as the Goldenberg scandal, leaving the country in a state worse than that which it was in before the IMF reforms were implemented.

That the IMF intervenes only in countries that experience years of dire economic conditions has certainly hurt its reputation. The financial collapses it intervenes in are products of uneven capitalist development sometimes exacerbated by government mismanagement, but mismanagement is often cited by rich nations as the source of the financial crises. These collapses tend to lead to years of economic difficulty that can be addressed in various ways, but IMF Structural Adjustment Policies consistently serve to open up or "liberalize" economies to foreign capital rather than provide for economic recovery through statist policies such as government financed projects to achieve full employment. Thus, IMF policies further the notion that economic development in underdeveloped countries is dependent on attracting foreign investment rather than through a state-managed approach centered on full employment and progressive taxation. It is also true that politicians have used the IMF as an easy target for blame when they themselves have erred, using nationalism to gain easy political points. Overall the IMF success record is limited. While it was created to help stabilize the global economy, since 1980 over 100 countries have experienced a banking collapse that reduced GDP by four percent or more, far more than at any previous time in history. The considerable delay in IMF response to a crisis, and the fact that it tends to only respond to rather than prevent them, has led many economists to argue for reform. Whatever the feelings people in the Western world have for the IMF, research by the Pew Research Center shows that more than 60 percent of Asians and 70 percent of Africans feel that the IMF and the World Bank have a positive effect on their country. Such research has made proponents of IMF claim the IMF-critique misleading, as it would be difficult to speak of suffering if the sufferers don't feel hurt. The documentary Life and Debt deals with the IMF's policies' influence on Jamaica and its economy, from a critical point of view.

PAST MANAGING DIRECTORS

An unwritten rule establishes that the IMF's managing director must be European and that the president of the World Bank must be from the United States. Executive Directors, who confirm the managing director are voted in by Finance Ministers from countries they represent.

The IMF is for the most part controlled by the major Western Powers, with voting rights on the Executive board based on a quota derived from a monetary stake in the institution. Rarely does the board vote and pass issues contradicting the will of the US or Europeans. There have been some exceptions in the past. Dr. Mohamed Finaish from Libya, the Executive Director representing the majority of the Arab World and Pakistan, was a tireless defender of the developing nations' rights at the IMF. He stood steadfast in his beliefs and principles for fourteen years until his defeat in the 1992 elections to an Egyptian IMF Staff Member.

FREE TRADE AREA

A free trade area is a designated group of countries that have agreed to eliminate tariffs, quotas and preferences on most (if not all) goods between them.

It is the second stage of economic integration.

Countries choose this kind of economic integration form, if their economical structures are complementary. If they are competitive, they will choose customs union.

Unlike a customs union, members of a free trade area do not have the same policies with respect to non-members, meaning different quotas and customs. To avoid evasion (through re-exportation) the countries use the system of certification of origin most commonly called Rules of Origin, where there is a requirement for the minimum extent of local material inputs and local transformations adding value to the goods. Goods that don't cover these minimum requirements are not entitled for the special treatment envisioned in the free trade area provisions.

Cumulation is the relationship between different FTAs regarding the Rules of Origin sometimes different FTAs supplement each other, in other cases there is no cross-cumulation between the FTAs.

The Free Trade Area is a result of a Free Trade Agreement (a form of trade pact) between two or more countries. Free Trade Areas/Agreements (FTA) are cascadable to some degree if some countries sign agreement to form free trade area and choose to negotiate together (either as a trade bloc or as a forum of individual members of their FTA) another free trade agreement with some external country (or countries) then the new FTA will consist of the old FTA plus the new country (or countries).

A Free Trade Area is a region in which obstacles to unrestricted trade have been reduced to a minimum.

Within an industrialized country there are usually few if any significant barriers to the easy exchange of goods and services between parts of that country. For example, there are usually no trade tariffs or import quotas; there are usually no delays as goods pass from one part of the country to another (other than those that distance imposes); there are usually no differences of taxation and regulation.

Between countries on the other hand, many of these barriers to the easy exchange of goods can and often do occur. It is commonplace for there to be import duties of one kind or another (as goods enter a country) and the levels of sales tax and regulation often vary by country.

The aim of a free trade area is to so reduce barriers to easy exchange that trade can grow as a result of specialisation, division of labour, and most importantly via (the theory and practice of) comparative advantage. The theory of comparative advantage argues that in an unrestricted marketplace (in equilibrium) each source of production will tend to specialize in that activity where it has comparative (rather than absolute) advantage. The theory argues that the net result will be an increase in income and ultimately wealth and well-being for everyone in the free trade area. However the theory refers only to aggregate wealth and says nothing about the distribution of wealth. In fact there may be significant losers, in particular among the recently protected industries with a comparative disadvantage. The proponent of free trade can, however, retort that the gains of the gainers exceed the losses of the losers.

FREE TRADE ZONE

A free trade zone (FTZ) or export processing zone is one or more areas of a country where tariffs and quotas are eliminated and bureaucratic requirements are lowered in order to attract companies by raising the incentives for doing business there.

Most FTZs are located in developing countries. They are special zones where (some) normal trade barriers such as import or export tariffs do not apply, bureaucracy is typically minimized by outsourcing it to the FTZ operator and corporations setting up in the zone may be given tax breaks as an additional incentive. Usually, these zones are set up in underdeveloped parts of the host country, the rationale being that the zones will attract employers and thus reduce poverty and unemployment and stimulate the area's economy. These zones are often used by multinational corporations to set up factories to produce goods (such as clothing or shoes).

Criticism

The creation of special free-trade zones is criticized as giving business which set up operations under influence of already corrupt governments, and as giving foreign corporations more economic liberty than is given ordinary citizens, who face large and sometimes insurmountable "regulatory" hurdles in most third-world nations. Because the multinational corporation is able to choose between many underdeveloped or depressed countries in setting up an overseas factory, and most of these countries do not have limited governments, bidding wars of sorts erupt between their governments. Often the government pays part of the initial cost of factory setup, loosens environmental protections and rules regarding negligence and the treatment of workers, and promises not to ask payment of taxes for the next few years. When the taxation-free years are over the corporation which set up the factory without fully assuming its costs is often able to set up operations elsewhere for less expense than the taxes to be paid, giving it leverage to take the host government to the bargaining table with more demands in order for it to continue operations in the country. The widespread use of free trade zones by companies such as Nike has received criticism from numerous writers such as Naomi Klein in her No logo book.

Free Trade Zones

* South American Community of Nations (planned for 2007)
* Mercosur
* Andean Community
* Jamaican Free Zones
* Jebel Ali Free Zone
* Shannon Free Zone

INTERNATIONAL TRADE

For other uses of that term, International trade is the exchange of goods and services across international boundaries or territories. In most countries, it represents a significant share of GDP. While international trade has been present throughout much of history, its economic, social, and political importance has been on the rise in recent centuries. Industrialization, advanced transportation, globalization, multinational corporations, and outsourcing are all having a major impact. Increasing international trade is the usually primary meaning of "globalization". International trade is also a branch of economics, which, together with international finance, forms the larger branch of international economics.

BRETTON WOODS SYSTEM

The Bretton Woods system of international monetary management established the rules for commercial and financial relations among the world's major industrial states. The Bretton Woods system was the first example of a fully negotiated monetary order intended to govern monetary relations among independent nation-states.

Preparing to rebuild the international economic system as World War II was still raging, 730 delegates from all 44 Allied nations gathered at the Mount Washington Hotel in Bretton Woods, New Hampshire for the United Nations Monetary and Financial Conference. The delegates deliberated upon and signed the Bretton Woods Agreements during the first three weeks of July 1944.

Setting up a system of rules, institutions, and procedures to regulate the international monetary system, the planners at Bretton Woods established the International Bank for Reconstruction and Development (IBRD) (now one of five institutions in the World Bank Group) and the International Monetary Fund (IMF). These organizations became operational in 1946 after a sufficient number of countries had ratified the agreement.

The chief features of the Bretton Woods system were an obligation for each country to adopt a monetary policy that maintained the exchange rate of its currency within a fixed value-plus or minus one percent-in terms of gold; and the ability of the IMF to bridge temporary imbalances of payments. In the face of increasing strain, the system collapsed in 1971, following the United States' suspension of convertibility from dollars to gold.

Until the early 1970s, the Bretton Woods system was effective in controlling conflict and in achieving the common goals of the leading states that had created it, especially the United States.

ORIGINS

The political bases for the Bretton Woods system are in the confluence of several key conditions: the shared experiences of the Great Depression, the concentration of power in a small number of states, and the presence of a dominant power willing and able to assume a leadership role in global monetary affairs.

THE GREAT DEPRESSION

A high level of agreement among the powerful on the goals and means of international economic management facilitated the decisions reached by the Bretton Woods Conference. The foundation of that agreement was a shared belief in capitalism. Although the developed countries differed somewhat in the type of capitalism they preferred for their national economies (France, for example, preferred greater planning and state intervention, whereas the United States favored relatively limited state intervention), all relied primarily on market mechanisms and on private ownership.

Thus, it is their similarities rather than their differences that appear most striking. All the participating governments at Bretton Woods agreed that the monetary chaos of the interwar period had yielded several valuable lessons.

The experience of the Great Depression, when proliferation of foreign exchange controls and trade barriers led to economic disaster, was fresh on the minds of public officials. The planners at Bretton Woods hoped to avoid a repeat of the debacle of the 1930s, when foreign exchange controls undermined the international payments system that was the basis for world trade. The "beggar thy neighbor" policies of 1930s governments-using currency devaluations to increase the competitiveness of a country's export products in order to reduce balance of payments deficits-worsened national deflationary spirals, which resulted in plummeting national incomes, shrinking demand, mass unemployment, and an overall decline in world trade. Trade in the 1930s became largely restricted to currency blocs (groups of nations that use an equivalent currency, such as the "Sterling Area" of the British Empire). These blocs retarded the international flow of capital and foreign investment opportunities. Although this strategy tended to increase government revenues in the short run, it dramatically worsened the situation in the medium and longer run.

Thus, for the international economy, planners at Bretton Woods all favored a liberal system, one that relied primarily on the market with the minimum of barriers to the flow of private trade and capital. Although they disagreed on the specific implementation of this liberal system, all agreed on an open system.

ECONOMIC SECURITY

Also based on experience of interwar years, U.S. planners developed a concept of economic security-that a liberal international economic system would enhance the possibilities of postwar peace. One of those who saw such a security link was Cordell Hull, the U.S. secretary of state from 1933 to 1944.1 Hull believed that the fundamental causes of the two world wars lay in economic discrimination and trade warfare. Specifically, he had in mind the trade and exchange controls (bilateral arrangements) of Nazi Germany and the imperial preference system practiced by Britain (by which members or former members of the British Empire were accorded special trade status). Hull argued

Unhampered trade dovetailed with peace; high tariffs, trade barriers, and unfair economic competition, with warif we could get a freer flow of tradefreer in the sense of fewer discriminations and obstructions so that one country would not be deadly jealous of another and the living standards of all countries might rise, thereby eliminating the economic dissatisfaction that breeds war, we might have a reasonable chance of lasting peace.

THE RISE OF GOVERNMENTAL INTERVENTION

The developed countries also agreed that the liberal international economic system required governmental intervention. In the aftermath of the Great Depression, public management of the economy had emerged as a primary activity of governments in the developed states. Employment, stability, and growth were now important subjects of public policy. In turn, the role of government in the national economy had become associated with the assumption by the state of the responsibility for assuring of its citizens a degree of economic well-being. The welfare state grew out of the Great Depression, which created a popular demand for governmental intervention in the economy, and out of the theoretical contributions of the Keynesian school of economics, which asserted the need for governmental intervention to maintain an adequate level of employment.

At the international level, these ideas evolved from the experience of the 1930s. The priority of national goals, independent national action in the interwar period, and the failure to perceive that those national goals could not be realized without some form of international collaboration resulted in "beggar-thy-neighbor" policies such as high tariffs and competitive devaluations which contributed to economic breakdown, domestic political instability, and international war. The lesson learned was that, as New Dealer Harry Dexter White, the principal architect of the Bretton Woods system, put it: the absence of a high degree of economic collaboration among the leading nations will inevitably result in economic warfare that will be but the prelude and instigator of military warfare on an even vaster scale.

To ensure economic stability and political peace, states agreed to cooperate to regulate the international economic system. The pillar of the U.S. vision of the postwar world was free trade. Free trade involved lowering tariffs and among other things a balance of trade favorable to the capitalist system.

Thus, the more developed market economies agreed with the U.S. vision of postwar international economic management, which was to be designed to create and maintain an effective international monetary system and foster the reduction of barriers to trade and capital flows.

THE RISE OF U.S. HEGEMONY

International economic management relied on the dominant power to lead the system. The concentration of power facilitated management by confining the number of actors whose agreement was necessary to establish rules, institutions, and procedures and to carry out management within the agreed system. That leader was the United States. As the world's foremost economic and political power, the United States was clearly in a position to assume the responsibility of leadership.

The United States had emerged from the Second World War as the strongest economy, experiencing rapid industrial growth and capital accumulation. The U.S. had remained untouched by the ravages of World War II and had built a thriving manufacturing industry and grown wealthy selling weapons and lending money to the other combatants; in fact, U.S. industrial production in 1945 was more than double that of annual production between the prewar years of 1935 and 1939. In contrast, Europe and East Asia were militarily and economically shattered.

As the Bretton Woods Conference convened, the relative advantages of the U.S. economy were undeniable and overwhelming. The U.S. held a majority of investment capital, manufacturing production and exports. In 1945, the U.S. produced half the world's coal, two-thirds of the oil, and more than half of the electricity. The U.S. was able to produce great quantities of ships, airplanes, vehicles, armaments, machine tools, chemicals, and so on. Reinforcing the initial advantage-and assuring the U.S. unmistakable leadership in the capitalist world-the U.S. held 80% of gold reserves and had not only a powerful army but also the atomic bomb.

As the world's greatest industrial power and one of the few nations unravaged by the war, the U.S. stood to gain more than any other country from the opening of the entire world to unfettered trade. The U.S. would have a global market for its exports, and it would have unrestricted access to vital raw materials.

The U.S. was not only able, it was also willing to assume this leadership role. Although the U.S. had more gold, more manufacturing capacity and more military power than the rest of the world put together, U.S. capitalism could not survive without markets and allies. William Clayton, the assistant secretary of state for economic affairs, was among myriad U.S. policymakers who summed up this point: "We need markets-big markets-around the world in which to buy and sell."

There had been many predictions that peace would bring a return of depression and unemployment, as war production ceased and returning soldiers flooded the labor market. Compounding the economic difficulties was a sharp rise in labor unrest. Determined to avoid another economic catastrophe like that of the 1930s, U.S. President Franklin D. Roosevelt saw the creation of the postwar order as a way to ensure continuing U.S. prosperity.

THE ATLANTIC CHARTER

Throughout the war, the United States envisaged a postwar economic order in which the U.S. could penetrate markets that had been previously closed to other currency trading blocs, as well as to expand opportunities for foreign investments for U.S. corporations by removing restrictions on the international flow of capital.

The Atlantic Charter, drafted during U.S. President Roosevelt's August 1941 meeting with British Prime Minister Winston Churchill on a ship in the North Atlantic, was the most notable precursor to the Bretton Woods Conference. Like Woodrow Wilson before him, whose "Fourteen Points" had outlined U.S. aims in the aftermath of the First World War, Roosevelt set forth a range of ambitious goals for the postwar world even before the U.S. had entered the Second World War.

The Atlantic Charter affirmed the right of all nations to equal access to trade and raw materials. Moreover, the charter called for freedom of the seas (a principal U.S. foreign policy aim since France and Britain had first threatened U.S. shipping in the 1790s), the disarmament of aggressors, and the "establishment of a wider and permanent system of general security."

As the war drew to a close, the Bretton Woods conference was the culmination of some two and a half years of planning for postwar reconstruction by the Treasuries of the U.S. and the UK. U.S. representatives studied with their British counterparts the reconstitution of what had been lacking between the two world wars: a system of international payments that would allow trade to be conducted without fear of sudden currency depreciation or wild fluctuations in exchange rates-ailments that had nearly paralyzed world capitalism during the Great Depression.

Without a strong European market for U.S. goods and services, most policymakers believed, the U.S. economy would be unable to sustain the prosperity it had achieved during the war. In addition, U.S. unions had only grudgingly accepted government-imposed restraints on their demand during the war, but they were willing to wait no longer, particularly as inflation cut into the existing wage scales with painful force. (By the end of 1945, there had already been major strikes in the automobile, electrical, and steel industries.)

Financier and self-appointed adviser to presidents and congressmen, Bernard Baruch, summed up the spirit of Bretton Woods in early 1945: if we can "stop subsidization of labor and sweated competition in the export markets," as well as prevent rebuilding of war machines, "oh boy, oh boy, what long term prosperity we will have." Thus, the United States would use its predominant position to restore an open world economy, unified under U.S. control, which gave all nations unhindered access to markets and raw materials.

WARTIME DEVASTATION OF EUROPE AND EAST ASIA

Furthermore, U.S. allies-economically exhausted by the war-accepted this leadership. They needed U.S. assistance to rebuild their domestic production and to finance their international trade; indeed, they needed it to survive.

Before the war, the French and the British were realizing that they could no longer compete with U.S. industry in an open marketplace. During the 1930s, the British had created their own economic bloc to shut out U.S. goods. Churchill did not believe that he could surrender that protection after the war, so he watered down the Atlantic Charter's "free access" clause before agreeing to it. Yet, U.S. officials were determined to break open the empire. Combined, British and U.S. trade accounted for well over half the world's exchange of goods. If the British bloc could be split apart, the U.S. would be well on its way to opening the entire global marketplace. But as the 19th century had been economically dominated by Britain, the second half of the 20th was to be one of U.S. hegemony.

A devastated Britain had little choice. Two world wars had destroyed the country's principal industries that paid for the importation of half the nation's food and nearly all its raw materials except coal. The British had no choice but to ask for aid. In 1945, the U.S. agreed to a loan of $3.8 billion. In return, weary British officials promised to negotiate the agreement.

For nearly two centuries, French and U.S. interests had clashed in both the Old World and the New World. During the war, French mistrust of the United States was embodied by General Charles de Gaulle, president of the French provisional government. De Gaulle bitterly fought U.S. officials as he tried to maintain his country's colonies and diplomatic freedom of action. In turn, U.S. officials saw de Gaulle as a political extremist. But in 1945 de Gaulle-the leading voice of French nationalism-was forced to grudgingly ask the U.S. for a billion-dollar loan. Most of the request was granted; in return France promised to curtail government subsidies and currency manipulation that had given its exporters advantages in the world market.

On a far more profound level, as the Bretton Woods conference was convening, the greater part of the Third World remained politically and economically subordinate. Linked to the developed countries of the West economically and politically-formally and informally-these states had little choice but to acquiesce to the international economic system established for them. In the East, Soviet hegemony in Eastern Europe provided the foundation for a separate international economic system.

In short, the confluence of these three favorable political conditions-the concentration of power, the cluster of shared interests and ideas, and the hegemony of the United States-provided the political capability to equal the task of managing the international economy.

Design

Free trade relied on the free convertibility of currencies. Negotiators at the Bretton Woods conference, fresh from what they perceived as a disastrous experience with floating rates in the 1930s, concluded that major monetary fluctuations could stall the free flow of trade.

The liberal economic system required an accepted vehicle for investment, trade, and payments. Unlike national economies, however, the international economy lacks a central government that can issue currency and manage its use. In the past this problem had been solved through the gold standard, but the architects of Bretton Woods did not consider this option feasible for the postwar political economy. Instead, they set up a system of fixed exchange rates managed by a series of newly created international institutions using the U.S. dollar (which was a gold standard currency for central banks) as a reserve currency.

INFORMAL REGIMES

Previous Regimes

In the 19th and early 20th centuries gold played a key role in international monetary transactions. The gold standard was used to back currencies; the international value of currency was determined by its fixed relationship to gold; gold was used to settle international accounts. The gold standard maintained fixed exchange rates that were seen as desirable because they reduced the risk of trading with other countries.

Imbalances in international trade were theoretically rectified automatically by the gold standard. A country with a deficit would have depleted gold reserves and would thus have to reduce its money supply. The resulting fall in demand would reduce imports and the lowering of prices would boost exports; thus the deficit would be rectified. Any country experiencing inflation would lose gold and therefore would have a decrease in the amount of money available to spend. This decrease in the amount of money would act to reduce the inflationary pressure. Supplementing the use of gold in this period was the British pound. Based on the dominant British economy, the pound became a reserve, transaction, and intervention currency. But the pound was not up to the challenge of serving as the primary world currency, given the weakness of the British economy after the Second World War.

The architects of Bretton Woods had conceived of a system wherein exchange rate stability was a prime goal. Yet, in an era of more activist economic policy, governments did not seriously consider permanently fixed rates on the model of the classical gold standard of the nineteenth century. Gold production was not even sufficient to meet the demands of growing international trade and investment. And a sizable share of the world's known gold reserves were located in the Soviet Union, which would later emerge as a Cold War rival to the United States and Western Europe.

The only currency strong enough to meet the rising demands for international liquidity was the US dollar. The strength of the US economy, the fixed relationship of the dollar to gold ($35 an ounce), and the commitment of the U.S. government to convert dollars into gold at that price made the dollar as good as gold. In fact, the dollar was even better than gold: it earned interest and it was more flexible than gold.

THE BRETTON WOODS SYSTEM OF FIXED EXCHANGE RATES

The Bretton Woods system sought to secure the advantages of the gold standard without its disadvantages. Thus, a compromise was sought between the polar alternatives of either freely floating or irrevocably fixed rates-an arrangement that might gain the advantages of both without suffering the disadvantages of either while retaining the right to revise currency values on occasion as circumstances warranted.

The rules of Bretton Woods, set forth in the articles of agreement of the International Monetary Fund (IMF) and the International Bank for

Reconstruction and Development (IBRD), provided for a system of fixed exchange rates. The rules further sought to encourage an open system by committing members to the convertibility of their respective currencies into other currencies and to free trade.

The "pegged rate" or "par value" currency regime

What emerged was the "pegged rate" currency regime. Members were required to establish a parity of their national currencies in terms of gold (a "peg") and to maintain exchange rates within plus or minus 1% of parity (a "band") by intervening in their foreign exchange markets (that is, buying or selling foreign money).

The "reserve currency"

In practice, however, since the principal "reserve currency" would be the U.S. dollar, this meant that other countries would peg their currencies to the U.S. dollar, and-once convertibility was restored-would buy and sell U.S. dollars to keep market exchange rates within plus or minus 1% of parity. Thus, the U.S. dollar took over the role that gold had played under the gold standard in the international financial system.

Meanwhile, in order to bolster faith in the dollar, the U.S. agreed separately to link the dollar to gold at the rate of $35 per ounce of gold. At this rate, foreign governments and central banks were able to exchange dollars for gold. Bretton Woods established a system of payments based on the dollar, in which all currencies were defined in relation to the dollar, itself convertible into gold, and above all, "as good as gold." The U.S. currency was now effectively the world currency, the standard to which every other currency was pegged. As the world's key currency, most international transactions were denominated in dollars.

The U.S. dollar was the currency with the most purchasing power and it was the only currency that was backed by gold. Additionally, all European nations that had been involved in World War II were highly in debt and transferred large amounts of gold into the United States, a fact that contributed to the supremacy of the United States. Thus, the U.S. dollar was strongly appreciated in the rest of the world and therefore became the key currency of the Bretton Woods system.

Member countries could only change their par value with IMF approval, which was contingent on IMF determination that its balance of payments was in a "fundamental disequilibrium."

Formal Regimes

The Bretton Woods Conference led to the establishment of the IMF and the IBRD (now the World Bank), which still remain powerful forces in the world economy.

As mentioned, a major point of common ground at the Conference was the goal to avoid a recurrence of the closed markets and economic warfare that had characterized the 1930s. Thus, negotiators at Bretton Woods also agreed that there was a need for an institutional forum for international cooperation on monetary matters. Already in 1944 the British economist John Maynard Keynes emphasized "the importance of rule-based regimes to stabilize business expectations"-something he accepted in the Bretton Woods system of fixed exchange rates. Currency troubles in the interwar years, it was felt, had been greatly exacerbated by the absence of any established procedure or machinery for intergovernmental consultation.

As a result of the establishment of agreed upon structures and rules of international economic interaction, conflict over economic issues was minimized, and the significance of the economic aspect of international relations seemed to recede.

THE INTERNATIONAL MONETARY FUND

Officially established on December 27, 1945, when the 29 participating countries at the conference of Bretton Woods signed its Articles of Agreement, the IMF was to be the keeper of the rules and the main instrument of public international management. The Fund commenced its financial operations on March 1, 1947. IMF approval was necessary for any change in exchange rates. It advised countries on policies affecting the monetary system.

Designing the IMF

The big question at the Bretton Woods conference with respect to the institution that would emerge as the IMF was the issue of future access to international liquidity and whether that source should be akin to a world central bank able to create new reserves at will or a more limited borrowing mechanism.

Although attended by 44 nations, discussions at the conference were dominated by two rival plans developed by the U.S. and Britain. As the chief international economist at the U.S. Treasury in 1942-44, Harry Dexter White drafted the U.S. blueprint for international access to liquidity, which competed with the plan drafted for the British Treasury by Keynes. Overall, White's scheme tended to favor incentives designed to create price stability within the world's economies, while Keynes' wanted a system that encouraged economic growth.

At the time, gaps between the White and Keynes plans seemed enormous. Outlining the difficulty of creating a system that every nation could accept in his speech at the closing plenary session of the Bretton Woods conference on July 22, 1944, Keynes stated:

We, the delegates of this Conference, Mr. President, have been trying to accomplish something very difficult to accomplish.[...] It has been our task to find a common measure, a common standard, a common rule acceptable to each and not irksome to any.

Keynes' proposals would have established a world reserve currency (which he thought might be called "bancor") administered by a central bank vested with the possibility of creating money and with the authority to take actions on a much larger scale (understandable considering deflationary problems in Britain at the time).

In case of balance of payments imbalances, Keynes recommended that both debtors and creditors should change their policies. As outlined by Keynes, countries with payment surpluses should increase their imports from the deficit countries and thereby create a foreign trade equilibrium. Thus, Keynes was sensitive to the problem that placing too much of the burden on the deficit country would be deflationary.

But the U.S., as a likely creditor nation, and eager to take on the role of the world's economic powerhouse, balked at Keynes' plan and did not pay serious attention to it. The U.S. contingent was too concerned about inflationary pressures in the postwar economy, and White saw an imbalance as a problem only of the deficit country.

Although compromise was reached on some points, because of the overwhelming economic and military power of the U.S., the participants at Bretton Woods largely agreed on White's plan. As a result, the IMF was born with an economic approach and political ideology that stressed controlling inflation and introducing austerity plans over fighting poverty. This left the IMF severely detached from the realities of Third World countries struggling with underdevelopment from the onset.

Subscriptions and Quotas

What emerged largely reflected U.S. preferences: a system of subscriptions and quotas embedded in the IMF, which itself was to be no more than a fixed pool of national currencies and gold subscribed by each country as opposed to a world central bank capable of creating money. The Fund was charged with managing various nations' trade deficits so that they would not produce currency devaluations that would trigger a decline in imports.

The IMF was provided with a fund, composed of contributions of member countries in gold and their own currencies. The original quotas planned were to total $8.8 billion. When joining the IMF, members were assigned "quotas" reflecting their relative economic power, and, as a sort of credit deposit, were obliged to pay a "subscription" of an amount commensurate to the quota. The subscription was to be paid 25% in gold or currency convertible into gold (effectively the dollar, which was the only currency then still directly gold convertible for central banks) and 75% in the member's own currency.

Quota subscriptions were to form the largest source of money at the IMF's disposal. The IMF set out to use this money to grant loans to member countries with financial difficulties. Each member was then entitled to withdraw 25% of its quota immediately in case of payment problems. If this sum was insufficient, each nation in the system was also able to request loans for foreign currency.

Financing Trade Deficits

In the event of a deficit in the current account, Fund members, when short of reserves, would be able to borrow needed foreign currency from this fund in amounts determined by the size of its quota. In other words, the higher the country's contribution was, the higher the sum of money it could borrow from the IMF.

Members were obligated to pay back debts within a period of 18 months to five years. In turn, the IMF embarked on setting up rules and procedures to keep a country from going too deeply into debt, year after year. The Fund would exercise "surveillance" over other economies for the U.S. Treasury, in return for its loans to prop up national currencies.

IMF loans were not comparable to loans issued by a conventional credit institution. Instead, it was effectively a chance to purchase a foreign currency with gold or the member's national currency.

The U.S.-backed IMF plan sought to end restrictions on the transfer of goods and services from one country to another, eliminate currency blocs and lift currency exchange controls.

The IMF was designed to advance credits to countries with balance of payments deficits. Short-run balance of payment difficulties would be overcome by IMF loans, which would facilitate stable currency exchange rates. This flexibility meant that member states would not have to induce a depression automatically in order to cut its national income down to such a low level that its imports will finally fall within its means. Thus, countries were to be spared the need to resort to the classical medicine of deflating themselves into drastic unemployment when faced with chronic balance of payments deficits. Before the Second World War, European nations often resorted to this, particularly Britain.

Moreover, the planners at Bretton Woods hoped that this would reduce the temptation of cash-poor nations to reduce capital outflow by restricting imports. In effect, the IMF extended Keynesian measures-government intervention to prop up demand and avoid recession-to protect the U.S. and the stronger economies from disruptions of international trade and growth.

Changing the Par Value

The IMF sought to provide for occasional discontinuous exchange-rate adjustments (changing a member's par value) by international agreement with the IMF. Member nations were permitted first to depreciate (or appreciate in opposite situations) their currencies by 10%. This tends to restore equilibrium in its trade by expanding its exports and contracting imports. This would be allowed only if there was what was called a "fundamental disequilibrium." A decrease in the value of the country's money was called a "devaluation" while an increase in the value of the country's money was called a "revaluation".

It was envisioned that these changes in exchange rates would be quite rare. Regrettably the notion of fundamental disequilibrium, though key to the operation of the par value system, was never spelled out in any detail-an omission that would eventually come back to haunt the regime in later years.

IMF Operations

Never before had international monetary cooperation been attempted on a permanent institutional basis. Even more ground-breaking was the decision to allocate voting rights among governments not on a one-state, one-vote basis but rather in proportion to quotas. Since the U.S. was contributing the most, U.S. leadership was the key implication. Under the system of weighted voting the U.S. was able to exert a preponderant influence on the IMF. With one-third of all IMF quotas at the outset, enough to veto all changes to the IMF Charter on its own.

In addition, the IMF was based in Washington, D.C., and staffed mainly by its economists. It regularly exchanged personnel with the U.S. Treasury. When the IMF began operations in 1946, President Harry S. Truman named White as its first U.S. Executive Director. Since no Deputy Managing Director post had yet been created, White served occasionally as Acting Managing Director and generally played a highly influential role during the IMF's first year.

SPECIAL DRAWING RIGHTS

Special Drawing Rights (SDRs) is a potential claim on the freely usable currencies of International Monetary Fund members. It is neither a currency, nor a claim on the IMF.

SDRs are defined in terms of a basket of major currencies used in international trade and finance. At present, the currencies in the basket are the euro, the pound sterling, the Japanese yen and the United States dollar.

The amounts of each currency making up one SDR are chosen in accordance with the relative importance of the currency in international trade and finance. The determination of the currencies in the SDR basket and their amounts is made by the IMF Executive Board every five years. The weights of the currencies in the basket in the past were and currently are:

* 1981-1985: USD 42%, DEM 19%, JPY 13%, GBP 13%, FRF 13%
* 1986-1990: USD 42%, DEM 19%, JPY 15%, GBP 12%, FRF 12%
* 1991-1995: USD 40%, DEM 21%, JPY 17%, GBP 11%, FRF 11%
* 1996-2000: USD 39%, DEM 21%, JPY 18%, GBP 11%, FRF 11%
* 2001-2005: USD 45%, EUR 29%, JPY 15%, GBP 11%
* 2006-2010: USD 44%, EUR 34%, JPY 11%, GBP 11%

The value of one SDR in terms of United States dollars is determined daily by the IMF, based on the exchange rates of the currencies making up the basket, as quoted at noon at the London market. (If the London market is closed, New York market rates are used; if both markets are closed, European Central Bank reference rates are used.)

SDRs are used as a unit of account by the IMF and several other international organizations. A few countries peg their currencies against SDRs, and it is also used to denominate some private international financial instruments.

SDRs basically were created to replace gold in large international transactions. Being that under a strict (international) gold standard, the quantity of gold worldwide is relatively fixed, and worldwide the economies of all participating IMF members as an aggregate are growing, a need arose to increase the supply of the basic unit or standard proportionately. Thus SDRs, or "paper gold" are credits that nations with balance of trade surpluses can 'draw' upon nations with balance of trade deficits.

So-called "paper gold" is little more than an accounting transaction within a ledger of accounts, which eliminates the problem of shipping gold back and forth across borders to settle national accounts.

9

International Bank for Reconstruction and Development

INTRODUCTION

No provision was made for international creation of reserves. New gold production was assumed sufficient. In the event of structural disequilibria, it was expected that there would be national solutions-a change in the value of the currency or an improvement by other means of a country's competitive position. Few means were given to the IMF, however, to encourage such national solutions.

It had been recognized in 1944 that the new system could come into being only after a return to normalcy following the disruption of World War II. It was expected that after a brief transition period-expected to be no more than five years-the international economy would recover and the system would enter into operation.

To promote the growth of world trade and to finance the postwar reconstruction of Europe, the planners at Bretton Woods created another institution, the International Bank for Reconstruction and Development (IBRD)-now the most important agency of the World Bank Group. The IBRD had an authorized capitalization of $10 billion and was expected to make loans of its own funds to underwrite private loans and to issue securities to raise new funds to make possible a speedy postwar recovery. The IBRD was to be a specialized agency of the United Nations charged with making loans for economic development purposes.

READJUSTING THE BRETTON WOODS SYSTEM

The Dollar Shortages and the Marshall Plan

The Bretton Wood arrangements were largely adhered to and ratified by the participating governments. It was expected that national monetary reserves, supplemented with necessary IMF credits, would finance any temporary balance of payments disequilibria. But this did not however prove sufficient to get Europe out of the doldrums.

Postwar world capitalism suffered from a huge dollar shortage. The United States was running huge balance of trade surpluses, and the U.S. reserves were immense and growing. It was necessary to reverse this flow. Dollars had to leave the United States and become available for international use. In other words, the United States would have to reverse the natural economic processes and run a balance of payments deficit.

The modest credit facilities of the IMF were clearly insufficient to deal with Western Europe's huge balance of payments deficits. The problem was further aggravated by the reaffirmation by the IMF Board of Governors in the provision in the Bretton Woods Articles of Agreement that the IMF could make loans only for current account deficits and not for capital and reconstruction purposes. Only the United States contribution of $570 million was actually available for IBRD lending. In addition, because the only available market for IBRD bonds was the conservative Wall Street banking market, the IBRD was forced to adopt a conservative lending policy, granting loans only when repayment was assured. Given these problems, by 1947 the IMF and the IBRD themselves were admitting that they could not deal with the international monetary system's economic problems. Thus, the much looser Marshall Plan-the European Recovery Program-was set up to provide U.S. finance to rebuild Europe largely through grants rather than loans. The Marshall Plan was the program of massive economic aid given by the United States to favored countries in Western Europe for the rebuilding of capitalism. In a speech to Congress on June 5, 1946, U.S. Secretary of State George Marshall stated:

The breakdown of the business structure of Europe during the war was complete. Europe's requirements for the next three or four years of foreign food and other essential products principally from the United States are so much greater than her present ability to pay that she must have substantial help or face economic, social and political deterioration of a very grave character.

From 1947 until 1958, the U.S. deliberately encouraged an outflow of dollars, and, from 1950 on, the United States ran a balance of payments deficit with the intent of providing liquidity for the international economy. Dollars flowed out through various U.S. aid programs: the Truman Doctrine entailing aid to the pro-U.S. Greek and Turkish regimes, which were struggling to suppress socialist revolution, aid to various pro-U.S. regimes in the Third World, and most important, the Marshall Plan. From 1948 to 1954 the United States gave 16 Western European countries $17 billion in grants.

To encourage long-term adjustment, the United States promoted European and Japanese trade competitiveness. Policies for economic controls on the defeated former Axis countries were scrapped. Aid to Europe and Japan was designed to rebuild productive and export capacity. In the long run it was expected that such European and Japanese recovery would benefit the United States by widening markets for U.S. exports, and providing locations for U.S. capital expansion.

In 1956, the World Bank created the International Finance Corporation and in 1960 it created the International Development Association (IDA). Both have been controversial. Critics of the IDA argue that it was designed to head off a broader based system headed by the United Nations, and that the IDA lends without consideration for the effectiveness of the program. Critics also point out that the pressure to keep developing economies "open" has lead to their having difficulties obtaining funds through ordinary channels, and a continual cycle of asset buy up by foreign investors and capital flight by locals. Defenders of the IDA pointed to its ability to make large loans for agricultural programs which aided the "Green Revolution" of the 1960s, and its functioning to stabilize and occasionally subsidize Third World governments, particularly in Latin America.

Bretton Woods, then, created a system of triangular trade: the United States would use the convertible financial system to trade at a tremendous profit with developing nations, expanding industry and acquiring raw materials. It would use this surplus to send dollars to Europe, which would then be used to rebuild their economies, and make the United States the market for their products. This would allow the other industrialized nations to purchase products from the Third World, which reinforced the American role as the guarantor of stability. When this triangle became destabilized, Bretton Woods entered a period of crisis which lead ultimately to its collapse.

BRETTON WOODS AND THE COLD WAR

In 1945, Roosevelt and Churchill prepared the postwar era by negotiating with Joseph Stalin at Yalta about respective zones of influence; this same year U.S. and Soviet troops divided Germany into occupation zones and confronted one another in Korea.

Harry Dexter White succeeded in getting the Soviet Union to participate in the Bretton Woods conference in 1944, but his goal was frustrated when the Soviet Union would not join the IMF. In the past, the reasons why the Soviet Union chose not to subscribe to the articles by December 1945 have been the subject of speculation. But since the release of relevant Soviet archives, it is now clear that the Soviet calculation was based on the behavior of the parties that had actually expressed their assent to the Bretton Woods Agreements. The extended debates about ratification that had taken place both in the UK and the U.S. were read in Moscow as evidence of the quick disintegration of the wartime alliance. Facing the Soviet Union, whose power had also strengthened and whose territorial influence had expanded, the U.S. assumed the role of leader of the capitalist camp. The rise of the postwar U.S. as the world's leading industrial, monetary, and military power was rooted in the impact of the U.S. military victory, in the instability of the national states in postwar Europe, and the wartime devastation of the Soviet economy.

Thus, American power had to be used to rebuild U.S.-friendly regimes and free market capitalism, especially in Europe, and prevent Soviet-backed regimes from spreading across the war-torn countries of Europe. The conflict, however, was that European nations, which still nominally held large colonial possessions overseas, could not simultaneously rebuild their own economies, and hold on to their colonial empires. The fiscal discipline imposed by Bretton Woods made the U.S. the only nation that could afford large-scale foreign deployments within the Western alliance. Over the course of the late 1940s and early 1950s, the United Kingdom and France were gradually forced to accept abandoning colonial outposts, which would in the late 1950s and early 1960s, lead to revolt and finally independence for most of their empires.

The price paid for this position-especially in the Cold War climate-was the militarization of the U.S. economy, what U.S. President Dwight D. Eisenhower called the "armament industry" and "the military-industrial complex," and the related notion that the U.S. should assume a protective role in what was referred to as "the free world." Looking back at the origins of the Cold War, in a paper that Harry Dexter White was writing at the time of his death, he lamented the "tensions between certain of the major powers" that had brought "almost catastrophic" consequences, including an "acute lack of confidence in continued political stability and the crippling fear of war on a scale unprecedented and almost unimaginable in its destructive potentialities."

Despite the economic effort imposed by such a policy, being at the center of the international market gave the U.S. unprecedented freedom of action in pursuing its foreign affairs goals. A trade surplus made it easier to keep armies abroad and to invest outside the U.S. Because other nations could not sustain foreign deployments, U.S. power to decide why, when and how to intervene in global crisis increased. The dollar continued to function as a compass to guide the health of the world economy, and exporting to the U.S. became the primary economic goal of developing or redeveloping economies. This arrangement came to be referred to as the Pax Americana, in analogy to the Pax Britannica of the late 19th century and the Pax Romana of the first.

The late Bretton Woods System

The U.S. balance of payments crisis (1958-68).

After the end of World War II, the U.S. held $26 billion in gold reserves, of an estimated total of $40 billion (approx 65%). As world trade increased rapidly through the 1950s, the size of the gold base increased by only a few percent. In 1958, the U.S. balance of payments swung negative. The first U.S. response to the crisis was in the late 1950s when the Eisenhower administration placed import quotas on oil and other restrictions on trade outflows. More drastic measures were proposed, but not acted on. However, with a mounting recession that began in 1959, this response alone was not sustainable. In 1960, with Kennedy's election, a decade-long effort to maintain the Bretton Woods System at the $35/ounce price was begun.

The design of the Bretton Woods System was that only nations could enforce gold convertibility on the anchor currency-the United States'. Gold convertibility enforcement was not required, but instead, allowed. Nations could forgo converting dollars to gold, and instead hold dollars. Rather than full convertibility, it provided a fixed price for sales between central banks. However, there was still an open gold market, 80% of which was traded through London, which issued a morning "gold fix," which was the price of gold on the open market. For the Bretton Woods system to remain workable, it would either have to alter the peg of the dollar to gold, or it would have to maintain the free market price for gold near the $35 per ounce official price. The greater the gap between free market gold prices and central bank gold prices, the greater the temptation to deal with internal economic issues by buying gold at the Bretton Woods price and selling it on the open market. However, keeping the dollar because of its ability to earn interest was still more desirable than holding gold. In 1960 Robert Triffin noticed that the reason holding dollars was more valuable than gold was because constant U.S. balance of payments deficits helped to keep the system liquid and fuel economic growth. What would be later known as Triffin's Dilemma was predicted when Triffin noted that if the U.S. failed to keep running deficits the system would lose its liquidity, not being able to keep up with the world's economic growth, thus bringing the system to a halt. Yet, continuing to incur such payment deficits also meant that over time the deficits would erode confidence in the dollar as the reserve currency creating instability.

The first effort was the creation of the "London Gold Pool." The theory of the pool was that spikes in the free market price of gold, set by the "morning gold fix" in London, could be controlled by having a pool of gold to sell on the open market, which would then be recovered when the price of gold dropped. Gold's price spiked in response to events such as the Cuban Missile Crisis, and other smaller events, to as high as $40/ounce. The Kennedy administration began drafting a radical change of the tax system in order to spur more productive capacity, and thus encourage exports. This would culminate with his tax cut program of 1963, designed to maintain the $35 peg.

In 1967 there was an attack on the pound, and a run on gold in the "sterling area," and on November 17, 1967, the British government was forced to devalue the pound. U.S. President Lyndon Baines Johnson was faced with a brutal choice, either he could institute protectionist measures, including travel taxes, export subsidies and slashing the budget-or he could accept the risk of a "run on gold" and the dollar.

From Johnson's perspective: "The world supply of gold is insufficient to make the present system workable-particularly as the use of the dollar as a reserve currency is essential to create the required international liquidity to sustain world trade and growth." He believed that the priorities of the United States were correct, and that, while there were internal tensions in the Western alliance, that turning away from open trade would be more costly, economically and politically, than it was worth:

"Our role of world leadership in a political and military sense is the only reason for our current embarrassment in an economic sense on the one hand and on the other the correction of the economic embarrassment under present monetary systems will result in an untenable position economically for our allies."

While West Germany agreed not to purchase gold from the U.S., and agreed to hold dollars instead, the pressure on both the Dollar and the Pound Sterling continued. In January 1968 Johnson imposed a series of measures designed to end gold outflow, and to increase American exports. However, to no avail: on March 17, 1968, there was a run on gold, the London Gold Pool was dissolved, and a series of meetings began to rescue or reform the system as it existed. However, as long as the U.S. commitments to foreign deployment continued, particularly to Western Europe, there was little that could be done to maintain the gold peg.

The attempt to maintain that peg collapsed in November 1968, and a new policy program was attempted: to convert Bretton Woods to a system where the enforcement mechanism floated by some means, which would be set by either fiat, or by a restriction to honor foreign accounts.

STRUCTURAL CHANGES UNDERPINNING THE DECLINE OF INTERNATIONAL MONETARY MANAGEMENT

Return to Convertibility

In the 1960s and 70s, important structural changes eventually led to the breakdown of international monetary management. One change was the development of a high level of monetary interdependence. The stage was set for monetary interdependence by the return to convertibility of the Western European currencies at the end of 1958 and of the Japanese yen in 1964. Convertibility facilitated the vast expansion of international financial transactions, which deepened monetary interdependence.

The Growth of International Currency Markets

Another aspect of the internationalization of banking has been the emergence of international banking consortia. Since 1964 various banks had formed international syndicates, and by 1971 over three quarters of the world's largest banks had become shareholders in such syndicates. Multinational banks can and do make huge international transfers of capital not only for investment purposes but also for hedging and speculating against exchange rate fluctuations.

These new forms of monetary interdependence made possible huge capital flows. During the Bretton Woods era countries were reluctant to alter exchange rates formally even in cases of structural disequilibria. Because such changes had a direct impact on certain domestic economic groups, they came to be seen as political risks for leaders. As a result official exchange rates often became unrealistic in market terms, providing a virtually risk-free temptation for speculators. They could move from a weak to a strong currency hoping to reap profits when a revaluation occurred. If, however, monetary authorities managed to avoid revaluation, they could return to other currencies with no loss. The combination of risk-free speculation with the availability of huge sums was highly destabilizing.

The decline of U.S. Hegemony

A second structural change that undermined monetary management was the decline of U.S. hegemony. The U.S. was no longer the dominant economic power it had been for almost two decades. By the mid-1960s Europe and Japan had become international economic powers in their own right. With total reserves exceeding those of the U.S., with higher levels of growth and trade, and with per capita income approaching that of the U.S., Europe and Japan were narrowing the gap between themselves and the United States.

The shift toward a more pluralistic distribution of economic power led to increasing dissatisfaction with the privileged role of the U.S. dollar as the international currency. As in effect the world's central banker, the U.S., through its deficit, determined the level of international liquidity. In an increasingly interdependent world, U.S. policy greatly influenced economic conditions in Europe and Japan. In addition, as long as other countries were willing to hold dollars, the U.S. could carry out massive foreign expenditures for political purposes-military activities and foreign aid-without the threat of balance-of-payments constraints.

Dissatisfaction with the political implications of the dollar system was increased by dantente between the U.S. and the Soviet Union. The Soviet threat had been an important force in cementing the Western capitalist monetary system. The U.S. political and security umbrella helped make American economic domination palatable for Europe and Japan, which had been economically exhausted by the war. As gross domestic production grew in European countries, trade grew. When common security tensions lessened, this loosened the transatlantic dependence on defense concerns, and allowed latent economic tensions to surface.

The decline of the Dollar

Reinforcing the relative decline in U.S. power and the dissatisfaction of Europe and Japan with the system was the continuing decline of the dollar-the foundation that had underpinned the post-1945 global trading system. The Vietnam War and the refusal of the administration of U.S. President Lyndon B. Johnson to pay for it and its Great Society programs through taxation resulted in an increased dollar outflow to pay for the military expenditures and rampant inflation, which led to the deterioration of the U.S. balance of trade position. In the late 1960s, the dollar was overvalued with its current trading position, while the Deutsche Mark and the yen were undervalued; and, naturally, the Germans and the Japanese had no desire to revalue and thereby make their exports more expensive, whereas the U.S. sought to maintain its international credibility by avoiding devaluation. Meanwhile, the pressure on government reserves was intensified by the new international currency markets, with their vast pools of speculative capital moving around in search of quick profits.

In contrast, upon the creation of Bretton Woods, with the U.S. producing half of the world's manufactured goods and holding half its reserves, the twin burdens of international management and the Cold War were possible to meet at first. Throughout the 1950s Washington sustained a balance of payments deficit in order to finance loans, aid, and troops for allied regimes. But during the 1960s the costs of doing so became less tolerable. By 1970 the U.S. held under 16% of international reserves. Adjustment to these changed realities was impeded by the U.S. commitment to fixed exchange rates and by the U.S. obligation to convert dollars into gold on demand.

In sum, monetary interdependence was increasing at a faster pace than international management in the 1960s, leading up to the collapse of the Bretton Woods system. New problems created by interdependence, including huge capital flows, placed stresses on the fixed exchange rate system and impeded national economic management. Amid these problems, economic cooperation decreased, and U.S. leadership declined, and eventually broke down.

THE PARALYSIS OF INTERNATIONAL MONETARY MANAGEMENT

"Floating" Bretton Woods (1968-72)

By 1968, the attempt to defend the dollar at a fixed peg of $35/ounce, the policy of the Eisenhower, Kennedy and Johnson administrations, had become increasingly perishable. Gold outflows from the U.S. accelerated, and despite gaining assurances from Germany and other nations to hold gold, the "dollar shortage" of the 1940s and 1950s had become a dollar glut. In 1967, the IMF agreed in Rio de Janeiro to replace the tranche division set up in 1946. Special Drawing Rights were set as equal to one U.S. dollar, but were not usable for transactions other than between banks and the IMF. Nations were required to accept holding SDRs equal to three times their allotment, and interest would be charged, or credited, to each nation based on their SDR holding. The original interest rate was 1.5%.

The intent of the SDR system was to prevent nations from buying pegged dollars and selling them at the higher free market price, and give nations a reason to hold dollars by crediting interest, at the same time setting a clear limit to the amount of dollars which could be held. The essential conflict was that the American role as military defender of the capitalist world's economic system was recognized, but not given a specific monetary value. In effect, other nations "purchased" American defense policy by taking a loss in holding dollars.

They were only willing to do this as long as they supported U.S. military policy, because of the Vietnam war and other unpopular actions, the pro-U.S. consensus began to evaporate. The SDR agreement, in effect, monetized the value of this relationship, but did not create a market for it.

The use of SDRs as "paper gold" seemed to offer a way to balance the system, turning the IMF, rather than the U.S., into the world's central banker. The US tightened controls over foreign investment and currency, including mandatory investment controls in 1968. In 1970, U.S. President Richard Nixon lifted import quotas on oil in an attempt to reduce energy costs; instead, however, this exacerbated dollar flight, and created pressure from petro-dollars. Still, the U.S. continued to draw down reserves. In 1971 it had a reserve deficit of $56 Billion dollars; as well, it had depleted most of its non-gold reserves and had only 22% gold coverage of foreign reserves. In short, the dollar was tremendously overvalued with respect to gold.

THE "NIXON SHOCK"

By the early 1970s, as the Vietnam War accelerated inflation, the United States as a whole began running a trade deficit (for the first time in the twentieth century). The crucial turning point was 1970, which saw U.S. gold coverage deteriorate from 55% to 22%. This, in the view of neoclassical economists, represented the point where holders of the dollar had lost faith in the ability of the U.S. to cut budget and trade deficits.

In 1971 more and more dollars were being printed in Washington, then being pumped overseas, to pay for the government's military expenditures and private investments. In the first six months of 1971, assets for $22 billion fled the U.S. In response, on August 15, 1971 Nixon unilaterally imposed 90-day wage and price controls, a 10% import surcharge, and most importantly "closed the gold window," making the dollar inconvertible to gold directly, except on the open market. Unusually, this decision was made without consulting members of the international monetary system or even his own State Department, and was soon dubbed the "Nixon Shock".

The surcharge was dropped in December 1971 as part of a general revaluation of major currencies, which were henceforth allowed 2.25% devaluations from the agreed exchange rate. But even the more flexible official rates could not be defended against the speculators. By March 1976, all the major currencies were floating in other words, exchange rates were no longer the principal method used by governments to administer monetary policy.

THE SMITHSONIAN AGREEMENT

The shock of August 15 was followed by efforts under U.S. leadership to develop a new system of international monetary management. Throughout the fall of 1971, there was a series of multilateral and bilateral negotiations of the Group of Ten seeking to develop a new multilateral monetary system.

On 17 and 18 December 1971, the Group of Ten, meeting in the Smithsonian Institute in Washington, created the Smithsonian Agreement which devalued the dollar to $38/ounce, with 2.25% trading bands, and attempted to balance the world financial system using SDRs alone. It was criticized at the time, and was by design a "temporary" agreement.

It failed to impose discipline on the U.S. government, and with no other credibility mechanism in place, the pressure against the dollar in gold continued.

This resulted in gold becoming a floating asset, and in 1971 it reached $44.20/ounce, in 1972 $70.30/ounce and still climbing. By 1972, currencies began abandoning even this devalued peg against the dollar, though it took a decade for all of the industrialized nations to do so.

In February 1973 the Bretton Woods currency exchange markets closed, after a last-gasp devaluation of the dollar to $44/ounce, and reopened in March in a floating currency regime.

BRETTON WOODS II

A number of economists have referred to the system of currency relations which evolved after 2001, in which currencies, particularly the Renminbi, remain fixed to the US Dollar as Bretton Woods II. The argument is that a system of pegged currencies is both stable and desirable, a notion that causes considerable controversy.

CONCLUSIONS

The collapse of the Bretton Woods system is a subject of intense debate. There are a variety of theories as to why it did so, ranging from the budget deficit problems, to the Vietnam War, to marginal tax rates. The fundamental point of agreement is that the U.S. ran an increasing balance of trade deficit, and that, in the end, it could not establish credibility on reining this deficit in. This would lead to the study in economics of credibility as a separate field, and to the prominence of "open" macroeconomic models, such as the Mundell-Fleming model.

10

Monetary Policy and the Real Economy

INTRODUCTION

Monetary policy is the government or central bank process of managing money supply to achieve specific goals-such as constraining inflation, maintaining an exchange rate, achieving full employment or economic growth. Monetary policy can involve changing certain interest rates, either directly or indirectly through open market operations, setting reserve requirements, or trading in foreign exchange markets. Monetary policy is generally referred to as either being an expansionary policy, or a contractionary policy, where an expansionary policy increases the total supply of money in the economy, and a contractionary policy decreases the total money supply. Expansionary policy is traditionally used to combat unemployment in a recession by lowering interest rates, while contractionary policy has the goal of raising interest rates to combat inflation. Monetary policy rests on the relationship between the rates of interest in an economy, that is the price at which money can be borrowed, and the total supply of money.

Monetary policy uses a variety of tools to control one or both of these, to influence outcomes like economic growth, inflation, exchange rates with other currencies and unemployment. Where currency is under a monopoly of issuance, or where there is a regulated system of issuing currency through banks which are tied to a central bank, the monetary authority has the ability to alter the interest rate and the money supply in order to achieve policy goals. The beginning of monetary policy as such comes from the late 19th century, where it was used to maintain the gold standard. A policy is referred to as contractionary if it reduces the size of the money supply or raises the interest rate. An expansionary policy increases the size of the money supply, or decreases the interest rate. Further monetary policies are described as accomodative if the interest set by the central monetary authority is intended to spur economic growth, neutral if it is intended to neither spur growth or combat inflation, or tight if intended to reduce inflation or "cool" an economy.

There are several monetary policy tools available to achieve these ends. Increasing interest rates by fiat, reducing the monetary base or increasing reserve requirements all have the effect of contracting the money supply, and, if reversed, expand the money supply. Since the 1970s, monetary policy has generally been formed separately from fiscal policy. And even prior to the 1970s, the Bretton Woods system still ensured that most nations would form the two policies separately.

Within almost all modern nations, special institutions (like the European Central Bank or the Federal Reserve) exist which have the task of executing the monetary policy independently of the executive. In general, these institutions are called central banks and often have other responsibilities such as supervising the smooth operation of the financial system.

The primary tool of monetary policy is open market operations. This entails managing the quantity of money in circulation through the buying and selling of various credit instruments, foreign currencies or commodities. All of these purchases or sales result in more or less base currency entering or leaving market circulation.

Usually the short term goal of open market operations is to achieve a specific short term interest rate target. In other instances however monetary policy might instead entail the targeting of a specific exchange rate relative to some foreign currency or else relative to gold. For example in the case of the USA the Federal Reserve targets the federal funds rate, the rate at which member banks lend to one another overnight. However the monetary policy of China is to target the exchange rate between the Chinese renminbi and a basket of foreign currencies. The relationship between monetary policy and the real economy is uncertain. It is important to note that expansionary monetary policy should not be confused with economic expansion. The latter being an increase in economic output in the real economy.

Contractionary Monetary Policy

Contractionary monetary policy is monetary policy that seeks to reduce the size of the money supply. In most nations, monetary policy is controlled by either a central bank or a finance ministry. Neoclassical and Keynesian economics significantly differ on the effects and effectiveness of monetary policy on influencing the real economy; there is no clear consensus on how monetary policy effects real economic variables (aggregate output or income, employment). Both economic schools accept that monetary policy affects monetary variables (price levels, interest rates).

Monetary policy relies on a number of tools: monetary base, reserve requirements, discount window lending and interest rates.

Monetary Base

Contractionary policy can be implemented by reducing the size of the monetary base. This directly reduces the total amount of money circulating in the economy.

A central bank can use open market operations to reduce the monetary base. The central bank would typically sell bonds in exchange for hard currency. When the central bank collects this hard currency payment, it removes that amount of currency from the economy, thus contracting the monetary base.

Note that in the United States open market operations are a relatively small part of the total volume in the bond market, thus the Federal Reserve is not able to influence interest rates through this method.

Reserve Requirements

The monetary authority exerts regulatory control over banks. Contractionary policy can be implemented by requiring banks to hold a higher proportion of their total assets in reserve. Banks only maintain a small portion of their assets as cash available for immediate withdrawal; the rest is invested in illiquid assets like mortgages and loans. By requiring a higher proportion of total assets to be held as liquid cash, the Federal Reserve reduces the availability of loanable funds. This acts as a reduction in the money supply.

Discount Window Lending

Many central banks or finance ministries have the authority to lend funds to financial institutions within their country. The lent funds represent an expansion in the monetary base. By calling in existing loans the monetary authority can directly reduce the size of the money supply. By advertising that the discount window will reduce future lending, the monetary can also indirectly reduce the money supply by reducing risk-taking by financial institutions.

Interest Rates

Monetary authorities in different nations have differing levels of control of economy-wide interest rates. In the United States, the Federal Reserve can only indirectly set the Federal Funds Rate by open market operations, discount lending, and changes in reserve requirement. This rate has some effect on other market interest rates, but there is no direct, definite relationship. In other nations, the monetary authority may be able to mandate specific interest rates on loans, savings accounts or other financial assets. By raising the interest rate(s) under its control, a monetary authority can contract the money supply, because higher interest rates encourage savings and discourage lending. Both of these effects reduce the size of the money supply.

MONETARY BASE

Expansionary policy can be implemented by increasing the size of the monetary base. This directly increases the total amount of money circulating in the economy. In the United States, the Federal Reserve can use open market operations to increase the monetary base. The Federal Reserve would buy bonds in exchange for hard currency. When the Federal Reserve disburses this hard currency payment, it adds that amount of currency from the economy, thus increasing the monetary base. Note that open market operations are a relatively small part of the total volume in the bond market, thus the Federal Reserve is not able to influence interest rates through this method.

HISTORY OF MONETARY POLICY

Monetary policy is associated with currency and credit. For many centuries there were only two forms of monetary policy: decisions about coinage, and the decision to print paper money to create credit. Interest rates, while now thought of as part of monetary authority, were not generally coordinated with the other forms of monetary policy. Monetary policy was seen as an executive decision, and was generally in the hands of the authority with seniorage, or the power to coin. With the advent of larger trading networks came the ability to set the price between gold and silver, and the price of the local currency to foreign currencies. This official price could be enforced by law, even if it varied from the market price.

With the creation of the Bank of England in 1694, which acquired the responsibility to print notes and back them with gold, the idea of monetary policy as independent of executive action began to be established.

MONEY MARKET

The money market is the financial market for short-term borrowing and lending, typically up to thirteen months. This contrasts with the capital market for longer-term funds. In the money markets, banks lend to and borrow from each other, short-term financial instruments such as certificates of deposit (CDs) or enter into agreements such as repurchase agreements (repos). It provides short to medium term liquidity in the global financial system. Money market derivatives include forward rate agreements (FRAs) and short-term interest rate futures. Trading takes place between banks in the "money centers" (New York and London primarily, also Chicago, Frankfurt, Paris, Singapore, Hong Kong, Tokyo, Toronto, Sydney, San Francisco).

Common Money Market Instruments

* Bankers' acceptance-A draft or bill of exchange accepted by a bank to guarantee payment of the bill.
* Certificate of deposit-A time deposit with a specific maturity date shown on a certificate; large-denomination certificates of deposits can be sold before maturity.

* Commercial paper-An unsecured promissory note with a fixed maturity of one to 270 days; usually it is sold at a discount from face value.
* Eurodollar deposit-Deposits made in U.S. dollars at a bank or bank branch located outside the United States.
* Federal Agency Short-Term Securities-(in the US). Short-term securities issued by government sponsored enterprises such as the Farm Credit System, the Federal Home Loan Banks and the Federal National Mortgage Association.
* Federal funds-(in the US). Interest-bearing deposits held by banks and other depository institutions at the Federal Reserve; these are immediately available funds that institutions borrow or lend, usually on an overnight basis. They are lent for the federal funds rate.
* Municipal notes-(in the US). Short-term notes issued by municipalities in anticipation of tax receipts or other revenues.
* Repurchase agreements-Short-term loans-normally for less than two weeks and frequently for one day-arranged by selling securities to an investor with an agreement to repurchase them at a fixed price on a fixed date.
* Treasury bills-Short-term debt obligations of a national government that are issued to mature in 3 to 12 months.

MONEY CREATION

Money creation is the process by which the money supply of a country is increased. There are several ways that a government, in coordination with the country's commercial banks, can increase or decrease the money supply of a country.

If a country follows a fractional-reserve banking regime, as virtually all countries do, not all of the money in circulation needs to be backed by other currencies, physical assets such as gold, or government assets. Instead, the country's currency is backed by the economic potential of the country and is based on government fiat, or decree. This perceived potential puts a theoretical limit on the amount of money a country can prudently create.

DEPOSIT CREATION MULTIPLIER

The most common mechanism used to create money is typically called the deposit creation multiplier. It measures the amount by which the commercial banking system increases the money supply. To control the amount of money created by the system, central banks place strict reserve ratios on the commercial banks. For example, central banks generally restrict the proportion of primary deposits that commercial banks can lend out. This is called the cash reserve ratio.

For example, let's assume that a primary deposit of $1000 is made into bank A. If the cash reserve ratio is 12%, then $120 must be kept on hand by the bank and $880 is available to be lent to someone else (called the excess reserve). Now if bank A uses its $880 in excess reserve by lending it out, and that is deposited in bank B, it represents a primary deposit to the second bank.

Bank B must keep 12% of $880 on hand but can lend out $774.40. If that $774.40 is eventually deposited in bank C, the third bank must keep $92.93 on hand but can lend out $681.47. The process continues until there is no excess reserve left (For simplicity we will ignore safety reserves.). By adding all the derivative deposits we can calculate the amount of money created. Alternatively we can use the deposit multiplier equation: TD = ID/crr

Where:

*TD = change in Total Deposits

*ID = Initial change in Deposit

*crr = cash reserve ratio

The initial change in deposit of $1000 will increase total deposits by $8333.33 given a reserve ratio of 12% (1000/.12=8333.33).

An Example of the Creation of New Money

The following steps describe one way that new money can be created. It is an example from the US. The government issues a Treasury security. This is simply an IOU, a promise to pay the holder a specified sum of money on a particular date. In this example, let's say the government issues $1,000,000 worth of bonds. Individual investors, pension funds, mutual funds, insurance agencies, banks, foreign government central banks, can all buy the bonds, effectively loaning money to the treasury. They do this to invest their money and receive interest in return. The Federal Reserve prints a check, in the amount of $1,000,000 and makes it payable to the government. This check is the proceeds from the sale of the bonds.

The $1,000,000 is recorded as an asset by the Fed. (money owed to the central bank is called an "asset" by the bank) It is assumed the government, with its power to tax, will make good on its debt (this is why the people buying the bonds from the fed consider it a risk-free investment). The government deposits the check in its own account. The government hires employees and buys things with the $1,000,000, and it does so by writing government checks. These government checks are then deposited in commercial banks. For the sake of simplicity, assume it all goes into one commercial bank, which has a zero balance to begin with.

The commercial bank now claims $1,000,000 in new liabilities (the amount on deposit in a bank is called a "liability" by the bank, because the bank has to pay interest to it, amongst other things). In the US, the law allows the bank to lend out 90% of what it has on deposit. This lending of money that it has on deposit is the precise point at which new money is created, because the depositor still has his money, and the person getting the loan now has money too. $900,000 is lent out on Friday for someone to buy a house. This loan is in the form of a check.

The home buyer signs the check and gives it to the seller, who deposits it right back into the bank on Monday. Note however, in real life that money would only come from the bank temporarily, which then would issue its own bonds or use a company like Fannie Mae to issue its own bonds, so that again investors can actually lend the money while the bank is simply a middleman, called a "servicer".

The commercial bank now claims $900,000 in new liabilities. 10 percent of that money is put into reserves, and 90% of that, or $810,000 is lent out. As soon as the $810,000 is deposited back into the bank, the cycle repeats and repeats until there is no more money to lend. The total amount lent out to borrowers is $9,000,000. Add that to the $1,000,000 that it still has on deposit and the total is $10,000,000. Commercial banks make profit by charging fees for transactions, and by charging a higher interest rate to those they lend to, than what they pay for the funds. If the commercial bank charges 6% interest on the $9,000,000 it will earn $540,000 per year. If the bank making the loan pays 1% interest to the person who put the money on deposit in the first place it will cost them $100,000 per year.

With 90% of that money lent out, if the original depositor wants their money back, the bank has to borrow that money from another bank (or maybe from another source), at rate of interest set by the government (the overnight rate, or the federal funds rate in the US). This is called "asset-liability bouncing", and is a delicate balancing act all banks must work on every day.

A more Realistic Model of Money Creation

In actual fact, the money creation multiplier is more complex than this simple, small description. We must add to the equation the currency drain ratio (the propensity of the public to hold cash rather than deposit it in the banking system), the clearing house drain (the loss of deposits from the system due to interactions between banks), and the safety reserve ratio (excess reserves beyond the legal requirement that commercial banks voluntarily hold-usually a very small amount). Also, most jurisdictions require different levels of reserves for different types of deposits. Foreign currency deposits, domestic time deposits, and government deposits often have different cash reserve ratios.

FEDERAL RESERVE SYSTEM

The Federal Reserve System (also the Federal Reserve; informally The Fed) is the central banking system of the United States.

The Federal Reserve System is a quasi-governmental banking system composed of (1) a presidentially-appointed Board of Governors of the Federal Reserve System in Washington, D.C.; (2) the Federal Open Market Committee; (3) twelve regional Federal Reserve Banks located in major cities throughout the nation; and (4) numerous private member banks, which own varying amounts of stock in the regional Federal Reserve Banks. Ben Bernanke serves as the current Chairman of the Board of Governors of the Federal Reserve System.

Legal Status and Position in Government

The various components of the Federal Reserve System have differing legal statuses.

The Board of Governors of the Federal Reserve System is an independent government agency. The Board is subject to laws like the Freedom of Information Act and the Privacy Act which cover Federal agencies and not private entities. Like most other independent agencies, its decisions do not have to be ratified by the President or anyone else in the executive or legislative branches of government. The Board of Governors does not receive funding from Congress, and the terms of the members of the Board span multiple presidential and congressional terms. Once a member of the Board of Governors is appointed by the president, he or she is relatively independent (although the law provides for the possibility of removal by the President "for cause" under).

The Federal Reserve Banks are nominally "owned" by the private member banks. In Lewis v. United States, 680 F.2d 1239 (9th Cir. 1982), the United States Court of Appeals for the Ninth Circuit stated that the "the Reserve Banks are not federal instrumentalities for purposes of the FTCA [the Federal Tort Claims Act], but are independent, privately owned and locally controlled corporations." The opinion also stated that "the Reserve Banks have properly been held to be federal instrumentalities for some purposes."

The member banks are generally privately-owned corporations. The stocks of many of the member banks are publicly traded.

The Federal Reserve System was created via the Federal Reserve Act of December 23rd, 1913. All national banks were required to join the system and other banks could join. The Reserve Banks opened for business on November 16th, 1914. Federal Reserve Notes were created as part of the legislation, to provide an elastic supply of currency. The notes were to be issued to the Reserve Banks for subsequent transmittal to banking institutions.

History

The first institution with responsibilities of a central bank in the U.S. was the First Bank of the United States, chartered in 1791 by Alexander Hamilton. Thomas Jefferson, in opposition to its proposed charter, wrote the following:

The bill for establishing a national bank, in 1791, undertakes, among other things,

(1) To form the subscribers into a corporation.

(2) To enable them, in their corporate capacities, to receive grants of lands; and, so far, is against the laws of mortmain.

(3) To make alien subscribers capable of holding lands; and so far is against the laws of alienage.

(4) To transmit these lands, on the death of a proprietor, to a certain line of successors; and so far, changes the course of descents.

(5) To put the lands out of the reach of forfeiture, or escheat; and so far, is against the laws of forfeiture and escheat.

(6) To transmit personal chattels to successors, in a certain line; and so far, is against the laws of distribution.

(7) To give them the sole and exclusive right of banking, under the national authority; and, so far, is against the laws of monopoly.

(8) To communicate to them a power to make laws, paramount to the laws of the states; for so they must be construed, to protect the institution from the control of the state legislatures; and so probably they will be construed.

I consider the foundation of the Constitution as laid on this ground--that all powers not delegated to the United States, by the Constitution, nor prohibited by it to the states, are reserved to the states, or to the people (12th amend.). To take a single step beyond the boundaries thus specially drawn around the powers of Congress, is to take possession of a boundless field of power, no longer susceptible of any definition.

The incorporation of a bank, and the powers assumed by this bill, have not, in my opinion, been delegated to the United States by the Constitution. (The Writings of Thomas Jefferson, ed. by H. E. Bergh, Vol. III, p. 145 ff.)

In 1816, the Second Bank of the United States was chartered, later to be dissolved under president Andrew Jackson. From 1837 to 1862, in the Free Banking Era there was no formal central bank, while from 1862 to 1913, a system of national banks was instituted by the 1863 National Banking Act.

A series of bank panics, in 1873, 1893, and 1907, caused by market speculation and the actions of international banks, provided public support for the creation of a centralized banking system, which it was thought would provide greater stability.

After the Panic of 1907, Congress created the National Monetary Commission to draft a plan for reform of the banking system. Senate Republican leader and financial expert Nelson Aldrich was the head of the Commission. In 1910, Aldrich attended a secret meeting at Jekyll Island, Georgia with leading bankers, including Paul Warburg, Frank Vanderlip of the National City Bank, Henry Davison of J.P. Morgan Company, and Benjamin Strong, also of J.P. Morgan, to draft the Aldrich Plan, which would later become the Federal Reserve Act.

It took the political clout of Woodrow Wilson to get the bankers' plan passed over the objections of agrarian leader William Jennings Bryan. Wilson started with the bankers' plan that had been designed for conservative Republicans by banker Paul Warburg.

Wilson had to outmaneuver the agrarian wing of the party, led by William Jennings Bryan, which strenuously denounced banks and Wall Street. They wanted a government-owned central bank which could print paper money whenever Congress wanted; Wilson convinced them that because Federal Reserve notes were obligations of the government, the plan fit their demands.

Southerners and westerners learned from Wilson that the system was decentralized into 12 districts and surely would weaken New York and strengthen the hinterlands. One key Congressman, Carter Glass, was given credit for the bill, and his home of Richmond, Virginia, was made a district headquarters.

Powerful Senator James A. Reed of Missouri was given two district headquarters in St. Louis and Kansas City. Congress passed the Federal Reserve Act in late 1913. Wilson named Warburg and other prominent bankers to direct the new system, pleasing the bankers. The New York branch dominated the Fed and thus the power of the banking system remained in Wall Street. The new system began operations in 1915 and played a major role in financing the Allied and American war efforts. [Link 1956 pp 199-240]

Roles and Responsibilities

According to the Board of Governors, the main tasks of the Federal Reserve System are:

Conducting the nation's monetary policy by influencing the monetary and credit conditions in the economy in pursuit of maximum employment, stable prices, and moderate long-term interest rates supervising and regulating banking institutions to ensure the safety and soundness of the nation's banking and financial system and to protect the credit rights of consumers maintaining the stability of the financial system and containing systemic risk that may arise in financial markets providing financial services to depository institutions, the U.S. government, and foreign official institutions, including playing a major role in operating the nation's payments system.

ORGANIZATION OF THE FEDERAL RESERVE SYSTEM

The basic structure of the Federal Reserve System includes:

* The Board of Governors
* The Federal Open Market Committee
* The Federal Reserve Banks
* The member banks.

Each privately owned Federal Reserve Bank and each member bank of the Federal Reserve System is subject to oversight by a Board of Governors. The 7 members of the board are appointed by the President and confirmed by the Senate. Members are selected to terms of 14 years (unless removed by the President), with the ability to serve for no more than one term. A governor may serve the remainder of another governor's term in addition to his or her own full term.

The current members of the Board of Governors are:

* Ben Bernanke, Chairman
* Donald Kohn, Vice-Chairman
* Susan Bies
* Frederic Mishkin
* Kevin Warsh
* Randall Kroszner.

The Federal Open Market Committee (FOMC) created under comprises the 7 members of the board of governors and 5 representatives selected from the Federal Reserve Banks. The representative from the 2nd District, New York, (currently Timothy Geithner) is a permanent member, while the rest of the banks rotate on two and three year intervals.

CONTROL OF THE MONEY SUPPLY

The Federal Reserve System controls the size of the money supply by conducting open market operations, in which the Federal Reserve engages in the lending or purchasing of specific types of securities with authorized participants, known as primary dealers. All open market operations in the United States are conducted by the Open Market Desk at the Federal Reserve Bank of New York with an aim to making the federal funds rate as close to the target rate as possible. For a detailed look at the process by which changes to a reserve account held at the Fed affect the wider monetary supply of the economy.

The Open Market Desk has two main tools to adjust the monetary supply: repurchase agreements and outright transactions.

To smooth temporary or cyclical changes in the monetary supply, the desk engages in repurchase agreements (repos) with its primary dealers. Repos are essentially secured, short-term lending by the Fed. On the day of the transaction, the Fed deposits money in a primary dealer's reserve account, and receives the promised securities as collateral. When the transaction matures, the process unwinds: the Fed returns the collateral and charges the primary dealer's reserve account for the principal and accrued interest. The term of the repo (the time between settlement and maturity) can vary from 1 day (called an overnight repo) to 65 days, though the Fed will most commonly conduct overnight and 14-day repos.

Since there is an increase of bank reserves during the term of the repo, repos temporarily increase the money supply. The effect is temporary since all repo transactions unwind, with the only lasting net effect being a slight depletion of reserves caused by the accrued interest (think one day of interest at a 4.5% annual yield, which is 0.0121% per day). The Fed has conducted repos almost daily in 2004-2005, but can also conduct reverse repos to temporarily shrink the money supply.

In a reverse repo the Fed will borrow money from the reserve accounts of primary dealers in exchange for Treasury securities as collateral. At maturity, the Fed will return the money to the reserve accounts with the accrued interest, and collect the collateral. Since this drains reserves, reverse repos temporarily contract the monetary supply, except, again, for the extremely small lasting increase caused by the accrued interest.

The other main tool available to the Open Market Desk is the outright transaction. Outrights differ from repos in that they permanently alter the money supply. Outright transactions overwhelmingly involve the purchase of Treasury securities in the secondary market.

In an outright purchase, the Fed will buy Treasury securities from primary dealers and finance these purchases by depositing newly created money in the dealer's reserve account at the Fed. Since this operation does not unwind at the end of a set period, the resulting growth in the monetary supply is permanent. The Fed also has the authority to sell Treasuries outright, but this has been exceedingly rare since the 1980s. The sale of Treasury securities results in a permanent decrease in the money supply, as the money used as payment for the securities from the primary dealers is removed from their reserve accounts, thus working the money multiplier process in reverse.

IMPLEMENTATION OF MONETARY POLICY

Buying and selling federal government securities. When the Federal Reserve System buys securities, it in effect puts more money into circulation and takes securities out of circulation. With more money around, interest rates tend to drop, and more money is borrowed and spent. When the Fed sells government securities, it in effect takes money out of circulation, causing interest rates to rise and making borrowing more difficult.

Regulating the amount of money that a member bank must keep in hand as reserves. A member bank lends out most of the money deposited with it. If the Federal Reserve System says that a member bank must keep in reserve a larger fraction of its deposits, then the amount that the member bank can lend drops, loans become harder to obtain, and interest rates rise.

Changing the interest charged to banks that want to borrow money from the federal reserve system. Member banks borrow from the Federal Reserve System to cover short-term needs. The interest that the Fed charges for this is called the discount rate; this will have an effect, though usually rather small, on how much money the member banks will lend.

DISCOUNT RATES

The Federal Reserve System implements monetary policy largely by targeting the federal funds rate. This is the rate that member banks charge each other for overnight loans of federal funds, which are the reserves held by banks at the Fed.

The Federal Reserve System also directly sets the discount rate, which is the interest rate that banks pay the Fed to borrow directly from it. However, a bank will prefer to borrow Fed funds from another bank, rather than from the Fed at the normally higher discount rate, which might suggest problems with the bank's credit-worthiness or solvency.

Both of these rates influence the prime rate which is usually about 3 percentage points higher than the federal funds rate. The prime rate is the rate that most banks price their loans at for their best customers.

Lower interest rates stimulate economic activity by lowering the cost of borrowing, making it easier for consumers and businesses to buy and build. Higher interest rates slow the economy by increasing the cost of borrowing.

The Federal Reserve System usually adjusts the federal funds rate by 0.25% or 0.50% at a time. From early 2001 to mid 2003 the Federal Reserve lowered its interest rates 13 times, from 6.25 to 1.00%, to fight recession. In November 2002, rates were cut to 1.75, and many interest rates went below the inflation rate. (This is known as a negative real interest rate, because money paid back from a loan with an interest rate less than inflation has lower purchasing power than it had before the loan.) On June 25, 2003, the federal funds rate was lowered to 1.00%, its lowest nominal rate since July, 1958, when the overnight rate averaged 0.68%. Starting at the end of June, 2004, the Federal Reserve System started to raise the target interest rate 17 straight times. The rate is 5.25% as of August 8, 2005; the Fed elected to keep the rate steady on its August 8 meeting after seventeen straight 0.25% increases. The Federal Reserve System might also attempt to use open market operations to change long-term interest rates, but its "buying power" on the market is significantly smaller than that of private institutions. The Fed can also attempt to "jawbone" the markets into moving towards the Fed's desired rates, but this is not always effective.

THE FEDERAL RESERVE BANKS AND THE MEMBER BANKS

The twelve regional Federal Reserve Banks (not to be confused with the "member banks"), which were established by the Congress as the operating arms of the nation's central banking system, are organized much like private corporations-possibly leading to some confusion about "ownership." For example, the Reserve Banks issue shares of stock to "member banks.

" However, owning Reserve Bank stock is quite different from owning stock in a private company. The Reserve Banks are not operated for profit, and ownership of a certain amount of stock by a "member bank" is, by law, a condition of membership in the system.

The stock may not be sold or traded or pledged as security for a loan; dividends are, by law, limited to 6% per year. The largest of the Reserve Banks, in terms of assets, is the Federal Reserve Bank of New York, which is responsible for the Second District covering the state of New York, the New York City region, Puerto Rico, and the U.S. Virgin Islands.

The dividends paid by the Federal Reserve Banks to member banks are considered partial compensation for the lack of interest paid on member banks' required reserves held at the Federal Reserve Banks. By law, banks in the United States must maintain fractional reserves, most of which are kept on account at the Fed. The Federal Reserve does not pay interest on these funds.

The Federal Reserve Districts are listed below along with their identifying letter and number. These are used on Federal Reserve Notes to identify the issuing bank for each note.: Boston A 1:New York B 2 :Philadelphia C 3 :Cleveland D 4 :Richmond E 5 :Atlanta F 6 :Chicago G 7 :St Louis H 8 :Minneapolis I 9 :Kansas City J 10 :Dallas K 11 :San Francisco L 12.

INFLUENCE OF GOVERNMENT

Central bank independence from political control is a crucial concept in both economic theory and practice. The problem arises as central banks strive to maintain a credible commitment to price stability, when the markets know that there is political pressure to keep interest rates low. Low interest rates tend to keep unemployment below trend, encourage economic growth, and allow for cheap credit and loans. Some models however say such a policy is not sustainable without accelerating inflation in the long term.

Thus, a central bank believed to be under political control cannot make a credible commitment to fight inflation, as the markets know that sitting politicians will lobby to keep rates low. This point was one of the major research topics of economist Edward C. Prescott's career. It is in this limited sense that the Federal Reserve System is independent. The members of the FOMC are not elected and do not answer to politicians in making their interest rate decisions.

The Federal Reserve System is financially independent because it runs a surplus, due in part to its ownership of government bonds. In fact, it returns billions of dollars to the government each year. However, the Fed is still subject to oversight by the Congress, which periodically reviews its activities and can alter its responsibilities by statute. To further communication with Congress, the Fed delivers a report to both houses semiannually. Its independence from the executive branch was strengthened by the 1951 Accord. In general, the Federal Reserve System must work within the framework of the overall objectives of economic and financial policy established by the government.

FRACTIONAL-RESERVE BANKING

In its role of setting reserve requirements for the country's banking system, the Fed regulates what is known as fractional-reserve banking. This is the common practice by banks of retaining only a fraction of their deposits to satisfy demands for withdrawals, lending the remainder at interest to obtain income that can be used to pay interest to depositors and provide profits for the banks' owners. Some people also use the term to refer to fiat money, which is money that is not backed by a tangible asset such as gold. The United States' rules and oversight are within limits and guidelines set by the Bank for

International Settlements, a banking agency which pre-dates the Bretton Woods financial and monetary system and its institutions.

Criticisms of the Fed

A large and varied group of criticisms are often directed against the Federal Reserve System. Some of these criticisms relate to inflation and fractional reserve banking more generally, and an in-depth treatment of these issues may be found in their respective articles. There were also specific issues relating to the former chairmanship of Alan Greenspan, specifically, that the Fed's credibility is based on a cult of personality around him and his successors. This line of argument is also more thoroughly addressed in this article. Nonetheless, critics still point to a number of specific criticisms about the methods and actions of the Fed; these are treated below.

HISTORICAL CRITICISMS

Criticisms of the Fed are not new, and some historical criticisms are reflective of current concerns.

At one extreme are a few economists from the Austrian School and the Chicago School who want the Fed abolished. They criticize the Fed's expansionary monetary policy in the 1920's, allowing misallocations of capital resources and supporting a massive stock price bubble.

Milton Friedman, leader of the Chicago School, argues that the Fed did not cause the Great Depression but made it worse by contracting the money supply at the very moment that markets needed liquidity. He believes the Fed should be abolished. The Austrian School argues that the expansion of money supply by the Federal Reserve caused malinvestment leading to the Great Depression.

Opacity

Another criticism of the Federal Reserve System is that it is shrouded in secrecy. Meetings of some components of the Fed are held behind closed doors, and the transcripts are released with a lag of five years. Even expert policy analysts are unsure as to the logic behind Fed decisions. Critics argue that such opacity leads to greater market volatility, as the markets must guess, often with only limited information, about how the Fed is likely to change policy in the future.

The jargon-laden fence-sitting opaque style of Fed communication is often called "Fed speak." It has also been known to be standoffish in its relations with the media in an effort to maintain its carefully crafted image and resents any public information that runs contrary to this notion.

For example, Maria Bartiromo reported on CNBC that during a conversation at the White House Correspondents' Dinner in April of 2006, Fed Chairman Ben Bernanke stated investors had misinterpreted his recent congressional remarks as an indication the Fed was nearly done raising rates. This triggered a drop in stock prices just as the market was about to close.

Furthermore, the lag in the release of FOMC transcripts, as well as the extremely limited and carefully worded minutes and statement, leads to the public being unaware of the issues of major concern to the Fed, and leaves it with an inadequate understanding of the logic and rationale behind the decisions. Some argue that this is a concerted attempt to keep Congress and the public at arm's length, but this criticism has not gained much widespread acceptance.

OPPOSITION TO FEDERAL RESERVE

In The Creature from Jekyll Island author G. Edward Griffin argues that the Federal Reserve System was planned in secret by several extremely rich and powerful people for the purposes of furthering their family wealth and political power.

Economists of the Austrian School such as Ludwig von Mises contend that it is the Federal Reserve's artificial manipulation of the money supply that leads to the boom/bust business cycle that has occurred over the last century. Many economic libertarians, such as Austrian School economists, believe that the Federal Reserve's manipulation of the money supply to stop "gold flight" from England caused, or was instrumental in causing, the Great Depression.

In general, laissez-faire advocates of free banking argue that there is no better judge of the proper interest rate and money supply than the market. Nobel Economist Milton Friedman says, he "prefer[s] to abolish the federal reserve system altogether. "Friedman and Freedom, Interview with Peter Jaworski. The Journal, Queen's University, March 15, 2002-Issue 37, Volume 129. Ben Bernanke, Chairman of the Board of Governors of Federal Reserve, stated: "Regarding the Great Depression. You're right, we did it. We're very sorry."

The Libertarian Party (United States) platform and the Constitution Party hold positions that the Federal Reserve should be abolished on legal and economic grounds.

OPEN MARKET OPERATION

Open market operations are the means of implementing monetary policy by which a central bank controls its national money supply by buying and selling government securities, or other instruments. Monetary targets, such as interest rates or exchange rates, are used to guide this implementation.

Since most money is now in the form of electronic records, rather than paper records such as banknotes, open market operations are conducted simply by electronically increasing or decreasing the amount of money that a bank has, e.g., in its reserve account at the central bank, in exchange for the bank selling or buying a financial instrument. Newly created money is used by the central bank to buy in the open market a financial asset, such as government bonds, foreign currency, or gold. If the central bank sells these assets in the open market, the amount of money that the bank holds decreases, effectively destroying money.

The process does not literally require the immediate printing of new currency. A central bank account for a member bank can simply be increased electronically. However this will increase the central bank's requirement to print currency when the member bank demands banknotes, in exchange for a decrease in its electronic balance.

Possible Targets of Open Market Operations

Under inflation targeting open market operations target a specific short term interest rate in the debt markets. This target is changed periodically to achieve and maintain an inflation rate within a target band. Many other variants of monetary policy also target interest rates. Both the US Federal

Reserve and the ECB use interest rate targets to guide open market operations.

Besides interest rate targeting there are other possible targets of open markets operations. A second possible target is the growth of the money supply, as was the case in the U.S. in the late 1970s through the early 1980s under Fed Chairman Paul Volcker.

Under a gold standard open market operations would be used to achieve and maintain a target gold price. The goal would be to keep the value of the currency constant relative to gold.

Under a currency board open market operations would be used to achieve and maintain a fixed exchange rate with relation to some foreign currency. A central bank can also use a mixture of policy settings that change depending on circumstances. A central bank may peg its exchange rate (like a currency board) with different levels or forms of commitment.

The looser the exchange rate peg, the more latitude the central bank has to target other variables (such as interest rates). It may instead target a basket of foreign currencies rather than a single currency. In some instances it is empowered to use additional means other than open market operations, such as changes in reserve requirements or capital controls, to achieve monetary outcomes.

Economist Robert Mundell has stated that when using open market operations it is only possible to pursue a single target at any given time. You can not use open market operations to target interest rates while being on a gold standard. Likewise if you are targeting interest rates then the exchange rates will fluctuate.

Current Goals and Procedures of Open Market Operations

In the United States, as of 2006 the Fed sets an interest rate target for the Fed funds (overnight bank reserves) market. When the actual Fed funds rate is higher than the target, the desk will usually increase the money supply via a repo (effectively lending). When the actual Fed funds rate is less than the target, the desk will usually decrease the money supply via a reverse repo (effectively borrowing). The European Central Bank has similar mechanisms for their operations; however, it uses a four-tiered approach with different goals: beside its main goal of steering and smoothing Euroland interest rates while managing the liquidity situation in the market the ECB also has the aim of signalling the stance of monetary policy with its operations.

The regular weekly "main refinancing operations" and the monthly "longer-term refinancing operations" provide liquidity to the financial sector, while ad-hoc "fine-tuning operations" (in the form of reverse or outright transactions, foreign exchange swaps and the collection of fixed-term deposits) aim to smooth interest rates caused by liquidity fluctuations in the market and "structural operations" are used to adjust the central banks' longer-term structural positions vis-a-vis the financial sector.

The Swiss National Bank currently targets the 3 month Swiss franc LIBOR rate, and borrows or lends Swiss francs directly with Swiss banks (in other words, without using repos) on an almost daily basis. These borrowings or loans are typically made for 1 day or 1 week, but may be as long as 1 month

RESERVE REQUIREMENTS

The monetary authority exerts regulatory control over banks. Expansionary policy can be implemented by requiring banks to hold a lower proportion of their total assets in reserve. Banks only maintain a small portion of their assets as cash available for immediate withdrawal; the rest is invested in illiquid assets like mortgages and loans. By requiring a lower proportion of total assets to be held as liquid cash the Federal Reserve increases the availability of loanable funds. This acts as an increase in the money supply.

DISCOUNT WINDOW LENDING

Many central banks or finance ministries have the authority to lend funds to financial institutions within their country. The lent funds represent an expansion in the monetary base. By extending new loans the monetary authority can directly increase the size of the money supply. By advertising that the discount window will increase future lending, the monetary authority can also indirectly increase the money supply by raising risk-taking by financial institutions. After the September 11, 2001 attacks in the United States, the Federal Reserve announced that it would extend discount window loans to any and all financial institutions who requested funds. This had the effect of preventing any panics due to fear of insufficient liquidity.

Interest Rates

Monetary authorities in different nations have differing levels of control of economy-wide interest rates. In the United States, the Federal Reserve can only indirectly set the Federal Funds Rate. This rate has some effect on other market interest rates, but there is no direct, definite relationship. In other nations, the monetary authority may be able to mandate specific interest rates on loans, savings accounts or other financial assets. By lowering the interest rate(s) under its control, a monetary authority can expand the money supply, because lower interest rates discourage savings and encourage lending. Both of these effects increase the size of the money supply.

MONETARY POLICY AND INFLATION

Monetary policy can be used to control inflation. Inflation is defined as continuing increases in price levels. Since price level is a monetary variable, monetary policy can affect it. Contractionary monetary policy has the effect of reducing inflation by reducing upward pressure on price levels.

Note that inflation can also be affected by fiscal policy. However, contractionary fiscal policy is often politically unpopular, because it involves spending cuts and tax increases. Thus, politicians favor the use of monetary policy to control inflation.

Expansionary Monetary Policy vs. Contractionary Monetary Policy

What Effects Does Monetary Policy Have?

Q. I'm having a little trouble trying to understand expansionary monetary policies and contractionary monetary policies. Can you help explain what impact expansionary monetary policies and contractionary monetary policies have on the economy?

A. Thanks for your great question. Students first learning economics often have trouble understanding what contractionary monetary policy and expansionary monetary policy are and why they have the effects they do.

Generally speaking contractionary monetary policies and expansionary monetary policies involve changing the level of the money supply in a country.

Expansionary monetary policy is simply a policy which expands (increases) the supply of money, whereas contractionary monetary policy contracts (decreases) the supply of a country's currency.

Expansionary Monetary Policy

In the United States, when the Federal Open Market Committee wishes to increase the money supply, it can do a combination of three things:

1. Purchase securities on the open market, known as Open Market Operations
2. Lower the Federal Discount Rate
3. Lower Reserve Requirements

These all directly impact the interest rate.

When the Fed buys securities on the open market, it causes the price of those securities to rise. In my article on the Dividend Tax Cut we saw that bond prices and interest rates are inversely related. The Federal Discount Rate is an interest rate, so lowering it is essentially lowering interest rates. If the Fed instead decides to lower reserve requirements, this will cause banks to have an increase in the amount of money they can invest. This causes the price of investments such as bonds to rise, so interest rates must fall. No matter what tool the Fed uses to expand the money supply interest rates will decline and bond prices will rise.

Increases in American bond prices will have an effect on the exchange market. Rising American bond prices will cause investors to sell those bonds in exchange for other bonds, such as Canadian ones. So an investor will sell his American bond, exchange his American dollars for Canadian dollars, and buy a Canadian bond.

This causes the supply of American dollars on foreign exchange markets to increase and the supply of Canadian dollars on foreign exchange markets to decrease. As shown in my Beginner's Guide to Exchange Rates this causes the U.S. Dollar to become less valuable relative to the Canadian Dollar. The lower exchange rate makes American produced goods cheaper in Canada and Canadian produced goods more expensive in America, so exports will increase and imports will decrease causing the balance of trade to increase.

When interest rates are lower, the cost of financing capital projects is less. So all else being equal, lower interest rates lead to higher rates of investment.

What We've Learned About Expansionary Monetary Policy:

1. Expansionary monetary policy causes an increase in bond prices and a reduction in interest rates.
2. Lower interest rates lead to higher levels of capital investment.
3. The lower interest rates make domestic bonds less attractive, so the demand for domestic bonds falls and the demand for foreign bonds rises.
4. The demand for domestic currency falls and the demand for foreign currency rises, causing a decrease in the exchange rate. (The value of the domestic currency is now lower relative to foreign currencies)
5. A lower exchange rate causes exports to increase, imports to decrease and the balance of trade to increase.

WHAT EFFECTS DOES MONETARY POLICY HAVE?

Contractionary Monetary Policy

As you can probably imagine, the effects of a contractionary monetary policy are precisely the opposite of an expansionary monetary policy. In the United States, when the Federal Open Market Committee wishes to decrease the money supply, it can do a combination of three things:

1. Sell securities on the open market, known as Open Market Operations
2. Raise the Federal Discount Rate
3. Raise Reserve Requirements.

These cause interest rates to rise, either directly or through the increase in the supply of bonds on the open market through sales by the Fed or by banks. This increase in supply of bonds reduces the price for bonds. These bonds will be bought up by foreign investors, so the demand for domestic currency will rise and the demand for foreign currency will fall. Thus the domestic currency will appreciate in value relative to the foreign currency. The higher exchange rate makes domestically produced goods more expensive in foreign markets and foreign good cheaper in the domestic market. Since this causes more foreign goods to be sold domestically and less domestic goods sold abroad, the balance of trade decreases. As well, higher interest rates cause the cost of financing capital projects to be higher, so capital investment will be reduced.

What We've Learned About Contractionary Monetary Policy:

1. Contractionary monetary policy causes a decrease in bond prices and an increase in interest rates.
2. Higher interest rates lead to lower levels of capital investment.
3. The higher interest rates make domestic bonds more attractive, so the demand for domestic bonds rises and the demand for foreign bonds falls.
4. The demand for domestic currency rises and the demand for foreign currency falls, causing an increase in the exchange rate. (The value of the domestic currency is now higher relative to foreign currencies)
5. A higher exchange rate causes exports to decrease, imports to increase and the balance of trade to decrease.

WHAT IS DEFLATION AND HOW CAN IT BE PREVENTED?

While I haven't polled every economist who has written an article on deflation this should give you a good idea of what the general consensus on the subject. A psychological factor that has been overlooked is how many workers look at their wages in nominal terms.

The problem with deflation is that the forces causing prices in general to drop should cause wages to drop as well. Wages, however, tend to be rather "sticky" in the downward direction. If prices rise 3% and you give your employees a 3% raise, they're roughly as well off as they were before. This is equivalent to the situation where prices drop 2% and you cut the pay of your employees by 2%. However, if employees are looking at their wages in nominal terms, they'll be much happier with a 3% raise than a 2% pay cut. A low level of inflation makes it easier to adjust wages in an industry whereas deflation causes rigidities in the labor market.

These rigidities lead to an inefficient level of labor usage and slower economic growth.

Now we've seen some of the reasons why deflation is undesirable, we must ask ourselves: "What can be done about deflation?" Of the four factors listed, the easiest one to control is number 1 "The supply of money". By increasing the money supply, we can cause the inflation rate to rise, so we can avoid deflation.

In order to understand how this works, we first need a definition of the money supply. The money supply is more than just the dollar bills in your wallet and the coins in your pocket. Economist Anna J. Schwartz defines the money supply as follows:

> *"The U.S. money supply comprises currency--dollar bills and coins issues by the Federal Reserve System and the Treasury--and various kinds of deposits held by the public at commercial banks and other depository institutions such as savings and loans and credit unions."*

There are three broad measures economists use when looking at the money supply:

> *"M1, a narrow measure of money's function as a medium of exchange; M2, a broader measure that also reflects money's function as a store of value; and M3, a still broader measure that covers items that many regard as close substitutes of money."*

The Federal Reserve has several options at its disposal in order to influence the money supply and thereby raise or lower the inflation rate. The most common way the Federal Reserve changes the inflation rate is by changing the interest rate. The Fed influences interest rates causes the supply of money to change. Suppose the Fed wishes to lower the interest rate. It can do this by buying government securities in exchange for money. By buying up securities on the market, the supply of those securities goes down. This causes the price of those securities to go up and the interest rate to decline. The relationship between the price of a security and interest rates is explained on the third page of my article The Dividend Tax Cut and Interest Rates. When the Fed wants to lower interest rates, it buys a security, and by doing so it injects money into the system because it gives the holder of the bond money in exchange for that security. So the Federal Reserve can increase the money supply by lowering interest rates through buying securities and decrease the money supply by raising the interest rates by selling securities.

Influencing interest rates is a commonly used method of reducing inflation or avoiding deflation. Gongloff at CNN Money sites a Federal Reserve study that says "Japan's deflation could have been dodged, for example, if the Bank of Japan (BOJ) had only cut interest rates by 2 more percentage points between 1991 and 1995." Colin Asher points out that sometimes that if interest rates are too low, this method of controlling deflation is no longer an option, as currently in Japan where interest rates are practically zero. Changing interest rates in some circumstances is an effective way of controlling deflation through controlling the money supply.

WHAT IS DEFLATION?

The Glossary of Economics Terms defines deflation as occurring "when prices are declining over time. This is the opposite of inflation; when the inflation rate (by some measure) is negative, the economy is in a deflationary period."

The article Why Does Money Have Value? explains that inflation occurs when money becomes relatively less valuable than goods. Then deflation is simply the opposite, that over time money is becoming relatively more valuable than the other goods in the economy. Following the logic of that article, deflation can occur because of a combination of four factors:

1. The supply of money goes down.
2. The supply of other goods goes up.
3. Demand for money goes up.
4. Demand for other goods goes down.

Deflation generally occurs when the supply of goods rises faster than the supply of money, which is consistent with these four factors. These factors explain why the price of some goods increase over time while others decline. Personal computers have sharply dropped in price over the last fifteen years. This is because technological improvements have allowed the supply of computers to increase at a much faster rate than demand or the supply of money. During the 1980's there was a sharp increase in the price of 1950's baseball cards, due to a huge increase in demand and a basically fixed amount of supply of both cards and money. So your suggestion to increase the money supply if we're worried about deflation is a good one.

Before we decide that the Fed should increase the money supply, we have to determine how much of a problem deflation really is and how the Fed can influence the money supply. First we'll look at the problems caused by deflation.

Why is Deflation Bad?

Most economists agree that deflation is both a disease and a symptom of other problems in the economy. In Deflation: The Good, The Bad and the Ugly Don Luskin at Capitalism Magazine examines James Paulsen's differentiation of "good deflation" and "bad deflation". Paulsen's definitions are clearly looking at deflation as a symptom of other changes in the economy. He describes "good deflation" as occuring when businesses are "able to constantly produce goods at lower and lower prices due to cost-cutting initiatives and efficiency gains". This is simply factor 2 "The supply of other goods goes up" on our list of the four factors which cause deflation.

Paulsen refers to this as "good deflation" since it allows "GDP growth to remain strong, profit growth to surge and unemployment to fall without inflationary consequence." "Bad deflation" is a more difficult concept to define. Paulsen simply states that "bad deflation has emerged because even though selling price inflation is still trending lower, corporations can no longer keep up with cost reductions and/or efficiency gains." Both Luskin and I have difficulty with that answer, as it seems like half an explanation. Luskin concludes that bad deflation is actually caused by "the revaluation of a country's monetary unit of account by that country's central bank". In essence this is really factor 1 "The supply of money goes down" from our list. So "bad deflation" is caused by a relative decline in the money supply and "good deflation" is caused by a relative increase in the supply of goods.

These definitions are inherently flawed because deflation is caused by relative changes. If the supply of goods in a year increases by 10% and the supply of money in that year increases by 3% causing deflation, is this "good deflation" or "bad deflation"? Since the supply of goods has increased, we have "good deflation", but since the central bank hasn't increased the money supply fast enough we should also have "bad deflation". Asking whether "goods" or "money" caused deflation is like asking "When you clap your hands, is the left hand or the right hand responsible for the sound?". Saying that "goods grew too fast" or "money grew too slowly" is inherently saying the same thing since we're comparing goods to money, so "good deflation" and "bad deflation" are terms that probably should be retired.

Looking at deflation as a disease tends to get more agreement among economists. Luskin says that the true problem with deflation is that it causes problems in business relationships: "If you are a borrower, you are contractually committed to making loan payments that represent more and more purchasing power--while at the same time the asset you bought with the loan to begin with is declining in nominal price. If you are a lender, chances are that your borrower will default on your loan to him under such conditions."

Colin Asher, an economist at Nomura Securities, told Radio Free Europe that the problem with deflation is that "in deflation [there's] a declining spiral. Businesses make less profits so they cut back [on] employment. People feel less like spending money. Businesses then don't make any profits and everything works itself into a declining spiral." Deflation also has a psychological element as it "becomes rooted in peoples' psychologies and becomes self-perpetuating. Consumers are discouraged from buying expensive items like automobiles or homes because they know those things will be cheaper in the future."

Mark Gongloff at CNN Money agrees with these opinions. Gongloff explains that "when prices fall simply because people have no desire to buy--leading to a vicious cycle of consumers postponing spending because they believe prices will fall further--then businesses can't make a profit or pay off their debts, leading them to cut production and workers, leading to lower demand for goods, which leads to even lower prices."

Curing Deflation by Printing Money

We finally get to the original question: "Is the problem that there is more to printing money than printing money? Is in fact the way printed money gets into circulation, that the fed buys bonds, and thus gets money into the economy?". That's precisely what happens. The money the Fed gets to buy government securities has to come from somewhere. Generally it is just created in order for the Fed to carry out its open market operations. So in most instances, when economists talk about "printing more money" and "the Fed lowering interest rates" they're talking about the same thing. If interest rates are already zero, as in Japan, there is little room to lower them further, so using this policy to fight deflation will not work well. Fortunately interest rates in the U.S. have not yet reached the lows of those in Japan.

The Federal Reserve and Interest Rates

The Federal Reserve is responsible for maintaining full employment (generally considered to be around 4 to 5 percent unemployment) while keeping inflation low. This task may sound simple but, in reality, it's a delicate balancing act.

The most powerful weapon in the Fed's arsenal is the ability to influence the direction of interest rates. When interest rates are low, capital is easier to acquire. This can spur economic development because, human nature being what it is, the more cash you have available, the more you are likely to pay for something you want-whether it is a car or that new plasma screen television. Left unchecked, however, and the result is "too much money chasing too few goods," as the saying goes.

This leads to inflation as businesses realize they can charge higher prices for their goods and services. Suddenly, it costs you more to fill up your gas tank and refrigerator.

If interest rates are too high, however, the result can be a recession and, in extreme cases, deflation; the result of which can be economically devastating-imagine going to pay off your mortgage and realizing that, although the balance has not increased, it's going to cost you more dollars in terms of purchasing power than it did before!

How can the Federal Reserve influence the direction of interest rates? In one of two ways:

1. By raising or lowering the discount rate.
2. By indirectly influencing the direction of the Federal funds rate.

The Discount Rate

The discount rate is the interest rate banks are charged when they borrows funds overnight directly from one of the Federal Reserve Banks. When the cost of money increases for your bank, they are going to charge you more as a result. This makes capital more expensive and results in less borrowing. Spending decreases, causing it to become more difficult for prices to rise; the opposite being true when capital becomes less expensive due to a decrease in the discount rate.

The Federal Funds Rate

The Federal funds rate is the rate that banks charge each other for overnight loans. "Why would one bank borrow cash from another?" you ask. The Fed can require banks to keep a certain percentage of assets in the form of cash on hand or deposited in one of the Federal Reserve banks. From time to time, it will establish a required ratio of reserves to deposits; when this ratio is increased, more cash must be kept in the vault at night, making it more difficult (and expensive) for funds to be acquired. When the reserve requirement is lowered, the money supply is loosened; because less cash has to be kept on hand it becomes easier to acquire capital.

The increased (or decreased) cost of acquiring funds is passed on to consumers as banks adjust their prime lending rate (the rate banks charge their best customers) to compensate. The prime lending rate is not uniform; Bank of America may have one rate while U.S. Bank has another. As a result, the most widely quoted prime rate figure in the United States is the one found in the Wall Street Journal. It represents a polling of the nation's thirty largest banks; when twenty-three of those institutions have changed their prime rates, the WSJ responds by updating the published rate. This ultimately affects your bottom line because many credit cards, for example, base the interest rate you pay on a premium above the WSJ prime rate.

Federal Reserve Board

Definition: The Federal Reserve Board, also know as the "Fed," controls the nation's interests rates by setting the key rates. Alan Greenspan has headed the Fed for many years. When he sneezes the market gets a cold, is an old Wall Street saying. Any change in interest rates will have a dramatic effect on the markets if it was not anticipated. Raising and lowering interest rates is analogous to turning up or down the heat while cooking.

Primary Dealers

Primary dealers are banks or brokerage firms who may trade directly with the Federal Reserve System of the United States. They are required to make bids or offers when the Fed conducts open market operations, provide information to the Fed's open market trading desk, and to actively participate in U.S. Treasury securities auctions. They consult with both the U.S. Treasury and the Fed about funding the budget deficit and implementing monetary policy. Many former employees of primary dealers work at the Treasury, because of their expertise in the government debt markets, though the Fed avoids a similar revolving door policy.

Between them, these dealers purchase the vast majority of the U.S. Treasury securities (T-bills, T-notes, and T-bonds) sold at auction, and resell them to the public. Their activities extend well beyond the Treasury market, for example, according to the Wall Street Journal Europe (2/9/06 p. 20), all of the top ten dealers in the foreign exchange market are also primary dealers, and between them account for almost 73% of forex trading volume. Arguably, this group's members are the most influential and powerful non-governmental institutions in world financial markets. Group membership changes slowly, with the current list available from the New York Fed.

The primary dealers form a worldwide network that is needed to distribute the huge amount of new U.S. government debt. For example, Daiwa Securities, Mizuho Securities, and Nomura Securities distribute the debt to Japanese buyers. BNP Paribas, Barclays, Deutsche Bank, and Greenwich Capital (a division of the Royal Bank of Scotland) distribute the debt to European buyers. Goldman Sachs, Lehman Brothers, and Citigroup account for many American buyers. Nevertheless, most of these firms compete internationally and in all major financial centers.

The newest primary dealer (effective on August 1, 2006) is Cantor Fitzgerald. The previous last major change to the list (excluding name changes and mergers) was Countrywide Securities, which joined in 1999. It is an American firm which focuses on mortgage markets and electronic or internet securities sales.

Repurchase Agreement

Repurchase agreements (RPs or Repos) are financial instruments used in the money markets. A more accurate and descriptive term is Sale and Repurchase Agreement, since what transpires is sale of securities now for cash by party

A (the cash borrower) to party B (the cash lender), with the promise made by A to B of repurchasing those securities later (with A paying the requisite implicit interest to B at the time of repurchase-the implicit interest rate is known as the repo rate). There is little that prevents any security from being employed in a repo; so, Treasury or Government bills, corporate and Treasury/ Government bonds, and stocks/shares, may all be used as securities involved in a repo. "' A Reverse Repo is the repo as seen from the point of view of the cash lender, since the cash lender does not repurchase, but rather has securities repurchased from (i.e. the cash lender is the passive party in the act of securities repurchasing).

Normally, both parties view the transaction from the trader's perspective. A trader looking to borrow money is transacting a repo, while a trader looking to obtain securities is executing a reverse repo. When a customer provides money to a trader in return for securities, the transaction is often termed a repo by both parties.

A repo is similar to a secured loan, with the lender of money receiving securities as collateral to protect against default. The legal title to securities passes from the seller to the investor. The one providing the cash is referred to as an "investor"; the provider of the collateral is the "seller". Coupons that are paid out on the securities during the life of the loan are generally passed directly onto the seller of the Repo. It is possible to instead pass on the coupon by altering the cash paid at the end of the agreement, though this is more typical of Sell/Buy Backs.

Typically, repos are short-term, either overnight, or with a maturity of few days. However, repo agreements up to 3 months are not uncommon; these can be used to cover futures contracts, and are commonly called term repos.

Motivations for Repos

For the customer, a repo is an opportunity to invest cash for a custom period of time (other investments typically involve whole numbers of months). It is a short-term and secure investment; in return for investing, the customer receives collateral. Market liquidity for repos is good and yields are competitive for investors.

For the trader, repos are used to finance long positions and reduce funding costs of other speculative investments.

There is a small credit risk with using repos. It is essentially a collateralized borrowing; but it is possible that the borrower of cash may fail to repurchase the securities sold at the promised date (in other words, default). In this case the lender may keep the security, but it may have lost value since the original transaction date. To prevent this minor amount of credit risk, some repos are over-collateralized. The credit risk is directly associated with the maturity of the repo: the longer the maturity, the greater the credit risk coming with the repo.

In addition to using repo as a vehicle to obtain cheap funding cost using secured financing, the best traders are also able to gain by making markets in repo using matched traders. The concept of a matched trade follows closely to that of a broker that takes both sides of an active trade, essentially having no risk. In the case of a matched repo trade, the trader engages in both a repo and a reverse repo within a short period of time. Profits can be obtained by traders who can take both sides of the market, but still leave themselves with a positive spread between the two repo rates. There are three types of repo maturities: overnight, term, and open repo. Overnight refers to a one-day maturity transaction. Term refers to a repo with a specified end date. Open simply has no end date.

Repo transactions occur in three forms: specified delivery, Triparty, and held in custody. The third form is quite rare. The first form requires the delivery of a pre-specified bond at the onset and maturity of the contractual period. Triparty allows for a wide range of instruments to satisfy a general pool in the repo contract.

Repo transactions came into focus within the financial press due to the technicalities of settlements following the collapse of Refco. Occasionally, a party involved in a repo transaction may not have a specific bond at the end of the repo contract. This may cause a string of failures from one party to the next, for as long as different parties have transacted for the same underlying instrument. The focus of the media attention centers on attempts to mitigate these failures.

Federal Reserve use of Repos

Repurchase agreements when transacted by the Federal Open Market Committee of the Federal Reserve in open market operations initially add reserves to the banking system and then withdraw them; reverse repos initially drain reserves and later add them back.

Under a repurchase agreement ("RP" or "repo"), the Federal Reserve (Fed) buys US Treasury securities, U.S. agency securities, or mortgage backed securities from a primary dealer who agrees to buy them back, typically within one to seven days; a reverse repo is the opposite. Thus the Fed describes these transactions from the counter-party's viewpoint rather than from their own viewpoint.

If the Fed is one of the transacting parties, the RP is called a "system repo," but if they are trading on behalf of a customer (e.g. a foreign central bank) it is called a "customer repo." Until 2003 the Fed did not use the term "reverse repo"-which it believed implied that it was borrowing money (counter to its charter)-but used the term "matched sale" instead.

Types of Repo and Related Products

Due Bill/Hold in Custody Repo: In a Due Bill repo, the collateral pledged by the (cash) borrower is not actually delivered to the cash lender. Rather, it is placed in an internal account ("held in custody") by the borrower, for the lender, throughout the duration of the trade. This has become less common as the Repo market has grown, particularly owing to the creation of centralized counterparties. Due to the high risk to the security lender, these are generally only transacted with large, financially stable institutions.

Tri-Party Repo: The distinguishing feature of a Tri-Party Repo is that a custodian bank or international clearing organization acts as an intermediary between the two parties to the Repo. The tri-party agent is responsible for the administration of the transaction including collateral allocation, marking to market and substitution of collateral. Both the lender and borrower of cash in transaction enter into these transactions to avoid the administrative burden of bi-lateral Repos. A Tri-Party repo may be seen as the outgrowth of the Due Bill repo, in which the collateral is held by a neutral third party.

Whole Loan Repo: A Whole Loan Repo is a form of Repo where the transaction is collateralized by a loan or other form of obligation (e.g. mortgage receivables) rather than a security.

Equity Repo: The underlying security for most Repo transactions are government or corporate bonds. Equity Repos are simply repos on Equity securities such as common (or ordinary) shares. Some complications can arise because of greater complexity in the tax rules for dividends as opposed to coupons.

Sell/Buy Backs and Buy/Sell Backs A Sell/Buy Back is the spot sale and a forward repurchase of a Security. The basic motivation of Sell/Buy Backs is generally same as for a Classic Repo i.e. attempting to benefit from the lower financing rates generally available for collateralized as opposed to non-secured borrowing. The economics of the transaction are also similar with the interest on the cash borrowed through the sell/buy back being implicit in the difference between the sale price and the purchase price.

There are a number of differences between the two structures. A Repo is technically a single transaction while a Sell/Buy Back is a pair of transactions (a sell and a buy). A Sell/Buy back does not require any special legal documentation while a Repo generally requires a master agreement to be in place between the buyer and seller (typically a GMRA/ISMA or PSA/ISMA).

Any coupon payment on the underlying security during the life of the Sell/Buy Back will generally be passed back to the seller of the security by adjusting the cash paid at the termination of the Sell/Buy Back. In a Repo the coupon will be passed on immediately to the seller of the security.

A Buy/Sell Back is the equivalent of a Reverse Repo.

Securities Lending: The general motivation of Repo is the borrowing or lending of cash. In securities lending, the purpose is to temporarily obtain the security for other purposes, such as covering short positions or for use in complex financial structures. Securities are generally lent out for a fee. Securities lending trades are governed by different types of legal agreements than Repos.

The size of the Repo Market: The US Federal Reserve and the European Repo Council (a body of the International Securities Market Association) both try to estimate the size of their respective repo markets. At the end of 2004, the US repo market reached USD 5 trillion and the European one passed EUR 5 trillion in outstandings. Both are growing at two-digit pace.

FACTOR PRICE EQUALIZATION

Factor price equalization is an economic theory, which states that the relative prices for two identical factors of production in the same market will eventually equal each other because of competition. The price for each single factor need not become equal, but relative factors will. Whichever factor receives the lowest price before two countries integrate economically and effectively become one market will therefore tend to become more expensive relative to other factors in the economy, while those with the highest price will tend to become cheaper.

An often-cited example of factor price equalization is wages. When two countries enter a free trade agreement, wages for identical jobs in both countries tend to approach each other. After NAFTA was signed, for instance, unskilled labor wages gradually fell in the United States, at the same time as they gradually rose in Mexico. The same force has applied more recently to the various countries of the European Union.

The result was first proven mathematically as an outcome of the Heckscher-Ohlin model assumptions.

FAIR TRADE MEANING

The Fair Trade movement promotes international labour, environmental and social standards for the production of labelled and unlabelled goods ranging from handicrafts to agricultural commodities. The movement focuses in particular on exports from developing countries to developed countries.

The most widely recognized definition of fair trade was created by FINE, an informal Association of the four main Fair Trade networks (Fair-trade Labelling Organizations International, International Fair Trade Association, Network of European Worldshops and European Fair Trade Association): European Fair Trade Association. (2006). Definition of Fair Trade URL accessed on August 2, 2006.: "Fair Trade is a trading partnership, based on dialogue, transparency and respect, that seeks greater equity in international trade. It contributes to sustainable development by offering better trading conditions to, and securing the rights of, marginalized producers and workers-especially in the South. Fair Trade organisations (backed by consumers) are engaged actively in supporting producers, awareness raising and in campaigning for changes in the rules and practice of conventional international trade. Fair Trade's strategic intent is:

* deliberately to work with marginalised producers and workers in order to help them move from a position of vulnerability to security and economic self-sufficiency
* to empower producers and workers as stakeholders in their own organisations
* to actively to play a wider role in the global arena to achieve greater equity in international trade."

Implicit and often explicit in fair trade is a criticism of the current organisation of international trade as being "unfair". When developing countries export to Northern markets, they often face tariff barriers that can be as much as four times higher than those encountered by Northern countries. Poverty advocates claim that those barriers cost poor countries $100 billion a year-twice as much as they receive in aid. Oxfam International. (n.d.) Rigged Rules and Double Standards URL accessed on August 2, 2006. Advocates of fair trade practices also hold that the fluctuation of commodity prices does not guarantee a living wage for many producers in developing countries, forcing many into crippling debt. The Fair-trade Foundation. (n.d.) What is Fair-trade? URL accessed on August 2, 2006. Market prices may not properly reflect the true costs associated with producing the product due to economic externalities such as environmental and social costs.

HISTORY

Origins

The first attempts to commercialize fair trade goods in Northern markets were initiated in the 1940s and 1950s by religious groups and various politically-oriented non-governmental organizations (NGOs). The Mennonite Central Committee (MCC) and the Church of the Brethren were the first, in 1946 and 1949 respectively, to develop fair trade supply chains in Third World countries.

International Fair Trade Association. (2005). Crafts and Food. URL accessed on August 2, 2006. The products, almost exclusively handicrafts ranging from jute goods to cross-stitch work, were mostly sold in World Shops. The goods themselves had often no other function than to indicate that a donation had been made. Hockerts, K. (2005).

SOLIDARITY TRADE

The Fair Trade movement as we know today was however shaped in Europe in the 1960s. Fair trade during that period was often seen as a political gesture against neo-imperialism: radical student movements began targeting multinational corporations and concerns that traditional business models were fundamentally flawed started to emerge.

The global free market economic model came under attack during that period and fair trade ideals, built on a post-Keynesian approach to economics where price is directly linked to the actual production costs and where all producers are given fair and equal access to the markets, gained in popularity. Redfern A. & Snedker P. (2002) Creating Market Opportunities for Small Enterprises: Experiences of the Fair Trade Movement. International Labor Office. p4 The slogan at the time,

"Trade not Aid", gained international recognition in 1968 when it was adopted by the UNCTAD (United Nations Conference on Trade and Development) to put the emphasis on the establishment of fair trade relations with the developing world. International Fair Trade Association. (2005). Where did it all begin? URL accessed on August 2, 2006.

Throughout the 1960s and 1970s, important segments of the Fair Trade movement worked to find markets for products from countries that were excluded from the mainstream trading channels for political reasons. The work conditions of the producers were then rarely emphasized. The first fair trade effort to import fair trade coffee to Northern markets, for example, was a solidarity initiative with the Sandinista government in Nicaragua. Renard, M.-C., (2003). Fair Trade: quality, market and conventions. Journal of Rural Studies, 19, 87-96. At the time however, the overwhelming majority of fair trade goods sold in World Shops remained handicrafts.

Handicrafts vs. Agricultural Goods

In the early 1980s, alternative trading organizations faced a major challenge: the novelty of their fair trade products started wearing off, demand reached a plateau and the handicrafts began to look "tired and old fashioned" in the marketplace. Redfern A. & Snedker P. (2002) Creating Market Opportunities for Small Enterprises: Experiences of the Fair Trade Movement. International Labor Office. p6 The decline of the handicrafts market forced fair trade supporters to rethink their business model and find innovative remedies to the ongoing crisis in the industry.

Agricultural commodities provided alternative trading organizations the perfect substitute to the declining handicrafts market: they offered a renewable source of income while being easily marketable as virtually every single consumer can become a potential buyer. The first traded agricultural products were tea and coffee, quickly followed by dried fruits, cocoa, sugar, fruit juices, rice, spices and nuts. Coffee quickly became the main growth engine behind Fair Trade: between 25 to 50 % of the total alternative trading organization turnover in 2005 came from coffee sales. International Fair Trade Association. (2005). Market Access and Fair Trade Labeling. URL accessed on August 2, 2006.

Rise of Labelling Initiatives

Sales of fair trade products however only really took off with the arrival of the first Fair-trade labelling initiatives. Although buoyed by ever growing sales, fair trade had been generally contained to relatively small World shops scattered across Europe and to a lesser extent, North America. Many felt that these shops were too disconnected from the rhythm and the life-style of contemporary developed societies.

The inconvenience of going to them to buy only a product or two was too high even for the most militant customers. The only way to increase sale opportunities was to start offering fair trade products where consumers normally shop, in large distribution channels. Renard, M.-C., (2003). Fair Trade: quality, market and conventions. Journal of Rural Studies, 19, 87-96. The problem was to find a way to expand distribution without compromising consumer trust in fair trade products and in their origins. Following long debates within Fair

Trade circles, the first Fair-trade label, Max Havelaar, was created in 1988 by the Dutch ATO Solidaridad. The independent certification allowed the goods to be sold outside the World shops and into the mainstream, reaching a larger consumer segment and boosting fair trade sales significantly. The labeling initiative also allowed customers and distributors alike to track the origin of the goods to confirm that the products were really benefiting the farmers at the end of the supply chain. Redfern A. & Snedker P. (2002) Creating Market Opportunities for Small Enterprises: Experiences of the Fair Trade Movement. International Labor Office. The concept caught on: within years, similar Fair-trade labelling organizations such as the Fair-trade Foundation, Trans Fair and Rate wise market, emerged across Europe and North America in an effort to follow Max Havelaar's footsteps and boost Fair-trade sales. The organizations originally operated independently and launched their own campaigns and certification marks.

In 1997, these organizations created Fair-trade Labelling Organizations International (FLO), an umbrella organization whose mission is to set the Fair-trade standards, support, inspect and certify disadvantaged producers and harmonize the Fair-trade message across the movement. In 2002, FLO launched a new International Fair-trade Certification Mark: The goals of the launch were to improve the visibility of the Mark on supermarket shelves, convey a dynamic, forward-looking image for Fair-trade, facilitate cross border trade and simplify procedures for importers.

PRESENT STATUS OF FAIR TRADE

Global Fair Trade sales have boomed over the past decade. FINE estimated that in 2000, sales of Fair Trade products (labelled and non-labelled) in Europe amounted to approximately ,260 million; in 2005, the figure was estimated at ,660 million, a 154% jump, representing a sustained annual increase of about 20% a year. FINE. (2005) Fair Trade in Europe 2005: Facts and Figures on Fair Trade in 25 European countries. Brussels: Fair Trade Advocacy Office. p7 Similar sales patterns have emerged in the Americas and the Pacific Rim, as Fair Trade sales in both regions have jumped from $291 million in 2003 to $376 million in 2004. Fair Trade Federation. (2005). Fair Trade Trends in the Americas and the Pacific Rim.

Key Fair-trade Principles

Fair-trade advocates generally support the following principles and practices in trading relationships: International Fair Trade Association (2006). Key Principles of Fair Trade URL accessed on August 2, 2006. Creating opportunities for economically disadvantaged producers: Fair trade is a strategy for poverty alleviation and sustainable development. Its purpose is to create opportunities for producers who have been economically disadvantaged or marginalized by the conventional trading system.Transparency and accountability: Fair trade involves transparent management and commercial relations to deal fairly and respectfully with trading partners. Capacity building: Fair trade is a means to develop producers' independence.

Fair-trade relationships provide continuity, during which producers and their marketing organizations can improve their management skills and their access to new markets. Payment of a fair price: A fair price in the regional or local context is one that has been agreed through dialogue and participation. It covers not only the costs of production but enables production which is socially just and environmentally sound. It provides fair pay to the producers and takes into account the principle of equal pay for equal work by women and men.

Fair-traders ensure prompt payment to their partners and, whenever possible, help producers with access to pre-harvest or pre-production financing. Gender equity: Fair trade means that women's work is properly valued and rewarded. Women are always paid for their contribution to the production process and are empowered in their organizations. Working conditions: Fair trade means a safe and healthy working environment for producers. The participation of children (if any) does not adversely affect their well-being, security, educational requirements and need for play and conforms to the UN Convention on the Rights of the Child as well as the law and norms in the local context. Environment: Fair trade actively encourages better environmental practices and the application of responsible methods of production.

FAIR-TRADE CERTIFICATION AND LABELLING

Fair-trade labelling (usually simply Fair-trade or Fair Trade Certified) is a Certification system designed to allow consumers to identify goods which meet agreed standards. Overseen by an international umbrella organisation, the Fair-trade Labelling Organizations International (FLO), the system involves independent auditing of producers to ensure the agreed standards are met.

For a product to carry the International Fair-trade Certification Mark, it must come from FLO inspected and certified producer organizations. The crops must be grown and harvested in accordance with the International Fair-trade standards set by FLO e.V. The supply chain is monitored by FLO-Cert to ensure the integrity of labelled products.

Fair-trade certification guarantees not only fair prices, but also the principles of ethical purchasing. These principles include adherence to ILO agreements such as those banning child and slave labour, guaranteeing a safe workplace and the right to unionise, adherence to the United Nations charter of human rights, a fair price that covers the cost of production and facilitates social development, and protection and conservation of the environment. The Fair-trade certification system also promotes long-term business relationships between buyers and sellers, and greater transparency throughout the supply chain.

The FLO Fair-trade certification system covers a growing range of products, including bananas, honey, coffee, oranges, cocoa, cotton, dried and fresh fruits and vegetables, juices, nuts and oil seeds, quinoa, rice, spices, sugar, tea and wine. Companies offering products that meet the Fair-trade standards may apply for licences to use the International Fair-trade Certification Mark for those products.

The current international Fair-trade Mark was launched in 2002 by FLO. The goals of the launch were to improve the visibility of the Mark on supermarket shelves, convey a dynamic, forward-looking image for Fair-trade, facilitate cross border trade and simplify procedures for importers and traders. The Fair-trade Certification Mark harmonization process is still under way â" as of August 2006, all but three Labelling Initiatives (namely Trans Fair USA, Trans Fair Canada and Max Havelaar Switzerland) have adopted the new International Fair-trade Certification Mark. Full transition to the new Mark should become reality as it gradually replaces the old Certification Marks at various speeds in various countries. Fair-trade Labelling Organizations International (2006). About Fair Trade URL accessed on August 4, 2006. The

Mark is currently used in over 16 countries: Australia, Austria, Belgium, Denmark, Finland, France, Germany, Ireland, Italy, Luxembourg, the Netherlands, New Zealand, Norway, Spain, Sweden and the United Kingdom. In 2005, FLO labelled Fair-trade sales amounted to approximately, 1.1 billion worldwide, a 37 % year-to-year increase. As per December 2005, 508 certified producer organizations in 58 developing countries were Fair-trade certified. Fair-trade Labelling Organizations International. (2005) FLO Annual Report 2005. URL accessed on August 4, 2006.

FAIR TRADE IMPACT STUDIES

Several independent studies have recently measured the impact of Fair trade on disadvantaged farmers and workers.

In 2002, Loraine Ronchi of the Poverty Research Unit at the University of Sussex studied the impact of Fair Trade on the Coocafe cooperative in Costa Rica. Ronchi found that Fair Trade strengthened producer organizations and concluded that "in light of the coffee crisis of the early 1990s, Fair Trade can be said to have accomplished its goal of improving the returns to small producers and positively affecting their quality of life and the health of the organisations that represent them locally, nationally and beyond". Ronchi, L. (2002). The Impact of Fair Trade on Producers and their Organizations: A Case Study with Coocafe in Costa Rica. University of Sussex. p25-26.

In 2003, the Fair Trade Research Group at Colorado State University conducted seven case studies of Latin American Fair-trade coffee producers (UCIRI, CEPCO, Majomut, Las Colinas & El SincuyoLa Selva, Tzotzilotic and La Voz) and concluded that Fair Trade has "in a short time greatly improved the well-being of small-scale coffee farmers and their families" Murray D., Raynolds L. & Taylor P. (2003). One Cup at a time: Poverty Alleviation and Fair Trade coffee in Latin America. Colorado State University, p28 The various case studies most notably found that producers had under Fair Trade greater access to credit and external development funding. Taylor, Pete Leigh (2002). Poverty Alleviation Through Participation in Fair Trade Coffee Networks, Colorado State University, p18. The studies also found that Fair Trade producers had, compared to conventional coffee producers, greater access to training and enhanced ability to improve the quality of their coffee. Murray D., Raynolds

L. & Taylor P. (2003). One Cup at a time: Poverty Alleviation and Fair Trade coffee in Latin America. Colorado State University, p8. Families of Fair Trade producers were also said to be more stable and children had better access to education than in families growing conventional coffee. Murray D., Raynolds L. & Taylor P. (2003). One Cup at a time: Poverty Alleviation and Fair Trade coffee in Latin America. Colorado State University, p10-11

FAIR TRADE AND POLITICS

European Politics

In June 2006, Green MEP Frithjof Schmidt submitted the report Fair Trade and Development to the European Parliament Development Committee. The report stresses that the most significant part of the increase in Fair Trade sales has been achieved with respect to labelled products and that Fair Trade labelling initiatives have been developed in most European countries.

The Report was followed by a resolution which urged the Commission to issue a Recommendation on Fair Trade recognising its role in the pursuit of the EU's Development and Trade policy. The resolution also recommended to set up minimum criteria a certain product needs to comply with in order to be considered 'Fair Trade', in order to reduce the risk of abuse. European Parliament (2006). Fair Trade and Development-call for the Commission to act. URL accessed on August 5, 2006. "This resolution responds to the impressive growth of Fair Trade, showing the increasing interest of European consumers in responsible purchasing," said Green MEP Frithjof Schmidt during the plenary debate. Peter Mandelson, EU Commissioner for External Trade, responded that the resolution will be well-received at the Commission. "Fair Trade makes the consumers think and therefore it is even more valuable. We need to develop a coherent policy framework and this resolution will help us. "Frithjof Schmidt MEP (2006). Parliament in support of Fair Trade URL accessed on August 2, 2006.

The resolution was unanimously adopted on July 6, 2006.

ORIGIN OF THE TITLE

George Selgin in his paper "Gresham's Law" offers the following comments: The expression "Gresham's Law" dates back only to 1858, when British economist

Henry Dunning Macleod (1858, p. 476-8) decided to name the tendency for bad money to drive good money out of circulation after Sir Thomas Gresham (1519-1579). However, references to such a tendency, sometimes accompanied by discussion of conditions promoting it, occur in various medieval writings, most notably Nicholas Oresme's (c. 1357) Treatise on money, and can even be found in much earlier works, including Aristophanes' The Frogs, where the prevalence of bad politicians is attributed to forces similar to those favoring bad money over good.

The passage from The Frogs referred to is as follows; it is usually dated at 405 B.C.:: The course our city runs is the same towards men and money.: She has true and worthy sons.: She has fine new gold and ancient silver,: coins untouched with alloys, gold or silver,: each well minted, tested each and ringing clear.: Yet we never use them!: Others pass from hand to hand,: sorry brass just struck last week and branded with a wretched brand.: So with men we know for upright, blameless lives and noble names.: These we spurn for men of brass....

"Gresham's Law" was also earlier described by the astronomer Nicolaus Copernicus, in the year that Gresham was born in a treatise named Monetae cudendae ratio.

Gresham's Context

According to George Selgin in his paper "Gresham's Law": As for Gresham himself, he observed "that good and bad coin cannot circulate together" in a letter written to Queen Elizabeth on the occasion of her accession in 1558. The statement was part of Gresham's explanation for the "unexampled state of badness" England's coinage had been left in following the "Great Debasements" of Henry VIII and Edward VI, which reduced the metallic value of English silver coins to a small fraction of what that value had been at the time of Henry VII. It was owing to these debasements, Gresham observed to the Queen, that "all your fine gold was conveyed out of this your realm."

Gresham made his observations of good and bad money while in the service of Queen Elizabeth, with respect only to the observed poor quality of the British coinage. The previous monarchs, Henry VIII and Edward VI, forced the people to accept debased coinage by means of their legal tender laws. Gresham also made his comparison of good and bad money where the precious metal in the money was the same. He did not compare silver to gold, or gold to paper.

Gresham's Law in Reverse

In an influential theoretical article, Rolnick and Weber (1986) argued that bad money would drive good money to a premium rather than driving it out of circulation. However their research did not take into account the context in which Gresham made his observation. Rolnick and Weber ignored the influence of legal tender legislation which requires people to accept both good and bad money as if they were of equal value. They also focussed mainly on the interaction between different metallic moneys, comparing the relative "goodness" of silver to that of gold, which is not what Gresham was speaking of.

The experiences of dollarization in countries with weak economies and currencies (for example Israel in the 1980s, the Eastern European countries in the period immediately after the collapse of the Soviet bloc, or South American countries throughout the late twentieth and early twenty-first century) may be seen as Gresham's Law operating in its reverse form (Guidotti & Rodriguez, 1992), since in general the dollar has not been legal tender in such situations, and in some cases its use has been illegal.

These examples show that in the absence of legal tender laws, Gresham's law works in reverse. If given the choice of what money to accept, people will transact with money they believe to be of highest long-term value. However, if not given the choice, and required to accept all money, good and bad, they will tend to keep the money of greater perceived value in their possession, and pass on the bad money to someone else. Said in another way, in the absence of legal tender laws, the seller will not accept anything but money of real worth (good money), while the existence of legal tender laws will force the seller to accept money with no commodity value (bad money). Thus, the buyer will always try to spend his bad money first, but in the absence of legal tender laws, the seller will not accept money with no real worth.

Analogical Extensions of Gresham's Law

The Gresham's Law principle has been applied, by analogy, to many different fields.

For example, movie critics have invoked Gresham's law to explain why movies with innovative visuals and writing are rare but, once created, are much copied or made into sequels. The claim is that production companies and theaters see all movies as virtually interchangeable product, and prefer ones which are cheaper to make or that have less risk to promote.

In higher education, "diploma mills" have come into existence producing low-cost qualifications which are often of little or no market value. It may seem that according to Gresham's law these "bad" diplomas ought to drive out the "good diplomas". However, unlike money, there is no law requiring employers to accept all diplomas as being of equal value and each employer is free to assess the value of qualifications as they see fit. Therefore Gresham's law does not apply.

In business, bad managers and employees can drive out good ones.

In democracy, a less intelligent majority may be able to out-vote an exceptionally intelligent minority, effectively driving out the most intelligent voters by guaranteeing that their votes will be defeated.

In schools, curriculum is prone to "dumbing down" to make it accessible to the least academically prepared students, thereby leaving no meaningful academic challenges for the better prepared students, or even students of average academic preparedness.

In the market for second hand cars, lemon automobiles (analogous to bad currency) will drive out the good cars. This is because the seller of good cars will find that the "average" price of both lemons and good cars is less than the fair price of the good car.

In morality, a version exists positing that "the evil acts of bad men illicit from good men acts which, under better circumstances, would also be called evil".

WORLD BANK

The World Bank has taken a positive stance on fair trade. According to the Bank's 2003 Study of Sustainable Coffee Markets, sustainable coffees (both fair trade and organic) "can provide such benefits as improved natural resource management; fewer agrochemicals used in production, which decreases costs and health risks; and increased use of rural labour, which provides more jobs for those in desperate need. "The World Bank Group. (2003). The State of Sustainable Coffee: A Study of Twelve Major Markets.

FOREIGN DIRECT INVESTMENT

Foreign direct investment (FDI) is defined as a long term investment by a foreign direct investor in an enterprise resident in an economy other than that in which the foreign direct investor is based. The FDI relationship, consists of a parent enterprise and a foreign affiliate which together form a Transnational Corporation (TNC). In order to qualify as FDI the investment must afford the parent enterprise control over its foreign affiliate. The UN defines control in this case as owning 10% or more of the ordinary shares or voting power of an incorporated firm or its equivalent for an unincorporated firm.

In the years after the Second World War global FDI was dominated by the United States, as much of the world recovered from the destruction wrought by the conflict. The U.S. accounted for around three-quarters of new FDI (including reinvested profits) between 1945 and 1960. Since that time FDI has spread to become a truly global phenomenon, no longer the exclusive preserve of OECD countries.

FDI has grown in importance in the global economy with FDI stocks now constituting over 20% of global GDP. In the last few years, the emerging market countries such as China and India have become the most favoured destinations for FDI and investor confidence in these countries has soared. As per the FDI Confidence Index compiled by A.T. Kearney for 2005, China and India hold the first and second position respectively, whereas United States has slipped to the third position.

Types of FDI

* *Greenfield Investment*: Direct investment in new facilities or the expansion of existing facilities. Greenfield investments are the primary target of a host nation's promotional efforts because they create new production capacity and jobs, transfer technology and know-how, and can lead to linkages to the global marketplace. However, it often does this by crowding

out local industry; multinationals are able to produce goods more cheaply (because of advanced technology and efficient processes) and uses up resources (labor, intermediate goods, etc). Another downside of greenfield investment is that profits from production do not feed back into the local economy, but instead to the multinational's home economy. This is in contrast to local industries whose profits flow back into the domestic economy to promote growth.

* *Mergers and Acquisitions*: Occur when a transfer of existing assets from local firms to foreign firms takes place, this is the primary type of FDI. Cross-border mergers occur when the assets and operation of firms from different countries are combined to establish a new legal entity. Cross-border acquisitions occur when the control of assets and operations is transferred from a local to a foreign company, with the local company becoming an affiliate of the foreign company. Unlike greenfield investment, acquisitions provide no long term benefits to the local economy--even in most deals the owners of the local firm are paid in stock from the acquiring firm, meaning that the money from the sale could never reach the local economy. Nevertheless, mergers and acquisitions are a significant form of FDI and until around 1997, accounted for nearly 90% of the FDI flow into the United States.
* Horizontal Foreign Direct Investment is investment in the same industry abroad as a firm operates in at home.
* *Vertical Foreign Direct Investment*: Takes two forms (1) backward vertical FDI: where an industry abroad provides inputs for a firm's domestic production process (2) forward verticle FDI: in which an industry abroad sells the outputs of a firm's domestic production processes.

Gresham's Law

Gresham's law is commonly stated as: "Bad money drives good money out of circulation". A more correct rendering of Gresham's Law is that "Bad money drives out good if they exchange for the same price." This law was first formulated by Nicolaus Copernicus. Gresham's law applies specifically when there are two forms of commodity money in circulation which are forced, by the application of legal tender laws, to be respected as having the same face value in the marketplace. It is named after Sir Thomas Gresham, an English financier in Tudor times.

THEORY

Gresham's law says that any circulating currency consisting of both "good" and "bad" money, where both forms are required to be accepted at equal value under legal tender law, quickly becomes dominated by the "bad" money. This is because people spending money will hand over the "bad" coins rather than the "good" ones, keeping the "good" ones for themselves.

Consider a customer purchasing an item which costs five pence, who has in their possession several silver sixpence coins. Some of these coins are more debased, while others are less so â□" but legally, they are all mandated to be of equal value. The customer would prefer to retain the better coins, and so offers the shopkeeper the most debased one. In turn, the shopkeeper must give one penny in change â□" and has every reason to give the most debased penny. Thus, the coins that circulate in the transaction will tend to be of the most debased sort available to the parties.

If "good" coins have a face value below that of their metallic content, individuals may melt them down and sell the metal for its higher bullion value. For an example of this, consider the 1965 US Half-dollars which were made from only 40% silver. The previous year the half-dollar was 90% silver. With the release of the 1965 half, which was legally required to be accepted at the same value as the previous year's 90% halves, the older 90% silver coinage of the US quickly disappeared from circulation, and the debased money was allowed to circulate in its stead. As the price of bullion silver rose above the face value of the coins, many of those old half-dollars were melted down.

Bibliography

Angela Wood: *Structural Adjustment for the IMF: Options for Reforming the Governance Structures*, Bretton Woods Project, London, 2001.

Ariel Buira: *Challenges to the World Bank and IMF: Developing Country Perspectives*, London, Anthem Press, 2003.

Ashok, Vasant: *Indian Economy in the World Setting*, Bombay, Himalaya, 1988.

Bandow, Doug, and Ian Vasquez: *Perpetuating Poverty: The World Bank, the IMF, and the Developing World*, Washington, DC: Cato Institute, 1994.

Besley, T.: *How do Merket Failures Justify Interventions in Rural Credit Markets?*, Washington, D. C., World Bank, 1994

Bookman, Zarkovic: *The Political Economy of Discontinuous Development: Regional Disparities and Inter-regional Conflict*, New York, Praeger, 1991.

Bouman, F.J.A.: *Small, Short and Unsecured: Informal Rural Finance in India*, Delhi, Oxford University Press, 1989.

Cavanagh, John, and Mander, Jerry: *Alternatives to Economic Globalization : A Better World Is Possible,* San Francisco, CA : Berrett-Koehler, 2004.

Darrow, Mac: *Between Light and Shadow: The World Bank, the International Monetary Fund and International Human Rights Law,* Portland, Ore.: Hart Publishing, 2003.

Dhingra, C.: *The Indian Economy: Resources, Planning, Development, and Problems*, Delhi, Sultan Chand, 1983.

Eleanor B. Steinberg and Joseph A. Yager: *New Means of Financing International Needs: Possible Sources of Finance*, Washington D.C.: The Brookings Institution, 1978.

Ferraro, Gary P.: *The Cultural Dimension of International Business*, Englewood Cliffs, Prentice Hall, 1997.

Gerald, K.: *The Less Developed Countries in the International Economy*, Cambridge, Cambridge University Press, 1975.

Goldsmith, W.: *The Financial Development of India, 1860-1977*, New Haven, Yale University Press, 1983.

Guhan, S.: *The World Bank's Lending in South Asia*, Washington, Brookings Institution, 1995.

Kumar, Ajit : *New Economic Policy of India: Restructuring and Liberalizing the Economy for the 21st Century*, New Delhi, Deep and Deep, 1994.

Le Prestre, Philippe: *The World Bank and the Environmental Challenge*, London, Associated University Presses, 1989.

Magliveras, Konstantinos D. *Banks, Fraud and Crime*, Lloyd's of London Press, London, 2000.

McLellan, Elisabeth P.: *The International Monetary Fund: Overview, Issues and Bibliography*, Happague, NY: Nova Publishers, 2002.

Mowlana, H.: *Global Information and World Communication: New Frontiers in International Relations*, London, Sage Publications, 1997.

Musalem, Errico, Luca & Alberto: *Offshore Banking: An Analysis of Micro-and Macro-Prudential Issues*, IMF, Washington, D.C., 1999.

Peet, Richard, Born, Beate: *Unholy Trinity: The IMF, World Bank, and WTO*, New York, Zed Books, 2003.

Pettifor, Ann: *Real World Economic Outlook: The Legacy of Globalization: Debt and Deflation*, New York, Palgrave MacMillan, 2003.

Ranade, Sudhanshu: *Rural Banking Adrift*, Bombay, Jaico Publishing House, 1984.

Savla, Sandeep: *Money Laundering and Financial Intermediaries*, The Hague and Boston, Kluwer Law International, 2001.

Victor, David A.: *International Business Communication*, New York, Harper Collins Publishers, 1992.

Vines, David and Christopher Gilbert: *The IMF and its Critics: Reform of the Global Financial Architecture*, Cambridge, Cambridge University Press, 2004.

Index

L

M

N

O

P

R

❑❑❑